The US Antifascism Reader

Dear Catina,
Thank you so much
for sticking around
for the talk &
for your support!

The US Antifascism Reader

Edited by
Bill V. Mullen and Christopher Vials

VERSO
London • New York

First published by Verso 2020
Collection © Bill V. Mullen and Christopher Vials 2020
Contributions © The Contributors 2020

1 3 5 7 9 10 8 6 4 2

Verso
UK: 6 Meard Street, London W1F 0EG
US: 20 Jay Street, Suite 1010, Brooklyn, NY 11201
versobooks.com

Verso is the imprint of New Left Books

ISBN-13: 978-1-78873-350-2
ISBN-13: 978-1-78873-695-4 (HARDBACK)
ISBN-13: 978-1-78873-351-9 (UK EBK)
ISBN-13: 978-1-78873-352-6 (US EBK)

British Library Cataloguing in Publication Data
A catalogue record for this book is available from the British Library

Library of Congress Cataloging-in-Publication Data
A catalog record for this book is available from the Library of Congress

Typeset in Minion Pro by Hewer Text UK Ltd, Edinburgh
Printed and bound by CPI Group (UK) Ltd, Croydon CR0 4YY

Contents

Part II:
Antifascism and the State, 1941–1945

Part III:
Antifascism, Anticolonialism, and
the Cold War, 1946–1962

Acknowledgements

All books are collective, this one more than most. It reflects learning from, and organizing with, a wide range of people committed to the analysis of and fight against fascism. These would include: Joe Allen, Maximillian Alvarez, Megha Anwer, Chip Berlet, Tithi Bhattacharya, Will Biel, Marcel Bois, Jason Chang, Nigel Copsey, Mathew Dittman, Nada Elia, Amy Fehr, Sue Ferguson, Meleiza Figueroa, Evan Fritz, Hugo García, Micah Goodrich, Jane Gordon, Todd Gordon, Kate Doyle Griffiths, Alžbeta Hájková, Rebecca Hill, Aaron Jaffe, Alaina Kaus, Bre Leake, Fred Lee, Holly Lewis, Grant Mandarino, David McNally, Dana Mills, Adam Miyashiro, Wyatt Mund, Mimi Nguyen, David Palumbo-Liu, Ian Alan Paul, Jerry Phillips, Clayton Plake, Charlie Post, David Renton, Cathy Schlund-Vials, Malini Schueller, Dan Siegel, Hayley Stefan, G. M. Tamás, Enzo Traverso, Jarred Wiehe, and Anna Ziering.

We would especially like to thank the Humanities Institute at the University of Connecticut, particularly Michael Lynch and Alexis Boylan, for awarding us a grant to cover the permissions and copyright costs associated with this book. Without this crucial support, the scope of the book would have been very limited. We would also like to thank Alan Wald for his mentorship in helping us to find crucial individuals and artifacts of the antifascist left and to Benjamin Balthaser for his scholarly assistance. Jim Baggett at the Birmingham Public Library was also quite generous in helping us locate material on Asa Carter, and Jen Hoyer and Michelle Hardesty were true comrades for getting us the material on Anti-Racist Action from the Interference Archive in Brooklyn, New York. We owe a real debt of gratitude to Elyse Derounian Rogers for allowing us to use her father's writings, as well as to Marc Mamigonian at the National Association for Armenian Studies and Research for all his support with the Avedis Derounian Papers. A special thanks also to the American Studies Writing Group at the University of Connecticut, which provided valuable feedback on the introduction (Peter Baldwin, Kate Capshaw, Martha Cutter, Nina Dayton, Jeff Dudas, Clare Eby, Kathy Knapp, Shawn Salvant, Nancy Shoemaker, Manisha Sinha, David Yalof). Last but certainly not least, we would like to thank the living antifascists in this collection, not only for their contributions to real democracy, but for generously allowing us to use their work: Mark Bray, Kathleen Cleaver, Les Evans, Ken Lawrence, Sam Miller, Penny Nakatsu and Enzo Traverso.

A special shout-out goes to members of the Campus Antifascist Network (CAN). We helped found the group in June of 2017 after American fascists marched through Bay Area streets. Since then, a founding group of forty grew to include more than 2,000 people. The Network built chapters at more than a dozen campuses in the United States, the UK, and Canada. CAN organizers have helped build rallies against eugenics proponent Charles Murray at the University of Michigan, neo-Nazi Richard Spencer at Michigan State University, and alt-right hack Lucian Wintrich at the University of Connecticut. Those protests have slowed the momentum of a small but nascent fascist and neofascist movement. They have demonstrated a theory and practice of popular antifascism that this book seeks to remember, commemorate, and keep alive.

Introduction: Anti/Fascism and the United States

We assembled this collection because of fascism's loud return to the world stage as an animating political idea and an aspirant mode of political rule. Its return results from a complex weave of epochal shifts: the global economic slump of the 1970s and the attendant rise of neoliberal market ideologies; wide-scale attacks by elites and global financial institutions on working-class lives and social welfare; continuing deracination of workers' organizations, including trade unions; the collapse of "official" state communism in the Soviet Union and the Eastern bloc countries; 9/11, myriad "Wars on Terror" and Islamophobic panics generated across the capitalist West; population displacement from Middle Eastern, predominantly Muslim countries like Syria into Western Europe precipitated by the US invasion of Iraq and subsequent rise of ISIS into the resultant political vacuums; and the second global financial collapse of 2007–2008. In many traditionally democratic and capitalist Western states, these events have combined to erode lateral affiliations necessary for left-democratic politics and helped actuate a political third space, beyond conservativism and social democracy, a predominantly white, racist, nationalist, middle-class "backlash" that finds expression in a politics of resentment, victimhood, xenophobia and anti-leftism traditionally associated with classical fascism. In the United States, the return of fascist appeals relies on foundations much deeper in scope: namely, a history of white racial identification and settler colonial militarism, centuries in the making, without which the specter of an American fascism would be nearly unthinkable.

These historical coordinates are more durable in significance than the individual far-right figures and movements they have so far produced: individuals like Geert Wilders in the Netherlands, Marine Le Pen in France, and Jair Bolsonaro in Brazil, or movements such as CasaPound in Italy and Golden Dawn in Greece. They overwhelm in importance the "dog whistle" US politician of aspirant fascists—Donald Trump—whose election in 2016 was a tenuous constellation of the global currents enumerated above: a candidate who unconsciously rediscovered a fascist rhetorical style, rather than building a fascist-like movement. Yet Trump's election to the highest office of the world's most powerful militarized and capitalist state *did* demand reflection. Trump used classical-fascist tropes—an apocalyptic and hypermasculine language of nation, race, action, strength, power, authority, and violence—as calling cards for his campaign. A small portion of Trump's political base did and does perceive his political orientation as fascist. Even prior to his election, a hard-right populist turn was visible within the Tea Party movement, some of which evolved into Trumpism. Here, classical questions facing students of fascism were, for perhaps the first time in recent US history, practical ones—is fascism an independent right-wing movement from below, an extension of capitalist political authority at a moment of crisis, or an idea summoned by a singular political figure seeking to build power?—Yet is has become clear that even if Trump were a fascist, he lacks the political skill to be an effective one. His political rhetoric often uses a fascist grammar, but it lacks a properly fascist party or a fascist state.

However, Trump's election should also have the effect of forcing historical reflection on the role of the United States in relationship to global fascist movements of the past century, as well as its "native" traditions of fascism and the fight against them. The present volume might be seen as such a reflection. It is designed both as a response to the current conjuncture of global fascist renaissance, and as an intervention to help us understand why the United States has been integral to the historical formation of fascism and antifascist resistance while never realizing or sustaining a fascist state of its own.

In a general sense, we are motivated to compile this volume by our own political orientation to an antifascist tradition rooted primarily in Marxism, socialism, and anti-racism, but also in anticolonial, and (more recently) anarchist and "antifa," political practices. We find compelling the arguments by left-intellectual figures like Enzo Traverso in the

United States (included here) and G. M. Tamás in Hungary that, particularly since the collapse of the bipolar Cold War order, "post-fascist," "neofascist," "savage capitalist" and other recognizably protofascist formations have emerged globally as a condition of neoliberal, hypercapitalist, neocolonial global development.[1] The severe, violent resurgence of anti-Semitism (and conspiratorial anti-cosmopolitanism) in advanced capitalist Western states; the hardening of economic and racial nationalisms wedded to apartheid-style xenophobias ("border walls," "Fortress Europe" and otherwise); the viral Islamophobia that sutures together so many disparate forms of far-right political theory and practice today; these trends recall the contours of a modernity still beholden to Aimé Césaire's conception in his 1950 masterwork *Discourse on Colonialism*—excerpted here—that Occidental capitalism has yet to shed the violent, racist, authoritarian practices that helped constitute it: from the Muslim and Jewish purges of the fifteenth and sixteenth centuries foundational to European "civilization," to King Leopold II's severing of human hands in the Belgian Congo, to the gas chambers of the Nazi Holocaust. In the US context, the resurgence of antiblack, anti-immigrant racism in contemporary national fascist movements like the Traditionalist Worker Party, Patriot Front, and Identity Evropa rekindles the specters of white supremacy, eugenics and xenophobia that are as co-constitutive of American political culture as John Winthrop's designation of the New World as a "city on a hill."

The political mandate for this volume, if there is one, also lies in the creative theoretical and practical flowering of antifascist organizing that has marked the epochal shifts noted above. It is an important moment of historical remembrance when a small group of antifascists in Midwestern America in 2017—Indianapolis, Indiana, to be exact—launch a group called "Rock Against Racism." Specters of the Clash, Steel Pulse, X-Ray Spex, and other bands that stood down the renascent fascist National Front in 1976 London are welcome "images of the past," as Walter Benjamin might say, returning to confront a new fascist emergency. The march of more than 50,000 against fascism in Boston in August 2018; the street fights against white supremacists in East Lansing, Michigan, in March of the same year; the enduring viral meme of neo-Nazi Richard Spencer getting punched in the face: all of these flash

---

1 G. M. Tamás, "On Post-Fascism," *Boston Review,* June 1, 2000, bostonreview.net.

points stem from political roots at least as strong as those fueling white nationalism. These include anti-racist discourses and even institutions (ethnic studies education and cultural centers, for instance) that emerged from black freedom struggles and people of color movements throughout the twentieth century, feminist and LGBTQ mobilizations with their own histories of institution building, especially since the late 1960s, labor struggles for union power, and socialist and anarchist efforts to create alternative economies. Antifascists have persistently emerged from the ranks of these movements of democratic leveling. More fundamentally, these mobilizations also deeply influenced the political "common sense" (in Gramscian terms) of many millions of Americans—a common sense that has survived decades of neoliberal erosion and provided the basis for antifascism's public legibility.

This volume seeks to offer a backstory to this present: a history and historiography of popular engagement with the theory and practice of antifascism. The book is thus both a scholarly apparatus and a political handbook—a précis and a brick—meant for a wide range of readers and activists, and useful for courses on fascism and the antifascist tradition, as well as for study groups on campuses and in workplaces where fascism continues to try to penetrate. In this, the book seeks to build a textual consensus about the meaning of fascism, especially in the US context, inspired mainly by the historical materialist tradition on the subject and the socialist tradition of fighting against it.

Fascism and the United States

The gigantic growth of National Socialism is an expression of two factors: a deep social crisis, throwing the petty bourgeois masses off balance, and the lack of a revolutionary party that would be regarded by the masses of the people as an acknowledged revolutionary leader. If the Communist Party is the party of revolutionary hope, then fascism, as a mass movement, is the party of counter-revolutionary despair.

Leon Trotsky, 1930[2]

---

2 Leon Trotsky, "The Danger of German Fascism," *Marxists in Face of Fascism: Writings by Marxists on Fascism from the Inter-War Period*, ed. David Beetham (Manchester: Manchester University Press, 1993), 206.

Fascism in the United States, it may be said, has been both undertheorized and overimagined. Both problems stem from a liberal hegemony that has helped forestall "real existing fascism" in the United States while at the same time usurping analysis, especially class analysis, of the character of fascism. It is not just that the United States has no "Trotsky" to explain what fascism is, but that it lacks conditions favorable to either the emergence of a fascist state or to an astute analysis of its very real fascist potential. Be that as it may, the United States carries the ghosts of its own fascist and fascist-like traditions, as well as an unrecognized culture of antifascist resistance.

While historians of fascism tend to be deeply uncomfortable with loose applications of the term, there is a rough consensus among them that fascism, in some form or another, continued to survive after 1945. Here, it is important to distinguish between fascist rhetoric, a fascist movement, and a fascist state. A fully fascist state has yet to emerge anywhere in the world since the end of World War II, but fascist politics and fascist movements have resurfaced perennially across the world. As historian Roger Griffin stressed in 1993, "as a *political ideology* capable of spawning new movements [fascism] should be treated as a permanent feature of modern political culture."[3] The editors of this volume define fascism as a particular strand of right-wing politics, separate from classical conservatism or even other strands of right-wing authoritarianism (e.g., Pinochet's Chile, the Somozas' Nicaragua), in that it is not driven primarily by traditional elites wishing to preserve their economic interests. Rather, it is a largely middle-class movement animated by a highly symbolic, populist, and mythic drive for national renewal, grounded in militarism or male violence, anti-Marxism, racism, and authoritarianism. In addition, it actively mobilizes the population in a culture war against national minorities and/or the political left. While elites are not its main agents, they have crucially enabled fascism in the historical fascist states because of their fears of the left and the working classes.[4] Fascist rhetoric is not grounded in liberal

---

3 Roger Griffin, *The Nature of Fascism* (London: Routledge, 1993), xii.

4 This definition of fascism owes a debt to major works in the field of fascist studies. These include Stanley Payne, *A History of Fascism, 1914–1945* (Madison: University of Wisconsin Press, 1995); Ernst Nolte, *Three Faces of Fascism: Action Française, Italian Fascism, National Socialism* (New York: Holt, Rinehart & Winston, 1966); Robert Paxton, *The Anatomy of Fascism* (New York: Alfred Knopf, 2004); Griffin, *The Nature of Fascism*; Ian Kershaw, *The Nazi Dictatorship: Problems and Perspectives of Interpretation* (London: Edward Arnold, 1993 [1985]); and Richard Bessel, ed., *Life in the Third Reich* (Oxford: Oxford University Press, 1987).

Enlightenment themes of progress, liberty, democracy, or freedom; rather, it manifests as an apocalyptic, aggrieved language of nation, action, strength, power, vengeance, leadership, and race.

Enlightenment liberalism—the belief in free speech, freedom of association, individual property rights—is deeply embedded in US institutions and in the country's national narrative. For this reason, it is often assumed that Americans are immune to fascist appeals. Yet in the 1930s, influential sections of the US public were able to reconcile their faith in liberalism and the US Constitution with an admiration for Hitler, Mussolini, and Franco, in part because of contradictions inherent in liberalism itself.[5] As many on the American left have labored to warn us since the 1930s, these contradictions have persistently generated neofascist movements and currents.

While the United States, like other liberal democracies, is founded on a principle of formal legal equality and liberal rights, this leveling impulse was undercut at its roots by a capitalist political economy that has necessitated social hierarchy across a number of fronts. As Theodore W. Allen reminds us, "the white race" was created in the late seventeenth century as a means to maintain social order and hierarchy within an emergent capitalist world system, and race retained this function when the new nation of the United States was born. Plantation elites responded to the multiracial revolt of Bacon's Rebellion in 1676 with slave codes that introduced divisions among laborers, establishing black skin as the marker of the most degraded forms of labor. The corollary to this new social system was the creation of a white buffer class—what Allen terms the "intermediate stratum"—whose members would be given police roles, the right to bear arms, and other relative privileges. This buffer class would ally with the bourgeoisie on the basis of race and help them enforce their system of capitalist accumulation.[6]

At the same time, a settler colonial militarism worked to cement this cross-class alliance even more firmly by defining indigenous peoples as irredeemably savage and hence dispensable to settler land claims. An early colonial and US history of "Indian Wars" created a racial boundary

---

5   Chris Vials, *Haunted by Hitler: Liberals, the Left, and the Fight against Fascism in the United States* (Amherst, MA: University of Massachusetts Press, 2014), 45–6, 172–4.
6   Theodore Allen, *The Invention of the White Race, Volume 2: The Origin of Racial Oppression in Anglo-America* (London: Verso, 1994).

at the edge of the frontier that required as much maintenance as the labor-based color lines within, and it established a concept of war as inherently apocalyptic and racial. As cultural historian Nikhil Pal Singh has written, "Both [black and indigenous] populations featured in the development of a racialized narrative of security, one that invested every white person with the sovereign right to kill and blurred the lines between military and police action."[7] Out of this milieu emerged American liberalism, which, not unlike European liberalisms, produced a dual system of subjects: "citizens" invested with rights of property, free association, and the franchise on the basis of whiteness and masculinity; and rightless "bare life," often consigned to spaces of superexploitation or dispossessed from their land.[8]

Consequently, the United States has had a long history of racial violence that has not required the instigation of a fascist dictator. Its racial violence has often served to maintain the boundaries and exclusions within a liberal system of rights and to preserve its class rule. Unlike Nazi policies toward Jews and the Roma, for example, the lynching of African Americans never aimed at the total extermination of the black population: its violence toward the "part" was intended to discipline the whole, whose superexploited labor was required for its model of capitalist accumulation. Because so many of its racial formations were initially developed, in part, to manage the superexploited labor of large numbers of people of color, it is unlikely that a US fascist state would take the racially genocidal blueprint provided by Nazi eugenics. However, those who experienced racial abjection in US liberalism offered powerful insights on the nature of fascism. For example, a recurrent motif within African American antifascism, represented most forcefully in this volume by Kathleen Cleaver, views fascism as a collapsing of this dual system of rights. That is to say, under fascism, the space of existential dread, reserved for some and not others by the liberal state, grows in size to the point of encompassing the social whole, at the same time that those marginalized in the old liberal state face intensified forms of terror. This *spatial* notion of fascism begins to explain how Penny Nakatsu, a former

---

7 Nikhil Pal Singh, *Race and America's Long War* (Berkeley: University of California Press, 2017), 27.

8 The term "bare life" is borrowed here from Giorgio Agamben, *Homo Sacer: Sovereign Power and Bare Life*, trans. Daniel Heller-Roazen (Stanford, CA: Stanford University Press, 1998).

internee represented in this volume, could say she actually endured fascism in California, and it illuminates Langston Hughes's assertion, in 1936, that "fascism is a new name for that kind of terror the Negro has always faced in America . . . This kind of terrorism is extending more and more to groups of peoples whose skins are not black."[9]

While it is difficult to imagine a eugenicist regime in the United States, the country's brand of capitalism has politically relied upon and helped constitute white racial identity, and this dismal fact has given fascist movements an opening. American capitalism has also benefited from a militarism rooted in anticommunism, and from a heteropatriarchy that works to maintain cross-class alliances, as we have seen with the Christian right. When combined with profound economic anxiety, these interlocking hierarchies of class, race, gender, and sexuality generate a set of "possessive investments" that American capitalism depends upon politically but are difficult for its ruling class to manage.[10] In this light, fascist and overtly racist politics could be seen as the buffer class striking out on its own. The grammar of fascism allows the white middle class to define the political in its own terms, and in a way that radically overidentifies with dominant hierarchies and potentially destabilizes the cross-class, white alliance originally forged to serve its system of capitalist accumulation. In other words, race, which was originally developed to manage a class hierarchy, eventually develops a demonic logic of its own that surpasses its original function. In this vein, Theodor Adorno, writing from the United States, used the term "pseudo-conservatism" to describe the country's extreme right. Unlike conservatives proper, who understand how capitalism functions and defend its class structures accordingly, Adorno's pseudo-conservative suffers from a failed identification with established structures and would thus compromise the very institutions they seek to defend.[11]

The term "middle class" does not adequately capture the precise class composition of the buffer group that has so often formed the political base of fascist movements in Europe and North America over the past

9   Hughes, quoted in *Proceedings: Third US Congress against War and Fascism* (New York: American League against War and Fascism, 1936), 8–9.

10   The concept of "possessive investment" is borrowed here from George Lipsitz, *The Possessive Investment in Whiteness: How White People Profit from Identity Politics* (Philadelphia: Temple University Press, 2006).

11   Rolf Wiggershaus, *The Frankfurt School: Its History, Theories, and Political Significance* (Cambridge, MA: MIT Press, 1995), 419–20.

century. For example, exit polls from the 2016 US election reported paradoxical data that has yet to be properly understood: that is, they revealed that most Trump voters enjoyed incomes above the national average, yet they lacked college degrees, confusing commentators seeking a class label to describe them. For the student of fascism, this is not a riddle. It indicates that the Trumpian base, much like the base of fascist movements across the twentieth century, is strongest in what is sometimes called "the old middle class." Occupationally, its constituents are less often white-collar professionals or office workers ("the new middle class"), and more often small business owners and skilled workers. They were artisans and small farmers in the early twentieth century and, often, independent contractors and skilled tradesmen in the twenty-first. Fascism, in other words, draws heavily from a group that some Marxists traditionally labeled with the disparaging term "petite bourgeoisie": one of middle income but often unstably so, and lacking cultural capital.

Whatever we choose to call it, the buffer class has indeed struck out on its own at a number of moments in US history, to devastating effect. The United States has never been home to viable fascist parties, but it has been home to fascist *movements*—or the functional equivalents thereof—and these movements have impacted the political mainstream at critical junctures. To be sure, the country has always been home to a galaxy of relatively small fascist-oriented groups at the fringes, from the North Carolina–based Silver Shirts in the 1930s to the Traditionalist Worker Party of today. But few of these organizations have been able to pull themselves out of the swamp long enough to reshape American policies or institutions. A select number, however, have been more fortunate. In the United States, fascist or protofascist sensibilities cohered most influentially in the Ku Klux Klan of the 1920s; in Father Charles Coughlin's "Christian Front" and media platforms in the 1930s; in the resurgence of overt, mobilized white supremacy during the era of civil rights, culminating in George Wallace's American Independent Party and his 1968 presidential campaign; and in the Christian reconstructionism fueling the Christian right in the 1970s and beyond.

Each of these currents impacted mainstream US politics in its day. The lobbying efforts of the Ku Klux Klan in the 1920s, for example, helped to rewrite US immigration law by creating immigration quotas for the first time, producing in the process the very category of "illegal alien." Coughlin, a Hitler apologist whose radio audience may have numbered up to 10 million, helped ensure that no US aid came to Spanish loyalists in the 1930s; and in the late 1960s, the Republican Party co-opted George Wallace's third-party, populist appeal to white racial anxiety in order to form its so-called "Southern strategy," which facilitated the system of mass incarceration that exists in the United States to this day. The crucial role of the Christian right in pushing anti-LGBTQ legislation and in the administration of George W. Bush is well known. Less familiar is the seminal role in the movement of Rousas John Rushdoony (1916–2002), a philosopher-activist who advocated a theocracy wherein the enemies of Christ—most notably homosexuals—would be "cleansed" in a patriarchal, authoritarian utopia not unlike the one imagined by Margaret Atwood in her novel *The Handmaid's Tale* (1985).[12] Sadly, many Americans who have seen fascism as the most pressing issue of their time have not been tilting at windmills.

In comparison to their European counterparts, these mobilizations have not been able to develop into their own parties; this has been due to the hegemony of the two-party system, which has also worked to obscure the history of American fascism and its impact. In a multiparty system, different ideological currents to the political right can congeal into parties with more specific programs and philosophies: in postwar Germany, for example, one has the free market, libertarian Free Democratic Party (FDP), the right-of-center conservatism of the Christian Democratic Union (CDU), and the fascism—or protofascism—of the National Democratic Party (NPD) and, more recently, the Alternative for Germany (AfD). In the United States, however, such constellations typically come together under the umbrella of the Republican Party, merging their platforms and their political rhetoric within a comparatively broad coalition. If the United States possessed a multiparty system featuring right-wing parties with titles such as the Christian Patriotic Party or the American Homeland First

---

12   On shifts in US immigration law in the 1920s, see Mae Ngai, *Impossible Subjects: Illegal Aliens and the Making of Modern America* (Princeton, NJ: Princeton University Press, 2004); on the Republican Party's co-optation of Wallace, see Dan T. Carter, *From George Wallace to Newt Gingrich: Race in the Conservative Counterrevolution, 1963–1994* (Baton Rouge, LA: Louisiana State University Press, 1996). On the fascist tendencies of Coughlin, Wallace, Rushdoony, and the Christian right, see Vials, *Haunted by Hitler*.

Party, then Americans likely would have had a very different public conversation about fascism. Confounding matters further is that since World War II, fascist movements in the United States have tended to publicly disavow connections to the historical fascist states, even when they reproduce a political platform or rhetoric that is functionally equivalent to a neofascist movement.

While effective fascist-like movements have cohered at a number of critical junctures in US history, often with devastating effects, none have ever taken full control of the state. We can ascribe this to a number of factors. First, a history of class conflict and class struggle that has remained, generally, within a terrain of reform, rather than one of revolution. If one of fascism's primary objectives is the destruction of socialism, the United States has rarely seen anything remotely like a working-class insurgency that threatens to topple the existing order of capital, as occurred in Italy and Germany before World War II. And if classical fascism emerged as the ruling class's destroying angel of communist and socialist movements, no such threat from the left has ever exceeded the realm of the right's paranoid imaginings. In the US context, the FBI, police, military and Cold War apparatus of the liberal state have also combined to do what fascism historically has achieved itself: namely, the obliteration of strong radical organizational opposition to a potential state program of racist, nationalist class rule.

Second, it is also true that at least since the turn of the twentieth century, the United States has acted as a planetary hegemon, diminishing the possibility of national grievance, or retribution, as a motivating fascist impulse. The United States—with the exception of its catastrophe in Vietnam, and, more recently, its endless bogging down in Iraq, Afghanistan and elsewhere in Western Asia and North Africa—has enjoyed imperial prosperity in proportions unmatched by any nation in the modern world. Its unparalleled military apparatus has yet to succumb to a catastrophic national defeat necessitating terms of surrender, or to multipolar military threat that could serve as a convenient rallying cry for a fascist nationalism. Fascism has not been necessary to achieve US "strategic" goals, even at the height of the Cold War, though, as this volume demonstrates, the US left did try to cast American McCarthyism as "fascism."

Finally, and significantly, is the factor of the antifascist resistance. While the United States has not been home to the vast socialist or communist movement cultures of Germany, Italy, or France—let alone those of China, Vietnam, or Russia—it has been home to left-wing and reformist traditions that have played a distinct role in blunting home-grown fascist mobilizations and checking the rise of a fascist state. In the wake of the late 1960s, for example, the US state and civil society were forced to accommodate the demands of the black freedom movement and its allies in the Yellow Power, Native American, Puerto Rican and Chicano movements by invoking multiculturalism. With all its limita-tions, all its watering down of radical redistributionist demands, multi-culturalism and the institutionalization of ethnic studies in education have nonetheless worked to blunt fascist appeals among large sections of the public, particularly among younger generations. But all the move-ments that generated the writings and writers of this collection had a hand in this blunting, as well. An unnamed attendee at the American League against War and Fascism conference in 1936 uttered a truth that is very close to the spirit of this collection: "Whether or not America goes fascist depends on who gets organized first."[13] From the 1930s to the present, antifascist writers and organizers successfully worked to create an antifascist common sense among broad sections of the American public—in a sense, "getting organized first." In this volume, we can only give a glimpse of their efforts and the range of individuals in their ranks.

Fighting the Good Fight: The Basics of Antifascism

If antifascist politics have been important to comprehending the course of US politics, it is crucial to understand their basis. What, in other words, is an antifascist? Simply put, an "antifascist" is not someone who merely dislikes fascism. Rather, they are a person who sees fascism as an immedi-ate threat to their political environment and devotes a significant amount of energy to stopping it. An antifascist is one who sees "fascism" as a central issue of their time. Thus we agree with historian Nigel Copsey, who, in his work on the British context, sees antifascism as a matter of both thought and action—and action that takes a broad range of political

---

13   American League against War and Fascism, *A Program against War and Fascism* (New York: American League against War and Fascism, 1936), 25.

forms, from physical confrontation to leafletting. We also agree with his "antifascist minimum": what politically unites antifascist forms, to Copsey, is a genuine commitment to democracy, be it liberal democracy, social democracy, or the direct democracy of a workers' state.[14]

The "anti" status of the movement has tended to give its activities a self-defensive character; historically, antifascists have devoted much of their activity to thwarting mobilizations of the far right. But as a democratic movement, antifascism has generally been linked to positive programs as well: its bearers tend to fight not only *against* fascism, but also *for* racial justice, for socialist (or anarchist) transformation, and for gender equality. For this reason, antifascists historically have been involved in multiple organizations and forms of political action at the same time: for instance, participating in the American League against War and Fascism on one day and building a union on the next. In the United States, antifascism was at its height during the 1930s and 1940s, a time when it structured the very terms of the political for many people on the left. In those years, the US left made unprecedented gains in institutional power and influence through the Congress of Industrial Organizations (CIO) unions, an emergent black public sphere, and the New Deal state. Yet, for organizers on the left, fascism remained the all-too-real atavism that threatened to undo everything at a moment's notice. For many liberals and leftists of this generation, "fascism" was less a concrete regime in Germany or Italy, and more a grammar to conceive the connectedness of seemingly divergent struggles. The labor question, the woman question, anti-imperialism, the fight against "race hate," and the struggle for peace were often conjoined as a part of a common fight against "fascism," a fight to preserve democratic gains while extending them into uncharted territory.[15] This sensibility, moreover, guided both "popular front" and "united front" appeals. To be antifascist, then, was not only to collapse distances across continents, but to move toward what we now call *intersectional* thought and action.

----

14 Nigel Copsey, "Preface," *Varieties of Anti-Fascism: Britain in the Inter-War Period*, Nigel Copsey and Andrzej Olechnowicz, eds. (New York: Palgrave Macmillan, 2010), xiv–xxi.

15 The best example of these political linkages can be found in *Fight* (1933–1939), the magazine of the American League against War and Fascism, which covered all of these issues, often without even mentioning the word "fascism."

Following the bombing of Pearl Harbor, antifascism, for the first and last time, became an official logic of the state. Encouraged by state sponsorship, antifascist cultural workers attained access to wider audiences during World War II than they ever had before, breaking into the more heavily vetted culture industries like network radio and Hollywood film with greater regularity.

Their narratives of the fascist enemy—which described Hitler, Mussolini, and Tojo as parts of a global political reaction—were pervasive across the public sphere but not fully hegemonic. They had to contend with incompatible wartime visions of "why we fight" grounded in anti-Japanese racism and republican notions of citizenship.[16] Antifascism survived in the United States after 1945 as what Marxist theorist Raymond Williams would call a "residual culture." That is to say, it was formed in the past within a once-pervasive cultural formation, yet it persisted as a lived experience of the present: a reservoir of oppositional energies fueled by a sense of unfulfilled dreams and broken promises from an earlier time, now inexpressible within the newly dominant logic.[17] In this sense, postwar antifascism is a politics that on some level always accesses the unfinished business of 1945.

If one sees fascism as an imminent threat, the question is *how* one goes about stopping it: What political forms does one use? After the election of Donald Trump, the so-called "Antifa"—a radical movement, largely comprised of young people and devoted to physically confronting white supremacists in the streets—enjoyed an unprecedented visibility in the United States, even becoming a household word. This street-fighting impulse has always been part of the history of antifascism, but as the mass mobilizations of the 1930s and 1940s remind us, antifascism has also been much larger than a brawl. Antifascist activity frequently takes up the more conventional, political forms of the liberal state, including lobbying, canvassing, holding forums, media work, community organizing, and so forth. Some of the selections in this volume reflect this more quotidian mode of antifascism, a mode that has gotten far less attention. For instance, the American League for Peace

---

16 Chris Vials, "Contending Narratives of World War II," *American Literature in Transition: 1940–1950,* ed. Chris Vials (Cambridge, UK: Cambridge University Press, 2017), 13–28.

17 Raymond Williams, *Marxism and Literature* (Oxford: Oxford University Press, 1977), 122.

and Democracy's 1938 *People's Program for Peace and Democracy* outlines an institution-forging antifascist strategy that includes legislative lobbying, fundraising, picketing, community organizing, and so on. Les Evans's piece, "Alliances and the Revolutionary Party" (1971), discusses the nuts and bolts of antifascist coalition building, reviving a debate around "united fronts" and "popular fronts" that is now largely forgotten to a new generation of activists.

"Antifa" as we know it is largely a post-1980 phenomena and a European import. In the newly reunified Germany, the term spread as a reference to punk and anarchist youth, with roots in squatter and subcultural scenes, who physically clashed with members of a resurgent neo-Nazi movement. The first major organization in the United States to form along these lines was the Minneapolis-based Anti-Racist Action in 1988, and it initially used the term "anti-racist" because its organizers saw "anti-fascist" as a word too dogmatic for an American context.[18] In the twenty-first century, Americans from anarchist, radical, and subcultural scenes began mimicking the substance and style of their European counterparts even more directly. They borrowed the symbols and imagery of "Antifaschistiche Aktion," the short-lived united front of socialists and communists who first organized in Weimar Germany and later in the postwar rubble of the Nazi regime.[19]

Yet the street-fighting mode of antifascism has a genealogy in the United States that predates the 1980s, and this collection attempts to flesh it out as well. The flash points here include the famous battle inside and outside of Madison Square Garden between antifascists and supporters of the pro-Nazi German American Bund in 1939, captured in Felix Morrow's "All Races, Creeds Join Picket Line." Robert F. Williams provides a theoretical justification for armed self-defense in the excerpt from *Negroes with Guns* (1962)—a piece that has gone unrecognized as part of the antifascist tradition, even though Williams, a World War II veteran, repeatedly identified his white supremacist enemies as "fascists." Yet street-level action against fascists and protofascists was rarely articulated as a political philosophy before the 1980s. Moreover, the record of

---

18   Mark Bray, *Antifa: The Anti-Fascist Handbook* (Brooklyn, NY: Melville House, 2017), 67.

19   Loren Balhorn, "The Lost History of Antifa," *Jacobin*, May 8, 2017, jacobinmag. com.

fascist-versus-antifascist violence in the United States is actually quite long, and we have used the pieces by Morrow and Williams merely to index this history, rather than to catalog it. Other instances, not directly discussed in this volume, include the sometimes-lethal resistance from immigrant communities to marches by the Ku Klux Klan in the 1920s; Italian American antifascist clashes with Mussolini supporters in the 1920s and 1930s; Jewish American self-defense units formed to fight back against the anti-Semitic violence of the Christian Front in Boston and New York during World War II; the mass brawls inside and outside George Wallace's Madison Square Garden rally in October 1968; and the shoot-out at the so-called "Greensboro Massacre" of 1979, discussed in outline in the Ken Lawrence piece, "The Ku Klux Klan and Fascism" (1982).[20]

Yet most authors included in this reader attempt to name, identify, and subject to critique the face of fascism in their contemporary moment, rather than prescribe particular strategies for stopping it. In this sense, this volume, in part, puts forward a US antifascist *analytic* as it has developed across time: a conversation between generations about the nature of fascism that has largely gone unrecognized as coherent discourse. German antifascists developed a useful term for political interpretations of fascism: *Faschismustheorie.* The word is more than its rough English translation of "fascism theory." It refers to an interpretation of fascism and its nature that guides one's strategy and actions against it in the field. We set out to curate analytical writings in this vein, and we found that the vast majority emerged not from the academy, but from antifascist movement cultures and their organizations. Few of these pieces included in this volume were written for an academic audience, and only in a few instances were they composed from the site of the academy. Some are testaments to the autodidact culture of the political left, a space where individuals like Julius Jacobson or Robert F. Williams developed profound social and historical insights from the feedback loop between movement literature, independently selected books, and political organizing in the field. Yet whether the pieces in

---

20   Rory McVeigh, *The Rise of the Ku Klux Klan: Right-Wing Movements and National Politics* (Minneapolis: University of Minnesota Press, 2009), 142; John Diggins, *Mussolini and Fascism: The View from America* (Princeton, NJ: Princeton University Press, 1972); Stephen Norwood, "Marauding Youth and the Christian Front: Antisemitic Violence in Boston and New York During World War II," *American Jewish History* 91:2 (2003), 253.

this collection were written by organic intellectuals like Jacobson or by PhDs like Franz Neumann, they all take seriously Karl Marx's famous dictum that the point of philosophy is not simply to interpret the world but to change it. Their insights are of value to any antifascist, regardless of their field of action or their choice of tactics.

The Historical Arc of This Collection

The pieces we have included in this volume fall into three main categories: (a) analyses of fascist currents and their political potential; (b) tactics and strategies for fighting fascism and their moral justification; and (c) writings from American fascists and protofascists.

Most of the writers and organizations included here are American by nationality, but not all. We have also included writings by individuals publishing in the United States, sometimes in exile, and a few pieces written outside this country that were deeply influential on American and global antifascist thought: namely, the entries from Dimitrov and Césaire.

We have organized this material chronologically, and our largest section is Part I, entitled "Can It Happen Here? US Antifascism in the Time of Dictators, 1932–1941." The 1930s and 1940s were the era of the fascist states: consequently, it was a time when the word "fascism" appeared constantly in political discourse, producing rich and extensive debates over its nature and manifestations. As the reader will note, these decades were also a time when the US left was deeply suffused with Marxism, hence class questions come to the fore in discussions of fascism. Yet, as the selections reveal, it was not merely the left that focused on class when approaching fascism: in fact, an emphasis on the class dimensions of fascism was ubiquitous across the political field. Such a focus was the spirit of an age in which economic collapse and an organized workers' movement kept class frames at the center of public debate.

Well into the 1960s, those on the left often argued that capitalists were the true power behind the thrones of Hitler and Mussolini, an inadequate interpretation that we have labeled elsewhere the "puppet master theory."[21] But historians of fascism have also overlooked the various

---

21 Vials, *Haunted by Hitler*, 75–7.

ways in which the pre-1968 left produced more layered analyses of their archenemy—ones that did not always make race, gender, or ideology epiphenomenal. Even before 1945, they focused on the dynamics of fascist racism, militarism, empire, and nationalism far more than has been acknowledged, and other theories of fascism's class politics quite frequently contended with the "puppet master theory," especially by the late 1930s. Represented by pieces in this volume by Vincenzo Vacirca, Sinclair Lewis, and Avedis Derounian, these other views ascribed far more agency to fascism's middle-class base; or, like the entries from Harry Ward, W. E. B. Du Bois, George Padmore, and Franz Neumann, they placed far more formative power on its racial and nationalist dimensions.

Part II, "Antifascism and the State, 1941–1945," offers artifacts that help to shed light on the question: To what extent did the United States become an antifascist state during the war? After the United States entered World War II following the bombing of Pearl Harbor, US anti-fascists had a much wider arena in which to make their case. This was also the period when the US government employed members of the Frankfurt School, then in exile mainly in New York and California, as intelligence analysts and propaganda experts, as the entry from Neumann illustrates. Yet, even if we were to limit ourselves to political rhetoric, the US state and American civil society were inconsistent and contradictory in this period: in this milieu, one can find the bona fide antifascisms of Henry Wallace and Neumann alongside the Yellow Peril imagery of race war directed against the Japanese, with its tragic and well-known consequences at home and abroad. W. E. B. Du Bois makes a tally of these contending forces in his short piece, "Negro's War Gains and Losses" (1945).

Part III, "Antifascism, Anticolonialism, and the Cold War, 1946–1962," documents the left's continuing use of antifascist frames as it fought the domestic battles of the Cold War era. During the early part of the Cold War, there was a rich debate on the left as to whether or not McCarthy and McCarthyism represented a new face of American fascism. In the 1950s, what alarmed the veterans of earlier antifascist struggles was the emergent rhetoric of conspiracy and racism within investigative bodies like the House Un-American Activities Committee and the Senate Internal Security Subcommittee, along with their very real erosion of civil liberties in the name of anticommunism. They read this repression in the context of a larger postwar social transformation that bore uncanny similarities to the very regimes they recently fought against in World War II: the permanent militarization of society necessitated by the Cold War; a growing anti-intellectualism, cultural homogenization and conformity; a violent, racial reaction against the nascent civil rights movement; and, perhaps most dramatically, the rehabilitation of Germany, Spain, and Japan as "bulwarks against communism," coupled with a disturbing silence about their recent victims (most notably, the millions who perished during the Holocaust). Readers will notice a shift in discussions of fascism in this period: to wit, an increasing readiness to discuss its noneconomic dimensions, especially its racial politics.

Anti-racism definitively moved to the center of antifascist politics by the late 1960s, as is visible in Part IV, "The Politics of Backlash and a New United Front, 1968–1971." In the earlier part of that decade, and for the first time, Americans began to discuss the Holocaust consistently as the most salient truth of fascism. While the televising of the Eichmann trial in 1961 by Israel was a catalyst, there were also deeper structures fueling this shift of focus: namely, the US civil rights movement and global anticolonial ferments abroad, which worked together to make "racism" legible as a determinant of history. Following the Holocaust "memory boom," fascism was much more relevant to activists of color and their allies, who began to access terms like "concentration camps" and "genocide" frequently when discussing the ultimate stakes of white supremacy.

In the late 1960s, antifascism became central to US left-wing politics for the second time in the twentieth century. In July 1969, the Black Panther Party hosted its "United Front against Fascism" conference in Oakland, which led to the formation of the National Committees to Combat Fascism (NCCFs) across the United States. The BPP's adoption of antifascism was important because the party exercised symbolic leadership over younger American leftists during that period. Conscious of the Popular Front of the 1930s, Bobby Seale and other Panther leaders intended the NCCFs to be a multiracial coalition of radical whites, Latinos, and Asian Americans, united in a common front to combat an emergent racial backlash. This return to antifascism emerged in the context of white political reaction against the black freedom struggle in the late 1960s. This reaction was embodied not only by the election of

Richard Nixon, but also by the rise to the national political stage of George Wallace, a segregationist strongman acknowledged by commentators across the political spectrum as the heir apparent to American fascism.

In Part V, "Anti/Fascism in the Age of Neoliberalism," we return to the themes we raised at the beginning of this introduction. Neoliberalism, while ostensibly "colorblind" and yoked to multiculturalism, nonetheless opened the door to right-wing extremism in various forms. First, given that arguments about restoring wealth to corporations and the rich have never been popular, even in the United States,[22] neoliberalism's most blatant proponents in the Republican Party relied on "dog whistle" politics (appeals to white racial anxiety)[23] and the anti-LGBTQ Christian right to forge the coalitions necessary to push through their politics of austerity. Overall, neoliberalism worked to hollow out lateral modes of political identification—faith in labor unions, cross-racial solidarity, the New Deal state—that so many antifascists in the 1930s and 1940s saw as crucial to any democratic ethos capable of resisting fascist appeals. At the same time, neoliberalism's assault on middle- and working-class living standards increased economic anxiety; its "neocon" implementation in the United States, moreover, maintained and even intensified American militarism and its attendant hypermasculinity. Rampant economic precarity, a highly militarized domestic culture, a retreat in official commitment to genuine racial justice, and the lack of a viable social democratic alternative combined to erode faith in the "demos," throwing open the door to deeply hierarchical and undemocratic politics.[24] Out of this matrix emerged an exponential rise of militia and "hate groups," a new form of homophobic extremism in the form of the Christian right, and more recently, the alt-right, Steve Bannon, and Donald Trump.

Antifascism continued the fight within this hostile environment, though the memory of fascism became increasingly obscure to so many

---

22   For a recent example, see Amanda Becker, "Three Quarters of Americans Favor Higher Taxes for Wealthy: Reuters/Ipsos Poll," *Reuters*, October 11, 2017, reuters.com; for Americans' longer-term attitudes toward wealth inequality, taxes, and redistribution, see "Taxes," Gallup official website, news.gallup.com/poll/1714/taxes.aspx.

23   Ian Haney López, *Dog Whistle Politics: How Coded Racial Appeals Have Reinvented Racism and Wrecked the Middle Class* (Oxford: Oxford University Press, 2014).

24   We owe a conceptual debt here to Wendy Brown's *Undoing the Demos: Neoliberalism's Stealth Revolution* (New York: Zone Books, 2015).

Americans living in amnesiac, strip mall landscapes further and further removed from Mussolini's March on Rome. As Stuart Marshall's piece reveals, LGBTQ activism took a distinctly antifascist turn in light of the AIDS crisis and the rise of the Christian right. At the same time, Americans developed their own "antifa" movement through organizations like the Anti-Klan Network, the Sojourner Truth Organization, Anti-Racist Action, and the post-Trump mobilizations that Mark Bray discusses in his piece. Indeed, Trump, as the first president to name "antifa" in public, made the term a household word in the United States for the first time. "Antifascist" sounded too foreign to be of any use to anti-racist activists of ARA in 1988, yet it is now a term known to virtually everyone in the United States, a flashpoint of debate from television screens to dinner tables across the country. To be clear, the state of affairs that made it so is an urgent one.

Indeed, "Who will get organized first?" is still an open question.

PART I

Can It Happen Here? US Antifascism in the Time of Dictators, 1932–1941

"Fascism after Ten Years,"
Wall Street Journal, October 29, 1932

This piece typifies the coverage of the Italian Fascist regime by the US business press, at least up until 1935. American business praised the dictatorship for turning a "basket case" nation into an exemplary economy and society. Mussolini, they argued, revived trade, established law and order, disciplined labor, stabilized the lira, and restored efficient management. Indeed, from the early 1920s into the 1930s, Mussolini created a more orthodox market economy using statist means. Yet business soured on Italian fascism in 1935, when Mussolini invaded Ethiopia, unsettling the colonial balance of power. By the late 1930s, many US elites also turned against statism as a solution to the Depression as Roosevelt's more redistributive "Second New Deal" appeared as a threat to their power. The Third Reich enjoyed a much shorter period of sympathy in the US business community, though its "openness" to the Nazi regime was never uniformly extinguished.

Another anniversary, the tenth, of the fascist march on Rome comes and goes, this time without shattering Europe's nerves or even distracting its attention from its grim bread-and-butter troubles. In contrast with the saber rattling on these anniversaries of a few years ago, Il Duce [Mussolini] this year opened a new railway, unveiled a memorial or two and extended political amnesties by way of observance.

So far from any longer regarding it as a menace to what is referred to as the peace of Europe, or invidiously comparing it with democracy or parliamentary rule, the world outside Italy is now interested only in the fact that fascism works. Whether it works, for Italians in their home country, better or worse than something else might or ought to, is Italy's own business, as the outside world is beginning to perceive.

Nearly seven years ago a parallel was drawn in this column between the then comparatively new fascist system in Italy and a receivership for a corporation. That parallel still holds good and has now extended itself to apply to the structural reorganization that takes place under a receiver. It is the purpose of receivership, political or corporate, to discover the altered means of carrying on a national civilization or a private undertaking under the altered conditions which surround it and set new tasks for management. The fact that its tenth anniversary finds fascism in Italy apparently firmly established among an apparently more tranquil people than Italy has contained for more than a decade speaks a great deal for the reorganization of the state that has taken place since 1922.

In the editorial of January 26, 1926, above referred to, the late William Peter Hamilton made this discerning observation: "A thoughtful Italian would not worry about Mussolini, but he ought to be much exercised about Mussolini's successor."

That, to be sure, remains for Italians the Italian problem. His grant of amnesty to political prisoners the other day can only mean that Mussolini himself is thinking of it and undertaking its solution, not because of any specific or immediate urgency, but because every political system requires time for its solidification. He cannot be unaware of the degree to which fascism remains an expression of his extraordinary but still human personality.

All of which perhaps sums up in the recognition that fascism has since 1922 undergone an evolution, as all successful institutions must. It is but reasonable to suppose that the process will be still more characteristic of fascism's second decade.

Vincenzo Vacirca, "The Essence of Fascism: A Marxian Interpretation," *American Socialist Quarterly* vol. 2, no. 2, spring 1933

Vincenzo Vacirca (1886–1956) was one of the most active Italian antifascist exiles in the United States, yet he is now only faintly remembered in the English-language world. In Italy, he had been a parliamentarian for the Socialist Party, which was democratic socialist in orientation. He lived in the United States from 1913 to 1919 and again from 1925 to 1946, where he survived multiple assassination attempts by Italian nationalists. In the 1920s, the Italian fascist state pressured the US State Department to silence Vacirca, along with other exiles. He returned to Italy in 1943 as an agent of the Office of Strategic Services (the precursor to the CIA), where he remained after the war.

Vacirca offers a complex class analysis of fascism's base of support and the ways this base shifts when fascist movements become fascist states. His class analysis, moreover, is roughly in line with those of a number of prominent contemporary historians of fascism. Vacirca also advances here the "gangster theory" of capitalism, a recurring motif in left antifascist writings during the 1930s and 1940s. The gangster metaphor rejected the idea that capitalists were the primary agents of fascism and instead described capitalists as enablers of fascism who could not control its direction once it assumed state power. It received elaborate expression in the literary modernisms of Bertolt Brecht and Dashiell Hammett, and it served as a digestible, popular metaphor for a generation reared in detective noir, one that crystallized a more complex theory of class structures under these regimes. Also of interest is Vacirca's analysis of the relationship between fascism and the liberal state, for it reflects views that were not unusual among socialists working within the parties of the Second International.

This essay appeared in the American Socialist Quarterly, *the theoretical journal of the militant wing of the American Socialist Party. The membership of the once-mighty SP had dwindled in the 1930s as that of the Communist Party USA rose, yet it continued to produce rich analytical texts on the nature of fascism.*

The exalting of Hitler to the German chancellorship has focused anew the attention of the world on the social phenomenon known under the name of Fascism. The former little Austrian corporal is trying to tread in the foot-steps of the former little Italian school teacher, just as the latter attempted to make himself a replica of the third Napoleon. A study of the policies, methods and system of government of the man of December the second, of Mussolini and Hitler, would show a striking similarity in these three historical movements—and in all probability the two contemporary ones will end, as their French predecessor, in the only possible way open to an oligarchic or a personal dictatorship: war.

Twenty-three centuries ago, the founder of political science wrote:

> The tyrant, who in order to hold his power, suppresses every superiority, does away with good men, forbids education and light, controls every movement of the citizens and, keeping them under a perpetual servitude, wants them to grow accustomed to baseness and cowardice, has his spies everywhere to listen to what is said in the meetings, and spreads dissension and calumny among the citizens and impoverishes them, is obliged to make war in order to keep his subjects occupied and impose on them permanent need of a chief.

From the time of Aristotle the psychology of the tyrant has not changed. And Hippias had nothing to learn from Hitler or Mussolini. But if the personal character and the external forms of a modern tyrant do not differ much from the most ancient ones, there are some social factors which are new and typical of the economic structure of our contemporary society. The analysis of these factors will help us to understand Fascism, in its double manifestations: as an accomplished fact in those countries where it has celebrated its triumphs, and as a menacing tendency in those countries where democratic forms of government still hold sway.

. . .

What is Fascism? A wave of supernationalism sweeping those countries which came out of the great war defeated, humiliated, enslaved and, what is more important, pauperized—as in the case of Germany? A reaction to the "excesses" of a briefly triumphant Bolshevism—as in Hungary? A revolt of the middle class, crushed in the struggle between proletarians and capitalists and succeeding for the first time in history in establishing an autonomous dominant power—as has been said of Italy? Or—according to the communist interpretation—a pure dictatorship of capitalism which attempts to solve its unsolvable crisis by discarding all democratic pretenses and entrenches itself beyond the machinery of the State used openly as a mere class instrument for the oppression of the proletariat and the brutal defense of its own interests and privileges? Or—as alleged psychologists and easy philosophers of history presume— a collective madness by which a free people surrenders its long-fought-for and hardly acquired liberties into the hands of a "man of destiny" to whom they assign the magic role of their savior in time of hardships and insurmountable difficulties?

None of these hypotheses is entirely valid, although in some of them there is a grain of truth.

The causes which brought on Fascism are several. Some of them are of general character and in a way permanent; some transitorial [sic] and local. Historically, Fascism is a phase of the old struggle started on the European continent the day the Parisian people demolished the Bastille, and continued with varying fortunes for 144 years.

A mystic would call it a struggle between light and darkness, liberty and reaction. An historical materialist would see in it a product of continually changing conditions begotten by the development of the capitalist society and of which wars, revolutions and counter-revolutions are simply episodic effects.

Fascism is not, therefore, a new social event, but simply a new name for an old thing. War, with a revival of the spirit of violence and cruelty, has been not a real cause of Fascism but an occasion which gave a peculiar color to that movement. The secret alliance between Italy, Hungary and Germany is a replica of the Holy Alliance that bound Austria, Prussia and Russia 118 years ago after the Napoleonic hurricane died down.

The later was an open league of victorious and dominant States for the enslavement of Europe and its sterilization from the epidemic spread of the ideas born with the French Revolution. The former is a conspiracy of privileged classes, of weak and partly defeated States which try to find a compensation for their weakness and poverty by intensifying the exploitation of their subjected masses and later in new war that would destroy the richer capitalism of the lately victorious nations. At the bottom of Fascism, therefore, we find a twofold conflict: one within the national frontiers, between wage-earners and property classes; and one over the national boundaries between different groups of international capitalists.

The first form of the conflict has been temporarily solved by the reduction to a condition of slavery of the workers of those countries where Fascism won its day. The second part has no possible solution, even if it will lead fatally to a war. In fact, a war could give one of these two results: either Fascist capitalism will emerge victorious—and that will provoke a revolution among defeated nations, which may spread in the ranks of the victorious; or—as is almost certain—the victory will be with the democratic nations and in this event all the Fascist regimes will be overthrown and the suppressed masses will conquer their lost liberty and something more. (It is inconceivable, for instance, that the German and Italian workers, once master again of their destiny, will limit themselves to the conquest of political freedom, instead of making a social revolution.)

Another aspect of Fascism is the large participation of the middle classes. The 12 millions who voted for Hitler cannot be called capitalist and cannot be disposed of easily as unconscious and ignorant masses.

It is true that in Italy and still more in Germany, Fascism started as a middle-class movement. It is true that it introduced itself (especially in Italy) with a quasi-socialist program. But a political movement, so rich in demagogic elements, cannot be judged by its program and promises. Those are the necessary catch-words to attract the most easily deceivable of all classes: the petty bourgeoisie, which never, in any country and in any period of history, has been capable of taking and keeping power alone. This poor middle class finds in Fascism an illusion of power and a promise of well-being, and follows it about blindly without even noticing that it becomes a tool in the hands of high finance and big industry in their game for the defeat of the workers. When the game is won, the middle class pay the cost together with the workers, and sometimes more than they. Then comes disillusion but usually it is too late to regret and amend the error. In Italy this has already happened. The middle class, ruined by the economic policy of Fascism, is spiritually in revolt against the monster that it helped so efficiently to snatch power. But spiritual revolt is of little use against men armed with guns and ready to use them pitilessly.

An important factor is the particular political moment and its psychological effect over a large part of the nation. In Italy, it was the abuses of general strikes in 1919–1920 and the revolutionary fever which exhausted itself without ever crystallizing in a concrete act which engendered a mad fear in the property classes and a sense of deluded expectancy and irritation in the middle classes, which contributed powerfully to create the political atmosphere that made possible the Mussolinian adventure. In Germany, the injustices of the Treaty of Versailles, the humiliation of the occupation of the left bank of the Rhine by colonial troops, and the occupation of the Ruhr four years after the end of the war helped not a little the Nazi movement which announced itself, among other things, as an avenger of the national honor.

Another element, the most faithful of all, typical of the old European society, which is always ready to rally to any reactionary movement and therefore has been a strong supporter of Fascism, is the military caste— a social group which is above any economic class and forms a world by itself. The military look instinctively with dismay at any democratic progress and especially at the march of the proletarian toward power. They know that labor and democracy are the natural enemy not only of war but of professional militarism. They like Fascism for its authoritarian spirit and for the prestige it gives to their caste. The military hierarchy is among the diversified forces that supported Fascism from the start, the only one which did not suffer any disillusionment. They got increased pay—while wages and salaries were enormously cut—and are extolled and flattered by the dictator as the flower and the columns of society.

As regards the big industrialists and rich landlords, even they are not well satisfied with the turn of affairs in Italy . . . The Fascist regime, initiated as a class dictatorship has, as it was fated to do, degenerated into an oligarchy and, worse, into personal tyranny. Mussolini has been quick in changing his position of hired gunman at the service of the Confederation of Industry, into that of boss. The onetime most powerful man in Italian industry, Commander Gualino, the Italian Henry Ford, a few years ago was deported without trial to one of the famous or infamous islands where many Socialists, Communists and Liberals are suffering. His crime: a show of independence in the face of Mussolini's power.

Fascism in Italy now takes towards capitalism the position of certain gangsters, hired by some American manufacturers for strike-breaking purposes, of whom they cannot rid themselves and who blackmail them without mercy. So, after all, Fascism has been no solution for the evils with which Italian capitalism was afflicted—and will not be for its German confrère.

In conclusion, we can say of Fascism: It is a reactionary movement camouflaged with socialistic coloration; formed principally and initially by elements of the middle class, but vigorously supported by capitalists, the military caste and all privileged groups; colored by political and sentimental contingencies. It begins when in control of the government as a class dictatorship supported by a large part of the population, although not by a majority; it transforms itself rapidly into a restricted oligarchy and then into a personal tyranny which may rule against the will and interests of all classes.

. . .

What has been said above belies the theory according to which Fascism is the last stand of capitalism, a kind of heroic remedy adopted when any other means prove to be inefficient to prevent its downfall.

The most natural political form of capitalism is liberalism. That does not mean that the capitalists are fond of liberal institutions and really love democratic regimes. Capitalists as individuals may have very reactionary inclinations, but the economic system to whose fortunes they are bound requires a regime of political democracy as the unavoidable conditions for its prosperous development. It is one of the many contradictions of the system. Capitalism in order to expand itself and increase its potentiality needs freedom of enterprise, of commerce, of individual initiative. It needs the right to move goods, men, labor freely, internally and internationally. It needs a base of security guaranteed by law. It must know in advance the amount of taxes to be paid and must have control in the expenditure of the money collected by the government through taxation. All that is a negation of personal despotic government. The "L'état c'est moi" of Louis XIV is inconsistent with a modern industrial organization. No vote, no tax—was the first battle-cry of capitalism in its cradle. The representative régime, with its constitutions and charters and bills of rights, was the natural outcome of that cry. It is not chance that England, the mother of modern capitalism, is also the mother of constitutionalism and parliamentary institutions. Of course, the bourgeoisie, in its struggle for freedom against the feudal caste and royalty, had in mind its particular freedom, that is, conquest of power for the protection of its own interests. But there are principles which have such universality of value, that once established they penetrate deeper than could have been foreseen by those who proclaimed them. The principle of representative government and personal rights, fostered by the pioneers of modern capitalists, became the aspiration of the working class which, in a century of struggle, succeeded in enlarging the base of democracy to include the proletarians. The first legislative bodies of America and Europe, elected nominally by the people, were at their beginning the true representative of those who possessed enough to pay direct tax. Universal suffrage is a relatively recent thing.

Once the machine of democratic government was set in motion it was almost impossible to stop it or to slow it, or, worse, to turn backward. Representative government, if it is not to be a mockery, presupposes public control, that is freedom of the press, of speech, of public meeting and organization. You cannot attack one of these freedoms without endangering the whole fabric. *Tout se tient*—all is linked—say the French.

Fascism, destroying public liberties and personal rights, under the false pretense of exalting the State, the new divinity to which all individual aspiration must be sacrificed, attacks the very roots of the political system under which in every country capitalism had an opportunity to develop.

Thus we can understand why these countries—e.g., England, France, Belgium, Holland, and the Scandinavian nations—where capitalism is vigorously developed and possesses a longer experience and a broader political wisdom, have almost no trace of Fascism and stick to democracy, although Socialism is so strong that it can be considered more than a menace.

Instead, it was in countries—like Italy, Hungary, Bulgaria, Yugoslavia, Poland—where modern industry is taking its first uncertain steps that Fascism exploded in all its fury. There is Germany, true, which seems to be an exception. But, besides the spiritual contagion—which must be taken into account in examining social phenomena—and the peculiar conditions brought to Germany by the lost war—the German experience is not yet concluded, and it is my humble opinion that, in spite of all the external and formal similarities, the Nazi movement differs fundamentally from the Italian Fascism. It embodies so many diversified elements that it will be very difficult to keep them united for very long, and it will meet such resistance (natural in a highly industrialized country, but almost impossible in an agricultural one) that all hopes for the cause of liberty in Germany are not yet lost.

M. David Gould, "What Can We Expect from Hitler? An Estimate of the Probable Economic Policies of Fascist Germany," *Barron's*, March 27, 1933

This piece appeared in Barron's, *a journal of the financial elite in the United States, less than two months after Hitler was named chancellor. Its crisp and surprisingly frank class analysis of fascism is not terribly distant from the kind of interpretation one might find in the left-wing press. Its prediction that Hitler would abandon his economic populism due to the pressures of global capital proved to be prescient, though the war would force Nazi Germany back into a kind of autarchy. Gould's analysis also illustrates how a focus on the class dynamics of fascism was not limited to the Marxist left but was widely shared across the public sphere in the 1930s, a decade when socialist and labor movements made class issues the most salient frames of the day.*

The Middle versus Two Extremes

This régime, whether we call it Hitlerism to emphasize its national German peculiarities, or Fascism to emphasize its resemblance to similar movements in other countries, and notably in Italy, is essentially this: the mobilization of the middle classes, of those who have or think they have a small stake in the existing order—the small business man, the professional man, the small farmer—behind big business and big (in Germany feudal) agriculture for the defense of the existing order against a threatened attack by those who have no stake in the existing order. This is necessary and even

possible only under conditions of extreme social pressure, when a political and economic crisis reaches such proportions that the existing system
cannot afford the ordinary concessions possible under a democratic form
of government—the rights of political expression, free speech, free assembly, trade unions, strikes, etc., while at the same time the working classes
are driven to press forward more and more sharply their economic and
political claims. The growing pressure of the crisis squeezes at democratic
institutions from both ends, forcing out the democratic, moderate,
reformistic groups in the middle, putting on the order of the day the question "Who shall be master of the household?" and compelling the re-establishment of the equilibrium through one extreme solution or the other,
through Fascism or Communism.

. . .

[From 1923] until 1929 the policy of supporting the moderate middle
against both extremes through stabilizing the economic situation by
borrowing was effective. With the outbreak of the world crisis, however,
the complete cessation of foreign support, the artificial and temporary
stabilization, broke down, and power began to flow to the extremes
again, deserting the middle. Both Fascism and Communism gained
heavily in the elections of 1930, at the expense of the Social Democrats
(representing the conservative element of labor) and the miscellaneous
republican and democratic moderate parties representing the middle
classes, respectively. Successive governments, moving ever further to
the right, expressed the increasing sharpness of the crisis and the
increasing inability of democratic institutions to sustain existing order
under the terrific tensions. Hitlerism represents the final collapse of
these institutions under strain.

. . .

Hitler Must Crush All Opposition

. . .

In less than two months Hitler has driven further ahead than
Mussolini did in two years. He has gone far toward suppressing both the
Communist and the Socialist working-class parties, along with their
press and their auxiliary organizations; his followers have seized local
branches of the central trade-union organizations, and it is clear that he
cannot stop until he has eliminated every possible nucleus for an

opposition to his policies, whether in the trade union or in the political field. Under the pressure of the crisis in Germany there is no margin left for any concessions; more than that, the final disruption of the opposition (assuming the continued absence of a unified mass counterattack), will mean a further reduction in wages and living standards, once the possibility of strikes is eliminated as in Italy.

In the domestic field, then, we can look toward an intensification of the trend toward reduction of production costs through reduction of wages. This renders unlikely a policy of inflation in the banking field. It was precisely the difficulty of carrying through successfully a direct reduction in wages during the stormy period of 1919–23 that led to the continuation of inflation as an invisible but effective form of wage cutting. The other major result of the inflation spree, the concentration of ownership in the hands of a small group of large capitalists through the impoverishment of large sections of the middle classes, also does not require inflation under present conditions in Germany with the power firmly established in the hands of the ruling group backed up solidly by the middle classes and with all effective working-class opposition being rapidly eliminated.

May Seek World Trade

There is more reason than ever to believe that some reduction in the stated payments on German loans will be pending within the next few months. There is another possibility, of course—a redoubled raid by Germany on the world export markets, based on the still-lower costs of production made possible by the lower wages which can be expected to follow the complete consolidation of the Hitler régime.

Exit the Spirit of Nationalism

True enough, this would contradict the program of "economic self-sufficiency" which was one of the bases of Hitler's propaganda before he came into power. This, however, seems one of the features of the Hitler program which seems most likely to go into the discard at an early date, along with the slogans of "break the slavery of interest" and "nationalization of big capital." To certain limited extent, "autarchy" serves a useful purpose to the feudal agricultural section of the present dominant bloc, because it has enabled it to exert pressure for higher tariffs on foodstuffs, and, by effectively reducing imports, has decreased the dependence of Germany on the outside world for products already grown in part in Germany. The German internal price of wheat, for instance, is two and a half to three times the world market price.

. . .

Industry May Balk at Nationalism

German industry is unlikely to consent to a further deliberate amputation of its possibilities of growth through a voluntary acceptance of the idea of national self-sufficiency. On the contrary, it is far more probable that it will make the fullest use of the powerful strategic position which it occupies under Hitlerism to assert its claims for a "place in the sun," continuing the Hohenzollern policy.[1] Without effective resistance from other elements of the population within Germany, with a strong trend toward the re-establishment of militarism and toward the revision of the Versailles Treaty, which means restoration of colonies and the right to re-arm, it is more than probable that German industry will bend every effort to solve its crisis through the expansion of foreign markets.

For it seems unlikely that further reductions of wages alone will suffice to bring Germany out of the crisis. They will undoubtedly increase the margin of profit, thus tending to stimulate business activity, but will at the same time aggravate the question of finding a market for the enormous potential production of the country.

. . .

A Gamble

Yet Hitlerism is essentially a gambling régime. The long efforts of the major economic interests in industry and agriculture to avoid putting Hitler into power, the effort to come through the crisis with the aid of

---

1   The "Hohenzollern policy" is a reference to the imperialist policy of Wilhelmine Germany (1890–1918). It was guided by Foreign Minister Bernhard von Bülow's notion that Germany deserved "a place in the sun" alongside other colonial powers.

Socialists, Centrists, even of the small but compact Nationalist Party which is the most direct representative in Germany of concentrated capital—all these indicate the fear and distrust which these classes felt toward such a movement as Hitler's, composed of heterogenous and, in part, unstable elements, led on by a violent demagogy which at times made use of anti-capitalist phraseology, certain to be costly and involving the risk of civil war and possibly complications abroad. Hitler was called in only as a desperate last resource.

If Hitlerism proves unable to solve its problems within Germany, there will be a strong temptation for it to tempt fortune abroad—in relatively peaceful forms through a struggle for foreign markets, possibly even through direct force of arms to recapture a colonial empire or to reduce the Soviet Union to submission, presumably not without the support of other powers. The violent antagonism between the two systems, the desperate need of a way out for Germany, the existence of well-trained forces in Germany running into the hundreds of thousands—all combine to render such a hypothesis far from fantastic, irrespective of the immediate developments of the day's news.

Harry Ward, "Fascism and Race Hate," *Fight*, July 1934

Harry Ward (1873–1966) was a British-born Methodist minister who was chairman of the American League against War and Fascism for most of its existence, from 1934 to 1939 (its name changed to the American League for Peace and Democracy in 1937). Before entering the league, he had played a major role in defining the politics of the Social Gospel movement and was the main author of the Social Creed of the Churches *(1908), a document that defined the domestic politics of the Federal Council of Churches for a generation. He was never a member of the Communist Party USA, but he visited the Soviet Union multiple times, returning from a 1932 visit as a true believer in the Soviet model. His presence and his efforts got a significant number of churches to affiliate with the American League.*

The following piece appeared in Fight, *the magazine of the American League. Contrary to many postwar assessments, the 1930s left quite often discussed the racial politics of fascism, and the pages of* Fight, *in particular, hammered on this theme consistently. The reader will have to decide whether or not the model Ward offers us for reading the relationship between race and class is a successful one, yet the historical significance of these artifacts of 1930s antifascism is their very attempt to map such intersections.*

Fascism is not always anti-Semitic. But always its inflated nationalism is joined with race pride. Mussolini rhapsodizes over the virtues and glorious future of the Italian people. Hitler enters the lists against him, proclaiming in more unctuous tones the superiority of German blood and German character, bolstering his claim by an absurd myth concerning the Aryan race. Wherever the conditioning circumstances are favorable, this egoistic race pride necessarily excites race prejudice and then fans that prejudice into race hate.

Old Order at Work

In its broadest aspect Fascism is the convulsive movement of an old order and its rulers in opposition to the coming of a new day. In its efforts to halt the future, it reaches back into the past and uses as weapons those blind, evil forces which have so long held back the development of humanity—absolutism, militarism, nationalism and race hate. The oldest of these evil spirits, born in the earliest days of tribal history but still terrible in its destructive power, is racial antagonism—the instinctive fear of the outlander, the man from another place, of another blood. Today, after all the centuries of human acquaintance, when this fear is excited by economic competition or lashed into fury by the threat of an oppressed class rising to power, it drives supposedly civilized men into deeds that are bestial. Both these conditions occasioned the hate and persecution of the Jews in Germany. Some of them were successful capitalists and some were ardent Communists, and some were neither. These contradictory facts clearly destroy racial responsibility, but as the old proverb has it, any stick will do to beat a dog with. Also, exciting crowds to beat innocent victims is an old device of the rulers to distract attention from their own misdeeds and failures.

In this country anti-Semitism will not go so far nor become so violent except in certain local situations. Here another victim has been historically prepared for the slaughter of a Fascist regime. The Negro has borne the brunt of our pogroms, and will again. It is true that our incipient economic Fascism is being accompanied by a whispering campaign against the Jews. It is mean and vicious, and as conditions grow worse it will gain headway in certain centers, but here the Jew will not be the main object of Fascist terrorism. This country is too big and too cosmopolitan for that; also the Jew has become too much a part of it. The real hate in this country is being expressed against and reserved for "the

dirty reds," the "outside agitators" who are leading the suffering unemployed, the protesting farmers, and the underpaid, company-union,
cheated workers. Some Jews will feel this hate and some will express it.
It will be used to incite a feeling against the race, but it is not in the
record that Jewish bankers in Germany or even Jewish department
storekeepers suffered as much as Jewish Communists.

The Target

It is the Negro who is getting and will get the full force of the race hate
with which the Fascist reaction incites the perpetrators of its outrages.
Jim-Crowed and lynched, segregated and shut out of most of the trade
unions, this victim of the white man's greed, pride and ignorance is now
to be feared as economic competitor and as rebel determined to get his
rights. The increase in the number of lynchings during the past year, the
beating and killing of Negroes by white men who wanted their jobs,
the Scottsboro and Herndon cases,[1] are all evidence of the impact of the
class struggle upon the racial conflict. The crossing of the color line by
the workers in united action at the bottom of society necessarily
increases race fear and hate at the top. In those sections of the South
where a Negro can be killed for any reason or no reason at all, and his
death go unreported or unnoticed by the law, what may we expect when
white and black workers together present a real threat to the power of
the dominant class! Its answer will be a terror beyond all restraint. This
will be the climax of Fascist brutality in the American scene.

---

1   The trials of Angelo Herndon and of the so-called "Scottsboro Boys" were major
rallying points for civil rights and labor activists during the 1930s. The Scottsboro
defendants were nine black teenagers accused of raping two white women in a train car
near Scottsboro, Alabama. Herndon, a black communist organizer, was arrested for
"insurrection" in Atlanta after leading a successful march of unemployed blacks and
whites to demand unemployment relief. Herndon and the Scottsboro youths were
defended by the International Labor Defense, an arm of the Communist Party USA,
which campaigned to ensure that the trials received international attention. All were
eventually acquitted of the original charges.

Unite against the Common Enemy

To avert this disgrace from the human record it is necessary for all the sufferers from race prejudice and all who have emancipated themselves from this evil spirit to unite their forces in time. None can save themselves except as they work to save all. Jew and Gentile, white and black, men and women of all colors and creeds must unite now—before it is too late—against the common enemy. The foe we have to fight is the Fascist state as the organized power of the capitalist economy. Against it we struggle with all our forces, not for ourselves but for the future of humanity, for a human society where all races can live, and build, and grow together.

Sinclair Lewis, from *It Can't Happen Here,* 1935

Sinclair Lewis's It Can't Happen Here *is a novel more often evoked than actually read. Since its publication in 1935, Americans have ironically used the phrase "it can't happen here" to call into question the presumed foreignness of fascism. Indeed, the book can be considered the literary urtext of US antifascism. It describes the transformation of the country under the regime of Berzelius "Buzz" Windrip, a politician who defeats Roosevelt in the 1936 election, quickly bans all political parties other than his own "American Corporate State and Patriotic Party," and then creates a police state complete with concentration camps for Jews and leftists. Its protagonist is Doremus Jessup, a small-town, liberal Vermont newspaper publisher who eventually becomes an enemy of the state.*

Sinclair Lewis (1885–1951) joined the Socialist Party in 1911 after graduating from Yale University. Though he quit paying dues within a year, he retained the general democratic socialist orientation of the SP for the rest of his days. His analysis of fascism was heavily informed by his second wife, Dorothy Thompson, a newspaper columnist who traveled extensively in Nazi Germany and spoke fluent German. Lewis won the Nobel Prize in Literature in 1930, yet he hastily wrote It Can't Happen Here *in only two months and did not regard it as his best work. Whatever its literary merits, its topicality quickly placed it on the bestseller list. Most reviewers did not see it as a particularly well-crafted novel, but they praised its analysis of fascism and lauded its relevance to American life. Despite its critical treatment of communists, even the communist press touted Lewis's chilling novel. It was adapted to the stage in 1936 through a grant from the New Deal's Federal Theatre Project, and met with both critical and commercial success as a play. Produced in English, Yiddish, and Spanish, the FTP production ran for 260 weeks (a five-year run) and was viewed by hundreds of thousands of people, many of whom had never been to the theater in their lives.*

Two chapters are excerpted here: The first, Chapter 9, describes the rhetoric and persona of Buzz Windrip when he is still a political candidate and not yet the head of a fascist state. The second excerpt, from Chapter 12, describes the cultural and political forms of his followers—the "Minute Men"—before their movement assumes state power. Lewis begins each chapter with an excerpt from Zero Hour, *Windrip's vapid autobiography.*

Chapter 9

Those who have never been on the inside in the Councils of State can never realize that with really high-class Statesmen, their chief quality is not political canniness, but a big, rich, overflowing Love for all sorts and conditions of people and for the whole land. That Love and that Patriotism have been my sole guiding principles in Politics. My one ambition is to get all Americans to realize that they are, and must continue to be, the greatest Race on the face of this old Earth, and second, to realize that whatever apparent Differences there may be among us, in wealth, knowledge, skill, ancestry or strength—though, of course, all this does not apply to people who are *racially* different from us—we are all brothers, bound together in the great and wonderful bond of National Unity, for which we should all be very glad. And I think we ought to for this be willing to sacrifice any individual gains at all.

—*Zero Hour*, Berzelius Windrip

Berzelius Windrip, of whom in late summer and early autumn of 1936 there were so many published photographs—showing him popping into cars and out of airplanes, dedicating bridges, eating corn pone and side-meat with Southerners and clam chowder and bran with Northerners, addressing the American Legion, the Liberty League, the YMHA, the Young People's Socialist League, the Elks, the Bartenders' and Waiters' Union, the Anti-Saloon League, the Society for the Propagation of the

Gospel in Afghanistan—showing him kissing lady centenarians and shaking hands with ladies called Madame, but never the opposite—showing him in Savile Row riding-clothes on Long Island and in overalls and a khaki shirt in the Ozarks—this Buzz Windrip was almost a dwarf, yet with an enormous head, a bloodhound head, of huge ears, pendulous cheeks, mournful eyes. He had a luminous, ungrudging smile which (declared the Washington correspondents) he turned on and off deliberately, like an electric light, but which could make his ugliness more attractive than the simpers of any pretty man.

His hair was so coarse and black and straight, and worn so long in the back, that it hinted of Indian blood. In the Senate he preferred clothes that suggested the competent insurance salesman, but when farmer constituents were in Washington he appeared in an historic ten-gallon hat with a mussy gray "cutaway" which somehow you erroneously remembered as a black "Prince Albert."

In that costume, he looked like a sawed-off museum model of a medicine-show "doctor," and indeed it was rumored that during one law-school vacation Buzz Windrip had played the banjo and done card tricks and handed down medicine bottles and managed the shell game for no less scientific an expedition than Old Dr. Alagash's Traveling Laboratory, which specialized in the Choctaw Cancer Cure, the Chinook Consumption Soother, and the Oriental Remedy for Piles and Rheumatism Prepared from a World-old Secret Formula by the Gipsy Princess, Queen Peshawara.[1] The company, ardently assisted by Buzz, killed off quite a number of persons who, but for their confidence in Dr. Alagash's bottles of water, coloring matter, tobacco juice, and raw corn whisky, might have gone early enough to doctors. But since then, Windrip had redeemed himself, no doubt, by ascending from the vulgar fraud of selling bogus medicine, standing in front of a megaphone, to the dignity of selling bogus economics, standing on an indoor platform under mercury-vapor lights in front of a microphone.

He was in stature but a small man, yet remember that so were Napoleon, Lord Beaverbrook, Stephen A. Douglas, Frederick the Great,

---

1   Travelling medicine shows were common forms of entertainment in rural America in the second half of the twentieth century. Their performers peddled generally fraudulent remedies in the wild days before Food and Drug Act (1906) and were generally understood to be scam artists who prayed on gullible or desperate rural people.

and the Dr. Goebbels who is privily known throughout Germany as "Wotan's Mickey Mouse."

Doremus Jessup, so inconspicuous an observer, watching Senator Windrip from so humble a Boeotia, could not explain his power of bewitching large audiences. The Senator was vulgar, almost illiterate, a public liar easily detected, and in his "ideas" almost idiotic, while his celebrated piety was that of a traveling salesman for church furniture, and his yet more celebrated humor the sly cynicism of a country store.

Certainly there was nothing exhilarating in the actual words of his speeches, nor anything convincing in his philosophy. His political platforms were only wings of a windmill. Seven years before his present credo—derived from Lee Sarason, Hitler, Gottfried Feder, Rocco, and probably the revue *Of Thee I Sing*—little Buzz, back home, had advocated nothing more revolutionary than better beef stew in the county poor farms, and plenty of graft for loyal machine politicians, with jobs for their brothers-in-law, nephews, law partners, and creditors.

Doremus had never heard Windrip during one of his orgasms of oratory, but he had been told by political reporters that under the spell you thought Windrip was Plato, but that on the way home you could not remember anything he had said.

There were two things, they told Doremus, that distinguished this prairie Demosthenes. He was an actor of genius. There was no more overwhelming actor on the stage, in the motion pictures, nor even in the pulpit. He would whirl arms, bang tables, glare from mad eyes, vomit Biblical wrath from a gaping mouth; but he would also coo like a nursing mother, beseech like an aching lover, and in between tricks would coldly and almost contemptuously jab his crowds with figures and facts—figures and facts that were inescapable even when, as often happened, they were entirely incorrect.

But below this surface stagecraft was his uncommon natural ability to be authentically excited by and with his audience, and they by and with him. He could dramatize his assertion that he was neither a Nazi nor a Fascist but a Democrat—a homespun Jeffersonian-Lincolnian-Clevelandian-Wilsonian Democrat—and (sans scenery and costume) make you see him veritably defending the Capitol against barbarian hordes, the while he innocently presented as his own warm-hearted Democratic inventions, every anti-libertarian, anti-Semitic madness of Europe.

Aside from his dramatic glory, Buzz Windrip was a Professional Common Man.

Oh, he was common enough. He had every prejudice and aspiration of every American Common Man. He believed in the desirability and therefore the sanctity of thick buckwheat cakes with adulterated maple syrup, in rubber trays for the ice cubes in his electric refrigerator, in the especial nobility of dogs, all dogs, in the oracles of S. Parkes Cadman, in being chummy with all waitresses at all junction lunch rooms, and in Henry Ford (when he became president, he exulted, maybe he could get Mr. Ford to come to supper at the White House), and the superiority of anyone who possessed a million dollars. He regarded spats, walking sticks, caviar, titles, tea-drinking, poetry not daily syndicated in news-papers and all foreigners, possibly excepting the British, as degenerate.

But he was the Common Man twenty-times-magnified by his oratory, so that while the other Commoners could understand his every purpose, which was exactly the same as their own, they saw him towering among them, and they raised hands to him in worship.

. . .

Chapter 12

I shall not be content till this country can produce every single thing we need, even coffee, cocoa, and rubber, and so keep all our dollars at home. If we can do this and at the same time work up tourist traffic so that foreigners will come from every part of the world to see such remarkable wonders as the Grand Canyon, Glacier and Yellowstone etc. parks, the fine hotels of Chicago, & etc., thus leaving their money here, we shall have such a balance of trade as will go far to carry out my often-criticized yet completely sound idea of from $3,000 to $5,000 per year for every single family—that is, I mean every real American family. Such an aspiring Vision is what we want, and not all this nonsense of wasting our time at Geneva and talky-talk at Lugano, wherever that is.

—*Zero Hour*, Berzelius Windrip

Election day would fall on Tuesday, November 3, and on Sunday even-ing of the first, Senator Windrip played the finale of his campaign at a mass meeting in Madison Square Garden, in New York. The Garden would hold, with seats and standing room, about 19,000, and a week before the meeting every ticket had been sold—at from fifty cents to five dollars, and then by speculators resold and resold, at from one dollar to twenty.

Doremus had been able to get one single ticket from an acquaintance on one of the Hearst dailies—which, alone among the New York papers, were supporting Windrip—and on the afternoon of November 1 he traveled the 300 miles to New York for his first visit in three years.

It had been cold in Vermont, with early snow, but the white drifts lay to the earth so quietly, in unstained air, that the world seemed a silver-painted carnival, left to silence. Even on a moonless night, a pale radiance came from the snow, from the earth itself, and the stars were drops of quicksilver.

But, following the redcap carrying his shabby Gladstone bag, Doremus came out of the Grand Central, at six o'clock, into a gray trickle of cold dishwater from heaven's kitchen sink. The renowned towers which he expected to see on Forty-Second Street were dead in their mummy cloths of ragged fog. And as to the mob that, with cruel disinterest, galloped past him, a new and heedless smear of faces every second, the man from Fort Beulah [Vermont] could think only that New York must be holding its county fair in this clammy drizzle, or else that there was a big fire somewhere.

He painfully hesitated before going out again from his small hotel in the West Forties, and when he did, when he muddily crept among the shrill shopgirls, the weary chorus girls, the hard cigar-clamping gamblers, and the pretty young men on Broadway, he felt himself, with the rubbers and umbrella which Emma had forced upon him, a very Caspar Milquetoast.

He most noticed a number of stray imitation soldiers, without side-arms or rifles, but in a uniform like that of an American cavalryman in 1870: slant-topped blue forage caps, dark blue tunics, light blue trousers, with yellow stripes at the seam, tucked into leggings of black rubberoid for what appeared to be the privates, and boots of sleek black leather for officers. Each of them had on the right side of his collar the letters "MM" and on the left, a five-pointed star. There were so many of them; they swaggered so brazenly, shouldering civilians out of the way; and upon insignificances like Doremus they looked with frigid insolence.

He suddenly understood.

These young condottieri were the "Minute Men": the private troops of Berzelius Windrip, about which Doremus had been publishing uneasy news reports. He was thrilled and a little dismayed to see them now—the printed words made brutal flesh.

Three weeks ago Windrip had announced that Colonel Dewey Haik had founded, just for the campaign, a nationwide league of Windrip marching-clubs, to be called the Minute Men. It was probable that they had been in formation for months, since already they had three or four hundred thousand members. Doremus was afraid the MMs might become a permanent organization, more menacing than the Ku Klux Klan.

Their uniform suggested the pioneer America of Cold Harbor and of the Indian fighters under Miles and Custer. Their emblem, their swastika (here Doremus saw the cunning and mysticism of Lee Sarason), was a five-pointed star, because the star on the American flag was five-pointed, whereas the stars of both the Soviet banner and the Jews—the Seal of Solomon—were six pointed.

The fact that the Soviet star, actually, was also five-pointed, no one noticed, during these excited days of regeneration. Anyway, it was a nice idea to have this star simultaneously challenge the Jews and the Bolsheviks—the MMs had good intentions, even if their symbolism did slip a little.

Yet the craftiest thing about the MMs was that they wore no colored shirts, but only plain white when on parade, and light khaki when on outpost duty, so that Buzz Windrip could thunder, and frequently, "Black shirts? Brown shirts? Red shirts? Yes, and maybe cow-brindle shirts! All these degenerate European uniforms of tyranny! No sir! The Minute Men are not Fascist or Communist or anything at all but plain Democratic—the knight-champions of the rights of the Forgotten Men—the shock troops of Freedom!"

Doremus dined on Chinese food, his invariable self-indulgence when he was in a large city without Emma, who stated that chow mein was nothing but fried excelsior with flour-paste gravy. He forgot the leering MM troopers a little; he was happy in glancing at the gilded wood carvings, at the octagonal lanterns painted with doll-like Chinese peasants crossing arched bridges, at a quartette of guests, two male and two female, who looked like Public Enemies and who all through dinner quarreled with restrained viciousness.

When he headed toward Madison Square Garden and the culminating Windrip rally, he was plunged into a maelstrom. A whole nation seemed querulously to be headed the same way. He could not get a taxicab, and walking through the dreary storm some fourteen blocks to Madison Square Garden he was aware of the murderous temper of the crowd.

Eighth Avenue, lined with cheapjack shops, was packed with drab, discouraged people who yet, tonight, were tipsy with the hashish of hope. They filled the sidewalks, nearly filled the pavement, while irritable motors squeezed tediously through them, and angry policemen were pushed and whirled about and, if they tried to be haughty, got jeered at by lively shopgirls.

Through the welter, before Doremus's eyes, jabbed a flying wedge of Minute Men, led by what he was later to recognize as a cornet of MMs. They were not on duty, and they were not belligerent; they were cheering, and singing "Berzelius Windrip went to Washington," reminding Doremus of a slightly drunken knot of students from an inferior college after a football victory. He was to remember them so afterward, months afterward, when the enemies of the MMs all through the country derisively called them "Mickey Mouses" and "Minnies."

An old man, shabbily neat, stood blocking them and yelled, "To hell with Buzz! Three cheers for FDR!"

The MMs burst into hoodlum wrath. The cornet in command, a bruiser uglier even than Shad Ledue, hit the old man on the jaw, and he sloped down, sickeningly. Then, from nowhere, facing the cornet, there was a chief petty officer of the navy, big, smiling, reckless. The CPO bellowed, in a voice tuned to hurricanes, "Swell bunch o' tin soldiers! Nine o' yuh to one grandpappy! Just about even—"

The cornet socked him; he laid out the cornet with one foul to the belly; instantly the other eight MMs were on the CPO, like sparrows after a hawk, and he crashed, his face, suddenly veal-white, laced with rivulets of blood. The eight kicked him in the head with their thick marching-shoes. They were still kicking him when Doremus wriggled away, very sick, altogether helpless.

He had not turned away quickly enough to avoid seeing an MM trooper, girlish-faced, crimson-lipped, fawn-eyed, throw himself on the fallen cornet and, whimpering, stroke that roustabout's roast-beef cheeks with shy gardenia-petal fingers.

There were many arguments, a few private fist fights, and one more battle, before Doremus reached the auditorium.

A block from it some thirty MMs, headed by a battalion leader—something between a captain and a major—started raiding a street meeting of Communists. A Jewish girl in khaki, her bare head soaked with rain, was beseeching from the elevation of a wheelbarrow, "Fellow travelers! Don't just chew the rag and 'sympathize'! Join us! Now! It's life and death!" Twenty feet from the Communists, a middle-aged man who looked like a social worker was explaining the Jeffersonian Party, recalling the record of President Roosevelt, and reviling the Communists next door as word-drunk un-American cranks. Half his audience were people who might be competent voters; half of them—like half of any group on this evening of tragic fiesta—were cigarette-sniping boys in hand-me-downs.

The thirty MMs cheerfully smashed into the Communists. The battalion leader reached up, slapped the girl speaker, dragged her down from the wheelbarrow. His followers casually waded in with fists and blackjacks. Doremus, more nauseated, feeling more helpless than ever, heard the smack of a blackjack on the temple of a scrawny Jewish intellectual.

Amazingly, then, the voice of the rival Jeffersonian leader spiraled up into a scream: "Come on, *you*! Going to let those hellhounds attack our Communist friends—friends *now*, by God!" With which the mild bookworm leaped into the air, came down squarely upon a fat Mickey Mouse, capsized him, seized his blackjack, took time to kick another MM's shins before arising from the wreck, sprang up, and waded into the raiders as, Doremus guessed, he would have waded into a table of statistics on the proportion of butter fat in loose milk in 97.7 percent of shops on Avenue B.

Till then, only half a dozen Communist Party members had been facing the MMs, their backs to a garage wall. Fifty of their own, fifty Jeffersonians besides, now joined them, and with bricks and umbrellas and deadly volumes of sociology they drove off the enraged MMs—partisans of Béla Kun side by side with the partisans of Professor John Dewey—until a riot squad of policemen battered their way in to protect the MMs by arresting the girl Communist speaker and the Jeffersonian.

Doremus had often "headed up" sports stories about "Madison Square Garden Prize Fights," but he did know that the place had nothing to do with Madison Square, from which it was a day's journey by bus, that it was decidedly not a garden, that the fighters there did not fight for "prizes" but for fixed partnership shares in the business, and that a good many of them did not fight at all.

The mammoth building, as in exhaustion Doremus crawled up to it, was entirely ringed with MMs, elbow to elbow, all carrying heavy canes, and at every entrance, along every aisle, the MMs were rigidly in line, with their officers galloping about, whispering orders, and bearing uneasy rumors like scared calves in a dipping pen.

These past weeks hungry miners, dispossessed farmers, Carolina mill hands had greeted Senator Windrip with a flutter of worn hands beneath gasoline torches. Now he was to face, not the unemployed, for they could not afford fifty-cent tickets, but the small, scared side-street traders of New York, who considered themselves altogether superior to clodhoppers and mine-creepers, yet were as desperate as they. The swelling mass that Doremus saw, proud in seats or standing chin to nape in the aisles, in a reek of dampened clothes, was not romantic; they were people concerned with the tailor's goose, the tray of potato salad, the card of hooks-and-eyes, the leech-like mortgage on the owner-driven taxi, with, at home, the baby's diapers, the dull safety-razor blade, the awful rise in the cost of rump steak and kosher chicken. And a few, and very proud, civil-service clerks and letter carriers and superintendents of small apartment houses, curiously fashionable in seventeen-dollar ready-made suits and feebly stitched foulard ties, who boasted, "I don't know why all these bums go on relief. I may not be such a wiz, but let me tell you, even since 1929, I've never made less than *2,000 dollars a year!*"

Manhattan peasants. Kind people, industrious people, generous to their aged, eager to find any desperate cure for the sickness of worry over losing the job.

Most facile material for any rabble-rouser.

Georgi Dimitrov, *Working Class Unity— Bulwark against Fascism*, Speech to the Seventh World Congress of the Communist International, Moscow, August 13, 1935

The importance of this speech in the history of the global antifascist left cannot be underestimated. It is the ultimate statement of the Popular Front turn in the international communist movement and marks the Communist International's break from its "Third Period" analysis (1928– 1935). The speech was widely circulated in pamphlet form in the United States and around the world.

Its key shifts from earlier communist positions include: (a) the call for a truce between Communist and Socialist parties in favor of a nonsectarian, united front against fascism; (b) a sidelining of communist revolution and a corresponding call to defend democratic advances within the bourgeois liberal state; (c) its openness to coalitions with the middle class (fascism's political base), and, implicitly, with some capitalists; (d) its demand to take seriously the nationalist and racial politics of fascism; and finally, (e) its call to appeal to national traditions and cultural forms familiar to workers and toilers.

During the Popular Front period (1935–1939) and again during World War II, American communists took up Dimitrov's call by using icons of the American past, from Thomas Jefferson to Frederick Douglass, in order to claim the nation for their political project rather than leave this terrain to their would-be fascist rivals. The US Popular Front indeed de-emphasized revolution and instead worked toward building the labor movement and expanding civil rights and the New Deal state. In the process, it more than doubled its membership. The Popular Front turn also enabled more intersectional analyses of fascism within the communist left—ones that probed its national, racial, and psychological appeals. Some within the left have criticized the Popular Front for turning away from the anti-imperialist politics of the Third Period, and Trotskyists have condemned it as "class collaboration" ever since.

Dimitrov's definition of fascism as "the open terrorist dictatorship of the most reactionary, most chauvinistic and most imperialist elements of finance capital" enjoyed a tremendous afterlife on the Marxist left globally, and it reappeared in Black Panther writings in the late 1960s. It is important to note that this definition was more of a political move than a grounded historical analysis. Finance capitalists were not the main players in fascist coalitions, and it would be highly reductive to read fascism as a "cultural logic" of finance capitalism given the fascists' very real investments in race and militarism. Nonetheless, Dimitrov's definition opened the door to a coalition with liberals and reformers who were more comfortable with a fight against the hard right and some capitalists than they were with a struggle against capitalism in general.

Georgi Dimitrov (1882–1949) was a Bulgarian communist and major figure within the Communist International. He earned world renown as a defendant in the Reichstag Fire Trials, mainly for his bold statements against his Nazi accusers in their own court in Leipzig.

Fascism and the Working Class

Comrades, as early as its Sixth Congress, the Communist International warned the world proletariat that a new fascist offensive was impending, and called for a struggle against it. The Congress pointed out that "in a more or less developed form, fascist tendencies and the germs of a fascist movement are to be found almost everywhere."

With the outbreak of the present, most profound, economic crisis, the sharp accentuation of the general crisis of capitalism and the revolutionization of the toiling masses, fascism has embarked upon a wide offensive. The ruling bourgeoisie is more and more seeking salvation in fascism, with the object of instituting exceptional predatory measures against the toilers, preparing for an imperialist war of plunder, attacking the Soviet Union, enslaving and partitioning China, and by all these means preventing revolution.

Imperialist circles are endeavoring to place the *whole* burden of the crisis on the backs of the toilers. *That is why they need fascism.*

They are trying to solve the problem of markets by enslaving the weak nations, by intensifying colonial oppression and repartitioning the world anew by means of war. *That is why they need fascism.*

They are striving to *forestall* the growth of the forces of revolution by smashing the revolutionary movement of the workers and peasants and by undertaking a military attack against the Soviet Union—the bulwark of the world proletariat. *That is why they need fascism.*

In a number of countries, Germany in particular, these imperialist circles have succeeded, *before* the masses have decisively turned toward revolution, in inflicting defeat on the proletariat and establishing a fascist dictatorship.

. . .

But what is characteristic of the victory of fascism is the fact that this victory, on the one hand, bears witness to the weakness of the proletariat, disorganized and paralyzed by the disruptive Social Democratic policy of class collaboration with the bourgeoisie, and, on the other, expresses the weakness of the bourgeoisie itself, afraid of the realization of a united struggle of the working class, afraid of revolution, and no longer in a position to maintain its dictatorship over the masses by the old methods of bourgeois democracy and parliamentarism.

. . .

Comrades, as was correctly described by the Thirteenth Plenum of the Executive Committee of the Communist International, fascism in power is *the open terrorist dictatorship of the most reactionary, most chauvinistic and most imperialist elements of finance capital.*

The most reactionary variety of fascism is the *German type* of fascism. It has the effrontery to call itself National Socialism, though having nothing in common with socialism. Hitler fascism is not only bourgeois nationalism, it is bestial chauvinism. It is a government system of political banditry, a system of provocation and torture practiced upon the working class and the revolutionary elements of the peasantry, the petty bourgeoisie and the intelligentsia. It is medieval barbarity and bestiality, it is unbridled aggression in relation to other nations and countries . . .

Fascism is not a form of state power "standing above both classes—the proletariat and the bourgeoisie," as Otto Bauer,[1] for instance, has asserted. It is not "the revolt of the petty bourgeoisie which has captured the machinery of the State," as the British socialist [H. N.] Brailsford declares. No, fascism is not superclass government, nor government of the petty bourgeoisie or the lumpenproletariat over finance capital. Fascism is the power of finance capital itself. It is the organization of terrorist vengeance against the working class and the revolutionary section of the peasantry and intelligentsia. In foreign policy, fascism is chauvinism in its crudest form, fomenting the bestial hatred of other nations.

The accession to power of fascism is not an *ordinary succession* of one bourgeois government by another, but a *substitution* for one state form of class domination of the bourgeoisie—bourgeois democracy—of another form—open terrorist dictatorship. It would be a serious mistake to ignore this distinction, a mistake which would prevent the revolutionary proletariat from mobilizing the broadest strata of the toilers of town and country for the struggle against the menace of the seizure of power by the fascists, and from taking advantage of the contradictions which exist in the camp of the bourgeoisie itself. But it is a mistake no less serious and dangerous to *underrate* the importance, in establishing the fascist dictatorship, of the *reactionary measures of the bourgeoisie which are at present being increasingly initiated in bourgeois-democratic countries*—measures which destroy the democratic liberties of the toilers, falsify and curtail the rights of parliament and intensify the repression of the revolutionary movement.

Comrades, the accession to power of fascism must not be conceived of in so simplified and smooth a form, as though some committee or other of finance capital decided on a certain date to set up a fascist dictatorship. In reality, fascism usually comes to power in the course of a mutual, and at times severe, struggle against the old bourgeois parties, or a definite section of these parties, in the course of a struggle even within the fascist camp itself—a struggle which at times leads to armed clashes, as we have witnessed in the case of Germany, Austria and other

---

1   Otto Bauer (1881–1938) was an Austrian Social Democrat and leading intellectual of the "Austro-Marxist" school. His piece "The Essence of Fascism" was reprinted in the American *Socialist Review* in March–April 1939, and is quite similar in its analysis to the piece by Vincenzo Vacirca reprinted in this volume.

countries. All this, however, does not detract from the fact that before
the establishment of a fascist dictatorship, bourgeois governments
usually pass through a number of preliminary stages and institute a
number of reactionary measures which directly facilitate the accession
to power of fascism. Whoever does not fight the reactionary measures
of the bourgeoisie and the growth of fascism at these preparatory stages
*is not in a position to prevent the victory of fascism, but, on the contrary,
facilitates that victory.*

What is the source of the influence enjoyed by fascism over the
masses? Fascism is able to attract the masses because it demagogically
appeals to their *most urgent needs and demands.* Fascism not only
inflames prejudices that are deeply ingrained in the masses, but also
plays on the better sentiments of the masses, on their sense of justice,
and sometimes even on their revolutionary traditions. Why do the
German fascists, those lackeys of the big bourgeoisie and mortal enemies
of socialism, represent themselves to the masses as "socialists" and
depict their accession to power as a "revolution"? Because they try to
exploit the faith in revolution, the urge toward socialism, which lives in
the hearts of the broad masses of the toilers of Germany.

Fascism acts in the interests of the extreme imperialists; but it presents
itself to the masses in the guise of champion of an ill-treated nation, and
appeals to outraged national sentiments, as German fascism did—for
instance, when it won the support of the masses by the slogan "Against
the Versailles Treaty!"

Fascism aims at the most unbridled exploitation of the masses, but it
appeals to them with the most artful anti-capitalist demagogy, taking
advantage of the profound hatred entertained by the toilers for the pirat-
ical bourgeoisie, the banks, trusts and the financial magnates, and
advancing slogans which at the given moment are most alluring to the
politically immature masses.

. . .

It stages its accession to power as a "revolutionary" movement against
the bourgeoisie on behalf of "the whole nation" and for "the salvation" of
the nation. (Let us recall Mussolini's "march" on Rome, Pilsudski's
"march" on Warsaw; Hitler's National Socialist "revolution" in Germany,
and so forth.)

But whatever the masks which fascism adopts, whatever the forms in
which it presents itself, whatever the ways by which it comes to power—

Fascism is a most ferocious attack by capital on the toiling masses;
Fascism is unbridled chauvinism and annexationist war;
Fascism is rabid reaction and counterrevolution;
Fascism is the most vicious enemy of the working class and of all the
     toilers!
. . .

The United Front of the Working Class against Fascism

Comrades, millions of workers and toilers of the capitalist countries ask the question: How can fascism be prevented from coming to power and how can fascism be overthrown after it has been victorious? To this the Communist International replies: *The first thing that must be done, the thing with which to commence is to form a united front, to establish unity of action of the workers in every factory, in every district, in every region, in every country, all over the world. Unity of action of the proletariat on a national and international scale is the mighty weapon which renders the working class capable not only of successful defense but also of successful counteroffensive against fascism, against the class enemy.*

Is it not clear that joint action by the adherents of the parties and organizations of the two Internationals, the Communist and the Second International, would facilitate the repulse by the masses of the fascist onslaught and would enhance the political importance of the working class?

Joint action by the parties of both Internationals against fascism, however, would not be confined to influencing their present adherents, the Communists and Social Democrats; it would also exert a powerful influence on the ranks of the *Catholic, anarchist and unorganized workers, even on those who had temporarily become the victims of fascist demagogy.*

Moreover, a powerful united front of the proletariat would exert tremendous influence on *all other strata of the toiling people*, on the peasantry, on the urban petty bourgeoisie, the intelligentsia. A united front would inspire the wavering groups with faith in the strength of the working class.

But even this is not all. The proletariat of the imperialist countries has possible allies not only in the toilers of its own countries but also in the *oppressed nations of the colonies and semicolonies.* Inasmuch as the proletariat is split both nationally and internationally, inasmuch as one of its parts supports the policy of collaboration with the bourgeoisie, in particular its system of oppression in the colonies and semicolonies, this alienates from the working class the oppressed peoples of the colonies and semicolonies and weakens the world anti-imperialist front. Every step on the road to unity of action, directed toward the support of the struggle for the liberation of the colonial peoples on the part of the proletariat of the imperialist countries, denotes the transformation of the colonies and semicolonies into one of the most important reserves of the world proletariat.

. . .

The Communist International *attaches no conditions to unity of action except one, and that an elementary condition acceptable for all workers, that is, that the unity of action be directed against fascism, against the offensive of capital, against the threat of war, against the class enemy.* This is our condition.

Content and Forms of the United Front

What is and ought to be the basic content of the united front at the present stage? The defense of the immediate economic and political interests of the working class, the defense of the working class against fascism, must form the *starting point*.

We must not confine ourselves to bare appeals to struggle for the proletarian dictatorship, but must also find and advance those slogans and forms of struggle which arise out of the vital needs of the masses, and are commensurate with their fighting capacity at the given stage of development.

. . .

We must strive to establish the widest united front with the aid of joint action by workers' organizations of different trends for the defense of the vital interests of the toiling masses. This means:

First, joint struggle to really shift the burden of the consequences of the crisis onto the shoulders of the ruling classes, the shoulders of the capitalists, landlords—in a word, the shoulders of the rich.

Second, joint struggle against all forms of the fascist offensive, in defense of the gains and the rights of the toilers, against the liquidation of bourgeois-democratic liberties.

Third, joint struggle against the approaching danger of imperialist war, a struggle that will impede the preparations for such a war.

. . .

Communists of course cannot and must not for a moment abandon their own *independent work* of communist education, organization and mobilization of the masses. However, for the purpose of ensuring that the workers find the road to unity of action, it is necessary to strive at the same time both for short-term and for long-term agreements providing for *joint action with social democratic parties, reformist trade unions and other organizations of the toilers* against the class enemies of the proletariat. The chief stress in all this must be laid on developing *mass action* locally, *to be carried out by the local organizations* through local agreements.

It goes without saying that the concrete realization of the united front will take *various* forms in various countries, depending upon the condition and character of the workers' organizations and their political level, upon the concrete situation in the particular country, upon the changes in progress in the international labor movement, et cetera.

These forms may include, for instance: coordinated joint action of the workers to be agreed upon *from case to case* on definite occasions, on individual demands or on the basis of a common platform; coordinated actions in *individual enterprises* or by *whole industries*; coordinated actions on a *local, regional, national,* or *international scale*; coordinated actions for the organization of the *economic* struggle of the workers, for carrying out mass *political* actions, for the organization of joint *self-defense* against fascist attacks; coordinated action in the rendering of *aid to political prisoners and their families*, in the field of struggle against *social reaction*; joint actions in the defense of the *interests of the youth and women*, in the field of the *cooperative movement, cultural activity, sports, et cetera.*

. . .

A contract commission between the leaders of the Communist and Socialist Parties is necessary to facilitate the carrying out of joint action, but by itself it is far from adequate for a real development of the united front, for drawing the broadest masses into the struggle against fascism.

The Communists and all revolutionary workers must strive for the formation of elective . . . *nonpartisan class bodies of the united front* at the *factories*, among the *unemployed*, in the *working-class districts*, among the *small townsmen* and in the *villages*. Only such bodies will be able to embrace in the united front movement the vast masses of unorganized toilers as well . . .

Joint action of the *organized* workers is the beginning, the foundation. But we must not lose sight of the fact that the unorganized masses constitute the vast majority of workers . . .

The creation of nonpartisan class bodies is the *best form* for carrying out, extending and strengthening the united front among the rank and file of the broadest masses. These bodies will likewise be the best bulwark against every attempt of the opponents of the united front to disrupt the established unity of action of the working class.[2]

. . .

The Ideological Struggle against Fascism

One of the weakest aspects of the antifascist struggle of our parties lies in the fact that they *react inadequately and too slowly to the demagogy of fascism*, and to this day continue to look with disdain on the problems of the struggle against fascist ideology. Many comrades did not believe that so reactionary a variety of bourgeois ideology as the ideology of fascism, which in its stupidity frequently reaches the point of lunacy, was capable of gaining a mass influence at all. This was a great mistake. The putrefaction of capitalism penetrates to the innermost core of its ideology and culture, while the desperate situation of the broad masses of the people renders certain sections of them susceptible to infections from the ideological refuse of this putrefaction.

We must under no circumstances underrate this fascist capacity for ideological infection. On the contrary, we must develop for our part an extensive ideological struggle on the basis of clear, popular argumentation and a correct, well thought-out approach to the peculiarities of the national psychology of the masses of the people.

The fascists are rummaging through the entire *history* of every nation

---

2   In the following section, redacted in this volume, Dimitrov calls on communists in the United States to create a new, nonsectarian political party that would be its vehicle for an "Anti-Fascist People's Front." However, this particular form of "nonpartisan class body" was quickly scrapped as unworkable by American communists, given their political context of the two-party system. More influential in the United States was his call for umbrella organizations to coordinate antifascist activity, the most famous of which was the American League against War and Fascism.

so as to be able to pose as the heirs and continuators of all that was exalted and heroic in its past, while all that was degrading or offensive to the national sentiments of the people, they make use of as weapons against the enemies of fascism . . .

The new-baked National Socialist historians try to depict the history of Germany as if for the last 2,000 years, by virtue of some "historical law," a certain line of development had run through it like a red thread which lead to the appearance on the historical scene of a national "savior," a "Messiah," of the *German* people, a certain "corporal" of *Austrian* extraction! . . .

Mussolini makes every effort to capitalize the heroic figure of Garibaldi. The French fascists bring to the fore as their heroine Joan of Arc. The American fascists appeal to the traditions of the American War of Independence, the traditions of Washington and Lincoln. The Bulgarian fascists make use of the national liberation movement of the seventies and its heroes beloved of the people, Vassil Levsky, Stephen Karaj, and others.

Communists who suppose that all this has nothing to do with the cause of the working class, who do nothing to enlighten the masses on the past of their own people, in a historically correct fashion—in a genuinely Marxist, a Leninist-Marxist, a Lenin-Stalin spirit—who do nothing to *link up their present struggle with its revolutionary traditions and past*—voluntarily relinquish to fascist falsifiers all that is valuable in the historical past of the nation, that the fascists may bamboozle the masses. (*Applause.*)

. . .

We Communists are the *irreconcilable opponents, on principle*, of bourgeois nationalism of every variety. But we are not supporters of *national nihilism*, and should never act as such. The task of educating the workers and all toilers in the spirit of proletarian internationalism is one of the fundamental tasks of every Communist party. But whoever thinks that this permits him, or even compels him, to sneer at all the national sentiments of the broad toiling masses is far from genuine Bolshevism, and has understood nothing of the teaching of Lenin and Stalin on the national question. (*Applause*).

William Z. Foster, "Fascist Tendencies in the United States," *Communist*, October 1935

William Z. Foster (1881–1961) was one of the leading organizers and intellectuals of the Communist Party USA (CPUSA) and served as its general secretary from 1945 to 1947. He entered political work from a solidly working-class background, having struggled as a factory worker, lumberman, longshoreman, and sailor at job sites across the United States. Before joining the CPUSA in 1923, his political passion was union organizing. Though the CPUSA's formal membership was relatively small in number, it was a significant political force in the United States during the 1930s.

Foster's essay, which appeared in the theoretical journal of the party, illustrates the strengths and weaknesses of CP analyses of fascism. It suggests that capitalists were the primary agents behind fascist politics, an unproductive notion that was common, though far from universal, in leftist writings of the decade. The notion that finance capital was the ultimate driver of fascist politics is simply not true, and shows the influence of Dimitrov and the Comintern. Insights into fascism's racial nationalism are also undeveloped here, though communist writings on this theme would appear more frequently toward the end of the decade. Otherwise, the piece contains a number of rich observations about the US political scene, including its list of fascist groupings in the United States and the insight that they lacked coordination; its comparison of the American political situation in relation to Europe; its emphasis on the strength of the US left in the 1930s; and the distinction its author draws between fascism and the normal class violence of a capitalist state.

As an answer to the fascist threat, Foster prescribes the building of a third party—a Farmer-Labor Party. This idea also came from Dimitrov. When it proved unworkable in the field, the CPUSA quickly scrapped this strategy and instead put its electoral efforts behind prolabor antifascists in existing parties, running their own candidates only in races where such individuals did not exist. Increasingly, the party fought alongside labor and other progressive organizations to extend the New Deal as a domestic antidote to fascism. Its most visible antifascist project in the Popular Front period, however, was the American League.

Fascism, in its semi-developed American forms, is now beginning to loom up as a real danger in the United States. This is a matter of grave concern, not only for the American revolutionary movement but also for the whole Communist International. For a serious advance of fascism in the United States would stimulate fascism in all capitalist countries and would gravely accentuate the danger of war against the USSR.

The immediate cause of the growth of American fascist tendencies is the inability of the capitalists to overcome the prolonged crisis and the present special type of depression. The capitalists have been quite unable to restore industry to a "prosperity" basis. Both the Hoover and Roosevelt governments have poured out billions of dollars "to prime the industrial pump," but industry stubbornly lags far below 1929 levels and farming remains in a profound crisis.

The deep and protracted economic crisis is rapidly sharpening all the inherent contradictions of capitalism in the United States, including antagonisms (a) between the working class and the capitalist class; (b) between the urban petty bourgeoisie and the capitalists; (c) between the farmers and the capitalists; (d) between various groups within the ranks of the monopoly bourgeoisie itself; (e) between the decisive part of finance capital and groups of the bourgeoisie representing local and state interests (silver, cotton, tobacco, etc.); (f) between the United States and other imperialist and colonial countries; (g) between the bourgeois world and the USSR.

These sharpening contradictions are intensifying the American struggle on every front. They are narrowing the social basis of the bourgeoisie by bringing it into conflict with growing millions of workers, farmers and city petty bourgeoisie. Thus the big capitalists are finding it more and more difficult to rule by their traditional methods of parliamentary democracy, concessions to the labor aristocracy, international diplomacy, et cetera. Consequently their most decisive section, finance capital, in order to reestablish its narrowing social base, is being compelled to strengthen its offensive against the masses by policies which tend in the direction of fascism.

The most decisive facts in gradually pushing monopoly capital toward a fascist course are its settled policy of thrusting the burden of the crisis upon the workers and other toiling masses and its fear of their growing resistance which it realizes is a serious threat to the bourgeois dictatorship.

With crassest brutality, the big capitalists have compelled the toiling masses to bear the brunt of the economic breakdown. Although they have greatly increased their own profits (the National City Bank reports that 1,453 companies with a deficit of $97,000,000 in 1932 made profits of $1,051,000,000 in 1934), they have forced the masses of workers and small farmers down to an unheard-of pauperization. Living standards have fallen catastrophically and continue to decline. From 12 to 15 million workers remain unemployed. Great multitudes of farmers and small businessmen have been utterly bankrupted, and this process continues. About 22 million toilers and their families are eking out a miserable existence upon the niggardly government relief, and at least one-third of the whole American people have been reduced to standards that mean not only hunger and misery, but actual physical degeneration.

But the toiling masses have not submitted to this monstrous pauperization without resistance. On the contrary, the United States for the past three years has been a scene of intense and increasing class battles, both economic and political.

Among these struggles are: the most intense wave of strikes in American history; a broad struggle of the unemployed for unemployment insurance and relief; strikes and other struggles of the poorer farmers against low farm prices and monopoly control; a wide and insistent movement among war veterans for the soldiers' bonus; and a strong agitation among the Negro masses for equality; big anti-war strikes and other demonstrations among students; an extensive movement of the aged for government pensions; struggles of the petty bourgeoisie against trustification and high taxes; wide radicalization among intellectuals; et cetera.

Never were the masses so stirred. They are conducting their struggles with unparalleled tenacity and bitterness. They are awakening politically and manifestly beginning to shed their capitalistic illusions. They are starting to think, however confusedly, in terms of revolution. The USSR gains in popularity among them. The trade unions have grown and strengthened their position in industry. A new spirit of unity and militancy grows on all sides.

In this rising wave of struggle the Communist Party is playing a considerable and an increasing role . . .

The Fascist Danger

The bourgeoisie are amazed and shocked by their inability to overcome the economic crisis and the multiplying political difficulties growing out of it. They are alarmed at the rapid radicalization of the workers, the rising tide of struggle, the growing strength and influence of the Communist Party. In years past, especially during the "prosperity" period of 1923–1929, the capitalists had confidently assured themselves that the workers were hopelessly poisoned with bourgeois illusions; and, as during the first three years of the crisis, the workers, misled and demoralized by their trade union and Socialist leaders, took blow after blow without resistance, [as] the capitalists hypocritically gloated over them, praising them for their patriotism, good sense and courage in accepting the crisis burdens placed upon them.

But now these same capitalists are astonished and alarmed to see the great American working class beginning to arouse itself and go to into battle with real militancy and solidarity. Such a situation interferes badly with the capitalists' plans to further slash living standards and to keep the whole weight of the crisis on the toilers' shoulders. So they are proceeding to try to crush the growing struggle by developing a demagogy and violence which takes on more and more of a fascist character . . .

Fascist Tendencies

What we have to deal with in the United States is not a well-defined fascist movement, but a series of more or less definite tendencies making toward fascism. These tendencies range from quite-conscious fascist groups to movements which, while not definitely fascist, nevertheless create favorable conditions for the growth of fascism.

Let us begin with the Roosevelt government. Today this government is increasingly under fire from the most reactionary groups of monopoly capital, which are the main source of fascist tendencies and organizers of the fascist movement; because these elements, in first line, resent Roosevelt's trade union policy, which they hold responsible for the many strikes. The liquidation of the National Recovery Administration (NRA)[1] means the victory of the most reactionary elements which demand the most unmerciful and open offensive against the working class. This victory strengthened the position of the fascist group among the monopolist capitalists. The most reactionary group of finance capital consider the NRA to have exhausted its benefits for them. But for the first two years of his term they gave Roosevelt substantial support. And despite Roosevelt's liberal trends, phrases and demagogic promises (and of the group of finance capitalist which he represents) there are tendencies also in his policies which give direct stimulus to fascist growth. Among these tendencies are: strengthening of finance capital through trustification, support of economic nationalism, increased war preparations, reductions of living standards of the masses, encouragement of company unionism, extensive use of legal and extralegal violence against the workers and farmers, discrediting of parliamentary government and popularization of the notion of a one-man savior of the country, pouring out a flood of demagogy about the "forgotten man," et cetera. And it is significant to note that the Roosevelt industrial code policies (the NRA) originated in the United States Chamber of Commerce (organ of

---

1   The National Recovery Administration was the prime New Deal agency of Roosevelt's "first New Deal." Established by executive order, it allowed the president to set industry-wide codes over trade, minimum wages, and workers' rights. As Foster rightly notes, however, US business played a critical role in drafting its policies. After the NRA was ruled unconstitutional by the Supreme Court in 1935, Roosevelt sought other vehicles for wage and hour legislation that labor played a stronger role in designing, and that ultimately proved more durable.

finance capital) and were hailed by many of their supporters as first steps toward a fascist corporate state in the United States.[2]

But the main stream of fascist development is at present to be found in a series of other more or less definitely fascist or semi-fascist demagogues, groupings and organizations of extended mass influence. Among these are:

The American Liberty League group of capitalist ultra-reactionaries, headed by Herbert Hoover and Al Smith.[3] This powerful organization, supported by DuPont, General Motors and other big capitalist concerns, has in its ranks many large Wall Street financial interests that are actively propagating fascist tendencies.

The American Legion.[4] The leadership of this strongest of the war veterans' organizations (769,908 members) is saturated with fascist spirit and constantly carries on violent anti-Red agitation.

W. R. Hearst, America's greatest newspaper publisher. He is a crony of Hitler and prosecutes a rabid anti-Communist, anti-Soviet campaign through his vast chain of publications with several million readers, especially among the city petty bourgeoisie and more backward workers.[5] With huge personal resources and powerful financial capitalist support, he tends to become the main center of the growing fascist

---

2   Foster's criticism of Roosevelt was indicative of critiques of the president in the Communist press up to 1935. In the second half of the decade, however, Communists increasingly aligned with Roosevelt, seeing him as an ally in the global fight against fascism. This support was put on hold during the period of the Hitler-Stalin Pact (1939–1941), but resumed in full force after the German attack on the Soviet Union in June 1941.

3   The membership of the American Liberty League was a roster of US corporate elites. Though some of these individuals had authoritarian and even fascist tendencies, the organization as a whole was more conservative and proto-neoliberal than fascist. Other than this organization, however, the other groups and individuals listed by Foster did in fact possess distinct fascist traits.

4   Founded in 1919, the American Legion—a veterans' organization—eagerly embraced Mussolini's Fascist movement as kindred spirits in the fight against "class conflict" and internationalism. In the 1930s, the national body was circumspect about embracing European fascism, yet, in that decade, it touted the Ku Klux Klan in its magazine, and local branches of the legion overlapped in their membership with the Klan and the Black Legion in Michigan.

5   Indeed, Hearst began calling for vigilante violence against the labor movement in 1934. That same year, he traveled to Nazi Germany, where he agreed to publish the writings of senior Nazi officials in his newspapers. After his visit, Hearst's US readers would encounter articles written by Hermann Goering and Alfred Rosenberg, both later sentenced to death at Nuremberg, without critical introductions or editorial rebuttal.

agitation. He has big influence among the leadership of the American Federation of Labor and American Legion, and he maintains working relations with the right-wing leaders of the SP [Socialist Party].

Father Coughlin, a Catholic priest. He speaks weekly over the radio to millions of listeners and claims (doubtless exaggerated) a definite membership of 200,000 and a following of 5 million in the National Union for Social Justice. A powerful and dangerous demagogue, he specializes in pseudo-attacks upon the great bankers and violent assaults upon the Communist Party and the Soviet Union. His cure-all is inflation and his motto is "Shoot the Communists." He has a huge influence among the farmers, city petty bourgeoisie and Catholic immigrant workers and is credited with having defeated Roosevelt in the latter's attempt to affiliate the United States to the World Court of the League of Nations.

Huey Long, US senator from Louisiana. This semi-fascist demagogue has a dictatorship in his own state, such as no other American state has ever seen before. His demagogic program is to expropriate partially the great capitalists and to "share the wealth," giving everybody an income of $5,000 yearly. He has behind him a nebulous organization of "share the wealth" clubs, with fabulous membership claims. He has a broad mass following throughout the South among the impoverished small farmers and workers. His popularity nationally is growing and he nourished presidential ambitions.

Matthew Woll, Major Berry and some other top leaders of the American Federation of Labor, who form a definitely reactionary clique. They are allied with various semi-fascist groups and, doubtless, as the fascist movement develops they will play a leading role in it.

Besides the foregoing, there are many more popular ultra-reactionary demagogues whose agitation goes to feed the growing fascist stream, such as: General Johnson, first chief of the NRA; Raymond Moley, former head of Roosevelt's "brain trust"; Hamilton Fish, wealthy New York congressman; Bernarr Macfadden, rich magazine publisher, et cetera.

Then there are various fascist and semi-fascist organizations of vague membership, but growing influence. Some of these, such as the Crusaders, Ku Klux Klan, Order of '76, Silver Shirts, Grey Shirts and many others with ambitious would-be Hitlers and Mussolinis at their heads, are made up chiefly of native American elements. Others, such as the Friends of

New Germany and similar organizations among the Italians, Poles, Bulgarians, Yugoslavs, et cetera, are more definitely fascist and are working energetically among their respective nationalities.

Besides all these fascist, semi-fascist and part-fascist tendencies and groupings, there have sprung up like mushrooms several broad mass bourgeois reformist movements, such as [Upton] Sinclair's "Epic," [Francis] Townsend's old age pension movement, the Utopians, et cetera. While the leaders of these organizations cannot be classed as fascists or even semi-fascists, undoubtedly their demagogic programs, denunciations of Communists, et cetera, create favorable conditions for fascist agitators.

The many fascist and semi-fascist demagogues and organizations penetrating the masses constitute a real menace. Vast numbers of the hungry, confused and politically unorganized and inexperienced masses, seeking a way out of their intolerable situation, are falling victims to the increasing flood of reactionary and fascist demagogy. These masses consist not only of the urban petty bourgeoisie and farmers, but also workers. No reliable statistics or other clear indications are yet at hand to show to what extent this specifically American fascist agitation has penetrated the masses, but that it has made such headway is manifest. The Communist Party is making considerable progress in winning the masses, but the fascists, semi-fascists and other reactionary capitalist demagogues are going much faster. They are undoubtedly establishing a broad mass base; the plain lesson of which is that we Communists must double and treble our united front against fascism.

The rapid growth of fascist tendencies in the United States emphasizes what a great error it is to suppose that there can be no real danger from fascism unless there is a far-advanced revolutionary crisis or unless the country is one of those defeated or semi-defeated in the war.

The Present Program of Fascism

The finance capitalist character of American fascism is plain. Many of the most outstanding fascists and semi-fascist demagogues, such as Hearst, Macfadden and Fish, are wealthy capitalists themselves and linked up with the most powerful financial interests in America; and the

others, such as Coughlin, Long, Woll, Johnson, et cetera, have had their
big capitalist connections fully exposed. Also the recent Dickstein
Congressional Committee (a very reactionary body) was compelled
reluctantly to show that big New York banking interests are permeated
with fascist sentiments and that some of them had actually planned a
mass march upon Washington, to be led by General Smedley Butler.
Wall Street is clearly the home address of American fascism.

The present-day activities of the fascist and semi-fascist agitators
and groupings conform to the interests of finance capital. It is true that
the American fascist trend, as I have already indicated, is unorganized
and not fully defined. Its status is one of confused ideas and loose
organizations. Often the fascist tendencies are contradictory and antagonistic to each other. These contradictions reflect the conflicts with the
bourgeoisie itself. They indicate that the bulk of monopoly capital has
not fully embarked on the road to fascism as the only way out of its
increasing difficulties. Nevertheless, there is a gradual process of
coming closer together and clarification of fascist aims going on. Out of
the welter of fascist and semi-fascist tendencies the following proposi-
tions, which dovetail generally with finance capitalist interests, may be
taken as the immediate, actual program of the incipient American
fascism.

a. A gigantic campaign of demagogy to hoodwink the toiling masses
   in order to prevent them developing programs, organizations and
   struggles of their own. Outstanding features of this demagogy are
   sharp verbal attacks on the trusts and "Wall Street," and the "international bankers"; programs of inflation; "share the wealth"; "soak
   the rich" tax measures; unemployed "self-help" schemes; fantastic
   old age pensions; illusory "security" programs; utopian plans to
   abolish poverty; ridiculing of parliamentary government; vague
   talk of a "new social order," et cetera.
b. Behind this barrage of radical demagogy, however, the fascists and
   semi-fascists pursue actual policies that result in direct or indirect
   support of the big bourgeoisie's program of wage slashing, strike-
   breaking, company unionism, trustification, [and] hostile labor
   legislation.
c. In general, they also display an intense economic and political
   nationalism, exemplified by intransigent support of all the major

objectives of American imperialism, including increased war preparations, high tariffs, collection of war debts, conquest of foreign markets, hostility to the League of Nations, et cetera.

d. The growth of fascist sentiments is marked by an increased use of violence against the masses in struggle, not only of troops and police, but also of vigilante groups, lynch mobs, et cetera.

e. Violent attacks upon the Communist Party and attempts to illegalize it or wreck it by violence.

f. [A] violent slander campaign against the Soviet Union.

g. Intensification of prejudices against Negroes, Jews and [the] foreign-born.

h. Cultivation of sectional chauvinism—Long's stimulation of anti-Northern prejudice in the South, which is still smarting from its defeat in the Civil War; and Coughlin's incitement of the agricultural West against the industrial East.

i. General cultural reaction, including intense cultivation of religion, reactionary trends in literature and science, and censorship of motion pictures, radio and theater.

Specific Characteristics of American Fascism

American fascism develops under its own special forms and slogans. It is vitally necessary that our party study these specific characteristics, their hidden and masked forms and maneuvers. This, however, it has not yet done adequately. It has not sufficiently analyzed the process of American fascization as a whole, especially to evaluate those features that are particularly American. Consequently, a number of wrong tendencies have developed in our fight against fascism, which the Central Committee strives to overcome. Among these are:

a. A tendency in our mass agitation to separate the question of fascism from that of the general employers' offensive program against wages, hours, working conditions, et cetera; that is, to make of fascism only an anti-Red issue, instead of a broad class issue. Such a tendency, if continued, would lead to the isolation of the party from the masses and make impossible a broad united front fight against fascism . . .

b. A tendency to class definitely as fascism all forms of bourgeoise reaction, including such movements as Sinclair's, Townsend's, et cetera, and also to apply the term "fascist" indiscriminately to reactionary and reformistic trade union leaders and organizations. This tendency would concede to the fascists valuable forces that we can readily win for struggle against fascism.

We must correct these theoretical weaknesses at once. We must look closely at the special features of American fascism; it is not enough to know the trend of fascism in general. Therefore, in the following pages I shall discuss four specific phases of American fascism. These are the questions of the tempo of fascist development, the central fascist slogans, the fascization of the state, and the organization of a fascist party.

1. The Question of the Tempo of American Fascist Development
A major specific feature of fascism, or semi-fascism, in the United States is its rapid tempo of development; that is, its appearance as a mass movement at a relatively earlier period in the class struggle than fascism occurred in either Italy or Germany. In those countries, when fascism assumed mass form the revolutionary crisis was far developed and the bourgeoisie faced a menacing threat of imminent proletarian revolution. But fascism, in its American forms, is developing on a mass basis in the United States under much less acute conditions of class struggle. Although in the United States the economic and political difficulties of the bourgeoisie are great and the class struggle is being rapidly intensified, and while the American capitalists are viewing with great alarm the stubborn economic crisis, the radicalization of the masses, the growing wave of struggle, the strengthening of the hated and feared Communist Party and the revolutionary example of the Soviet Union, they nevertheless do not yet possess the mortal fear of impending revolution to the extent that the Italian and German bourgeoisie did, nor the Spanish or Austrian capitalist classes.

The American imperialist bourgeoisie are gradually seizing upon fascist methods more for the purpose of intensifying their drive to reduce the present living standards of the toiling masses and break their growing resistance. It is chiefly in this sense that they are seeking to confuse the masses, isolate and destroy the Communist Party, weaken the trade unions, prevent the organization of a Labor Party, et cetera.

But more and more, also, they are coming to look upon fascism as the Italian, German, Spanish and other bourgeoisie do, as the only way to save them from proletarian revolution.

This growth of the American incipient fascism at a relatively earlier stage in the class struggle is to be explained chiefly by the following facts, taken in connection with the rapid sharpening of the economic and political situation.

a. Fascist demagogy and violence dovetails readily with the traditional ultra-ruthlessness of the American capitalist class in exploiting the toiling masses and repressing them politically; as evidenced by its longtime policies of extreme use of the police, army and gunmen in strikes; suppression of trade unionism and establishment of open shop and company unionism in the most basic sectors of American industry; brutal suppression of the Negro people; brutal herding and murderous exploitation of the foreign-born workers; refusal to set up even an elementary system of social insurance; crass methods to keep the toilers mobilized in two capitalized parties; ruthless elimination of the small businessmen and farmers; cynical corruption of elections, government officials, et cetera. A capitalist class historically guilty of such barbarities, in its hour of real need, turns easily to fascism for still more ruthless measures to maintain its rulership and exploitation.

b. American monopoly capital tends to adopt more readily fascist methods of demagogy and terrorism also because it is definitely conscious of the lack of a great, solidly entrenched reformist party on the model of German Social Democracy or the British Labour Party to paralyze the workers' resistance. To meet this deficiency in their situation of sharpening class struggle, the bourgeoisie displays two tendencies: some sections of it favor the development of the American Federation of Labor unions, but more decisive sections, noting the radicalization of the workers in the American Federation of Labor, the great wave of strikes (which they blame on Roosevelt) and the growing united front movement, tend to move more toward developing the mass basis of the bourgeoisie on fascist and semi-fascist lines.

c. Another important factor in pushing American big capitalism toward a fascist course is the fact that they have learned many lessons from Germany, or believe they have. They saw Hitler easily wreck the German political and trade union organizations and thus hamstring the working class. So, increasing numbers of them are coming to believe that his policies can be profitably used against the workers in the United States. Nor are they going to wait until they are confronted with a great revolutionary crisis. They are, so to speak, trying "to take time by the forelock" and by the early application of fascist methods throw the working class helplessly before their exploitation and nip the revolution in the bud.

An important result of the fast tempo of American fascist development, that is, its appearance as a mass movement at a relatively earlier stage in the class struggle, is to put a stamp of immaturity upon the entire fascist movement. This immaturity, which masks and makes more insidious the whole approach of American fascism, is evidenced by its theoretical and organizational incompleteness, such as: conflicting groupings, failure to develop more than embryonic theories of the corporate state (the NRA), failure to build up a separate fascist party, to develop a well-organized youth movement, to organize storm troops, et cetera.

These manifestations do not mean, however, that American fascism has limited objectives; that it will not develop beyond a sort of half fascism. On the contrary, American fascism already indicates that, like German, Italian, and other types of fascism, it is striving toward a fascist dictatorship, with all that this implies. Its specific features indicate simply that what we have in the United States is an undeveloped fascism, which, although playing an important role in sharpening the employers' offensive, has not yet fully developed its program and organization. As the class struggle sharpens, however, American fascism will mature with it.

The present immature state of American fascism and its important role in the employers' offensive make it all the more necessary for our party to understand the special forms the movement takes, and to link the fight against it closely with the everyday struggle of the workers. The main immediate fascist danger lies not in a victory of the ready-made mature types of fascist programs and organizations dogmatically patterned after fascist Germany or Italy or Poland, but in the raw, scattering and immature native American fascist growth, trends and tendencies, such as in the Hearst, Coughlin and Long movements . . .[6]

---

6   A section titled "The Question of the Central Fascist Slogan" was redacted here.

2. The Question of the Fascization of the State

Another specific characteristic of incipient American fascism to be remarked on is its concentration upon the fascization of the existing state. It is true that there is a growing agitation against parliamentary government, the Congress being widely ridiculed as an impotent body of babblers and the president's demand for more power in the crisis being willingly conceded; but still there is little talk, except among the smaller, more dogmatic and sectarian fascist tendencies, of abolishing the present form of government and establishing a corporate or totalitarian state.

This is chiefly because: (a) the structure of the American government, with huge powers in the hands of the president and the Supreme Court, lends itself readily to the development of a fascist dictatorship; and (b) the government is now almost completely in the hands of big capital and the upper bourgeoisie; there being no important Social Democratic, Communist, or militant trade union representatives for the fascists to contend with in utilizing the government for their purposes.

But because permeation of the present state apparatus is now the main political path of fascism, it does not follow that the fascists plan to pursue a legal road to power or to maintain the existing form of government. On the contrary, the vigilante terrorist gangs of the San Francisco general strike, the Wall Street planned march upon Washington, et cetera, should teach us that the fascists will use every form of violence, including, if they think it is practical, a coup d'etat, in their fight for power. And their present crassly expressed antidemocratic tendencies are enough proof that should the fascists and semi-fascists secure the power, they would find even the present undemocratic form of government too democratic for them and would supplant it by a state form leading toward a fascist dictatorship.

3. The Question of a Separate Fascist Party

It is another specific characteristic of incipient American fascism that the fascists and semi-fascists have not formed a party of their own, but are affiliated to the two old capitalist parties. The main reason for this is that the masses of workers, city petty bourgeoisie and farmers still follow these two parties, and the fascists find it necessary to work where these masses are. Furthermore, the decentralized character of these parties makes it relatively easy for fascist or semi-fascist demagogues to seize sections of them to use as their political organization. There is no maze of minority political parties struggling for control as in Italy and Germany, paralyzing the legislative branch of the government and offering a plausible pretext for organizing a fascist party to supplant all the others.

But the danger of the fascist tendencies forming a separate party becomes more and more imminent. Under the blows of the crisis and the consequent sharpening of class antagonisms, the traditional two-party system is now undergoing a great strain. It will face a severe test in the national elections of 1936. If the monopolist capitalists become convinced that they can no longer hold the masses of toilers under the hegemony of the old parties (either by a conservative Republican ticket, or a "left" demagogic Roosevelt program) they will probably have their fascist and semi-fascist demagogues (who can count on the support of such trade union leaders as Woll, Green and Lewis) either take the initiative in launching a semi-fascist party in order to canalize the toilers' rising discontent into counterrevolutionary channels; or, they will have these part-fascist agents go along with the toilers' mass breakaway movement from the old parties to try to capture or demoralize the new party from within.

The People's United Front against Fascism

The Seventh Congress of the Comintern correctly laid great stress upon the creation of a broad united front of workers and all other toilers against the fascist danger as the main immediate task of the international revolutionary movement. This policy applies with decisive force in the United States. There is urgent need for such a broad people's front against fascism and war, and awakening masses are at hand out of which to form it. Politically, the united front should take the form of a mass toilers' party, to bring into struggle the anti-fascist forces of the proletariat, the poorer farmers and the lower city petty bourgeoisie.

The reason why the anti-fascist united front must take the form of such a new mass party in the United States is because the American workers, petty bourgeoisie and small farmers have not yet broken with the bourgeois parties and formed a mass party, or parties, of their own, which could serve as the basis of such a united front of several parties as there is in France. In fact, the new mass party must be the crystallization of the historically necessary mass breakaway from the two capitalist parties.

The main cause why the American working class has not yet broken from the capitalist parties and formed a separate political party is the fact that the bourgeois revolution in the United States accorded the workers a relatively high degree of formal democratic rights, thereby sowing among them many capitalistic illusions. Consequently, they were not conscious (as for example, the workers of Germany, Austria, etc.) of a program of burning immediate political issues (right to vote, to organize, etc.) around which a mass party could be built. Their grievances, mostly over wages, hours, et cetera, loomed up to them chiefly as economic questions. Many other factors, such as relatively higher wage levels, free government land over a long period, the presence of a broad labor aristocracy, et cetera, also contributed to checking the class consciousness and political organization of the working class, but the question of democratic rights was the fundamental cause why the American workers formed no mass political party of their own and fought out the class struggle, historically, entirely on the economic field.

The city petty bourgeoisie, like the working class, has never been able to form its own party, although it has displayed much political activity, as evidenced by such movements as the [William Jennings] Bryan campaigns, the [Theodore] Roosevelt Bull Moose campaign of 1912, the support of [Franklin Delano] Roosevelt in 1932, et cetera. The explanation why the petty bourgeoisie has not differentiated itself politically from the two old parties is to be found, among other factors, in the fact that although considerable sections of it were being constantly crushed by the advance of the trusts, other and larger sections, the so-called "new" petty bourgeoisie in new and luxury industries, large numbers of people with petty bourgeois ideology (doctors, lawyers, technicians, chain store managers, etc.) were being created by the industrial expansion. This fact tended strongly to produce illusions among the petty bourgeoisie that it had common general political interests with the big capitalists.

The farmers have displayed much political activity. Confronted by sharp problems arising out of the intensely capitalistic character of American agriculture, they have conducted many organized political struggles, including such movements as the Greenback Party, Populist

Party, Nonpartisan League, the Farm Bloc, many state Farmer-Labor parties, et cetera. The chief reasons why they have not been able to break definitely with the two capitalist parties are: (a) because of the wide-spread system of small land holdings, fed for many decades by free government land, the basic question of the ownership of the land had not become sufficiently acute; and (b) because the decentralized nature of the two capitalist parties made it possible for the farmers to utilize these organizations to elect many representatives in the agricultural districts—an important reason also why the workers formed no sepa-rate mass party.

But the long, deep economic crisis has greatly politicalized the proletariat, the lower city petty bourgeoisie and the poorer farmers by throwing those masses increasingly into an intolerable pauperization. As for the workers, faced by huge mass unemployment, wage slashes and attacks upon their unions, they have developed a whole series of burning political and economic demands, chief among which are: unemployment insurance, unemployment relief, government works, thirty-hour week, government seizure and operation of closed facto-ries, government recognition of the right to organize, old age pensions, abolition of child labor, against the sales tax and the high cost of living, against fascism and war, et cetera. These political and economic demands have the support of millions of workers. Thus, for the first time in American history, there is in the minds of great masses of workers a series of urgent political demands, providing a sufficient basis upon which to organize a mass party. And for the first time also, a broad wave of revolutionary sentiment, confused but militant, is developing in the ranks of the proletariat . . .

Among the lower city petty bourgeoisie a rapid process of radicaliza-tion is also going on. The crisis has bankrupted vast numbers of them, the "new" petty bourgeoisie as well as the "old," forcing them down into the ranks of the workers and into the breadlines of the unemployed. Consequently, they are raising most urgent political demands against trustification, against the growing tax burden, for home owners' relief, for relief for impoverished professionals, against war preparations, against the curtailment of civil rights, et cetera . . .[7]

---

7   In a section redacted here, he also briefly covers the grievances of the farmers, and finally, of African Americans.

The task of leading the fight for the establishment of the new anti-fascist party falls largely upon the young Communist Party, and it is one that will require all its Bolshevik understanding, skill and strength. But it is in the carrying out of this task that the Communist Party will find its broad path to increased strength and mass prestige as the vanguard of the proletariat.

The Anti-Fascist Mass Party

The new mass party should constitute a great united front of the toiling masses against finance capital's program of hunger, fascism and war. It may be called the Workers' and Farmers' Party as Comrade Dimitro[v] suggests, or the Farmer-Labor Party, although it will probably have different names in various localities. The name Farmer-Labor Party has much prestige among the trade unions and farmers' organizations.

The anti-fascist mass party should be based on the trade unions and should include farmers' organizations, the Communist Party, the Socialist Party, state Farmer-Labor parties, veterans' organizations, working women's organizations, workers' and farmers' cooperatives, workers' fraternal societies, tenants' leagues, anti-war societies, groups of intellectuals, et cetera. It should pay especial attention to winning the youth, without whose ardent support victory over fascism is quite impossible, and whom the fascists and semi-fascists are now trying hard to capture. The party should also exert all efforts to win the Negro and foreign-born, especially the Germans, Italians, Poles and Jews. These groups, who number many millions, will be greatly stimulated to anti-fascist struggle by the fascists' anti-Negro, anti-Jew and anti-foreign-born agitation.

The new mass party of toilers should also strive to include sections of the sprouting fascist or partly fascist organizations and tendencies, such as: company unions, American Legion posts, and groups of the Coughlin and Long movements, et cetera. It should also pay special attention to winning the masses in the demagogic Sinclair, Townsend and similar movements. These groups are loosely organized and undisciplined, and many can be easily won over. It would be a great mistake to simply lump all these groupings together and concede them to the fascists.

The party program should be based upon the everyday demands and struggles of the masses, and the party should be the political united front expression of these struggles. It must oppose the fascists' anti–civil rights and government-centralizing tendencies by demands for limiting the powers of the president and Supreme Court, giving Negroes the right to vote, abolition of head tax and other voting qualifications, free right to place candidates on the ballot, et cetera. It must also raise the demand for a united front government upon the basis of the united front anti-fascist program.

In the fight to establish the new mass anti-fascist party, the Communist Party should by all means link up its struggle with the historical traditions of the American masses against capitalist oppression, which it is now beginning to do. Our party must ruthlessly expose the brazen fascist nationalist-chauvinist demagogy and show that the present anti-fascist struggle is the logical inheritor and carrier of these traditions and mass aspirations, and that only by the overthrow of capitalism and the establishment of socialism can the historical struggle of the American toiling masses for a fuller and richer life be realized. In this respect, the popularization of the revolutionary role and achievements of the Soviet Union become a matter of most vital importance. The large foreign-born membership and immigrant background of our party and its traditional narrow sectarianism in such matters make it doubly important that it pay close attention to the question of American mass traditions . . .

All efforts must be extended to get the new party in the field, or every possible local section or preliminary form of it, at the strategic period of the 1936 fall national elections. American workers, trained in the two capitalist parties, are not accustomed, like Social Democratic or Communist workers, to the slow building of a party. They want quick results and they object to "throwing away their votes" on weak parties. The new party must and easily can win many local victories in the 1936 elections. Our Communist Party was tardy in reissuing the Labor Party slogan, which it had shelved several years before, and this means that, by increased activity, it must make up for lost time.

In the United States there is now a race on between the fascists and the Communists for the leadership of the politically rapidly awakened masses. Despite some Communist Party united front successes, fascism in the United States develops with a fast tempo. Fascism has become a real danger. But it would be sheer madness to conclude therefrom that the victory of American fascism is inevitable. On the contrary, the political elements are at hand to deal fascism a decisive defeat. It is the task of our party to organize these anti-fascist forces.

In France, the Communist Party, correctly, applying the Comintern united front policy, has scored some real victories against fascism. As good or better can be achieved in the United States. The awakening masses will fight against fascism if we can give them proper leadership. We can confidently fight for victory in the United States that will deal a crushing defeat to fascism. And we can win that victory if the Communist Party knows how to apply in life the line and lessons of the Seventh World Congress of the Communist International.

W. E. B. Du Bois, Writings on National Socialism, *Pittsburgh Courier*, December 12, 1936

The two pieces by W. E. B. Du Bois in this volume are but a sample of his steady body of written work about fascism in the twentieth century. This piece is one of several reports by Du Bois (1868–1963) that were based on a 1936 visit to Berlin, part of a global excursion that included stops in China, Japan, and the Soviet Union. Du Bois's ardent admiration of nineteenth-century German nationalism—Kaiser Wilhelm was an early example for Du Bois of race leadership—was sharply redirected by his self-education in Marxism and the Russian Revolution. Here, for example, Du Bois aligns with contemporaries like Trotsky and other world communists in perceiving Nazism as the result of the destruction of the German Revolution of 1918, capitalist attacks on the German working class, and demonization of Bolshevism and Jews. The Marxist perspective continued its trajectory through Du Bois's work in his masterpiece Black Reconstruction, *published just a year earlier.*

The Hitler State

Hitler set up a tyranny: a state with a mighty police force, a growing army, a host of spies and informers, a secret espionage, backed by swift and cruel punishment, which might vary from loss of job to imprisonment, incommunicado and without trial, to cold murder. None used to the freedom and discussion of a modern state can endure Germany, save as a dire necessity or an ideal toward something better.

But this was not all that Hitler did. Had it been, he and his state would have disappeared long ere this. He showed Germany a way out when most Germans saw nothing but impenetrable mist, and he made the vast majority of Germans believe that his way was the only way and that it was actually leading to the promised land. Nine out of every ten Germans believe this today, and as long as they are convinced of this, they are going to uphold Hitler at any cost. They know the cost which they pay and they hate it. They hate war, they hate spying, they hate peace after a generation of wars and rumors of wars; they have a nation at work, after a nightmare of unemployment; and the results of this work are shown not simply by private profits, but by houses for the poor; new roads; an end of strikes and labor troubles; widespread industrial and unemployment insurance; the guarding of public and private health; great celebrations, organizations for old and young, new songs, new ideals, a new state, a new race. Have they paid, are they paying too much for all this? Would other and less dangerous roads lead to this same end? Germany is not asking this. She is simply saying, "HEIL HITLER!"

National Socialism

Before the war, Germany was planning the most gigantic industrial machine the world ever dreamed of. With a carefully planned economy, led by the greatest engineers of a new technical age, she was becoming the greatest manufacturing nation of the world. In 1913 she was making 29 percent of all the world's machines, and her methods and organization were the wonder of the world. The clouds in the sky were the bitter industrial rivalry of England, France and America, and the growing worldwide demand of the working classes for a higher wage—a larger share of the product of labor, which in the teaching of some amounted actually to the abolition of all private profit and the ownership of capital by the state. Germany held back the demands of her workers by state measures of insurance and help, careful education of workers to keep them out of unions, and patriotism. She went to war confidently expecting greatly increased command of raw materials and monopoly of world markets; and came out with the Russian communist revolution at her doors, her access to crucial raw material gone and her own land on the edge of communism. Had the German workers had a different training and leadership, Germany would have become communist. But her labor leaders quarreled, and the best of them were murdered. Thereupon capital made desperate effort to save German capital investment. They yielded to socialism—they had to, for the German state was already a larger owner of capital. But they sought to build a national, German socialism, to avoid international working-class movements, and to save capital and private profit by yielding enough to the German worker to keep him quiet and satisfied. This is the program of the Nazi Party, and it has to carry on a furious propaganda against communism, while on the other making every surrender to the German worker except the unearned increment.

The New Philosophy

There must be a dictatorship—that was absolutely necessary to put the state in order. If democratic forms persisted, this dictatorship might get in the hands of the workers. Democracy must go, and parliamentary institutions. The dictator must be a popular figure. Hitler filled the bill. He was an artisan, and a private in the war. He came from a part of Austria where the anti-Jewish feeling was strong, and his own economic rivalry with Jews as a worker had strengthened this. Here was an asset which would appeal to artisans, small shopkeepers and racial fanatics. He was a popular orator just at the time that the radio and loud speaker made speaking a possible state monopoly. All that was needed was a plausible philosophy, and propaganda.

The philosophy of Hitlerism is neither logical nor complete. Nor on the other hand is it wholly illogical and hypocritical. It is still a growing and developing body of thought, which large and larger bodies of Germans are following with strained ardor. Based on the old German idea of the state, it declares that the state, and not the working class, is the real unit to be developed. All opposition in the state must disappear. The interests of the capitalist and the worker are one. They must, by superior authority, be forced into unity, and then the resultant state must be conducted in the interests of all. Moreover, this new state which Germany is building is something holy and superior. It is composed of pure Nordics, with no contamination of Jews, nor of inferior races. Its inborn superiority is proven by history and experience. Germany was not beaten in the World War—she fought fourteen nations to a stand-still, and only succumbed when her own people betrayed her. This must never happen again. The new Germany must be one. This unity means national health, a living wage, public works, a planned economy with workers trained to fit into the plan, and capital subservient to the great end of building a united and happy people. The success of this plan depends on a strong government, obeyed without discussion or argument or hesitation, with the power in the hands of a supreme leader, who today is Adolf Hitler.

Propaganda

To secure such a government, and keep it in power, it is only necessary for the mass of the people firmly to believe that the thing works: that the Nazi state is doing what it promised, and nearing its goal. Part of such proof is a matter of plain sight—homes, roads, order. But the larger part of the work of a community or government is too subtle to be easily seen or measured. It is here that propaganda comes in. The greatest single invention of the World War was propaganda. This systematic distortion of the truth for the purpose of making larger numbers of people believe anything authority wishes them to believe, has grown into an art, if not a science. Nowhere is it being used to such tremendous advantage as in Germany today. Newspapers, public speakers, the radio, expositions, celebrations, books and periodicals; every possible vehicle of information and training, including schools, is being used today on German people to teach them that they are the most remarkable people on earth; that the National Socialist government is the best government for Germany, if not for the world; that other countries, especially Russia, are in the depths of misery, and that Jews are responsible for all criticism heaped on Germany and for most of the other ills of modern countries.

George Padmore, "Hitler, Mussolini and Africa," *Crisis*, September 1937

Aimé Césaire's argument in Discourse on Colonialism *that Western European fascism originated in colonial ideology and colonialist policy and practice (see his essay in Part III of this volume) was for some anticolonialists epitomized by the case of Ethiopia.*

They perceived fascist Italy's invasion of that country in 1935 as an extension of two prior events: the 1884 Berlin Conference, which divided up the African continent, and World War I, interpreted by both Lenin and W. E. B. Du Bois as an expression of European capital's "scramble for Africa."

The Trinidadian Marxist George Padmore (1903–1959) offered a striking distillation of these historical threads in his 1937 essay for the Crisis, *the magazine of the National Association for the Advancement of Colored People (NAACP). The essay also indicates something of a crossroads in the analysis of both fascism and communism by anticolonial intellectuals.*

Padmore joined the Communist Party USA in 1927. He attended the second congress of the League against Imperialism, a formation of the Communist International, or Comintern, in 1929. In 1934, Padmore quit the Comintern, alleging that it was failing to give adequate attention to African colonies and decolonization, especially in Liberia. The break with the Comintern hastened and deepened Padmore's commitment both to anticolonial work free of Soviet influence, and to his leadership within the Pan-African Movement.

Pan-Africanists frequently criticized the international Communist movement as an unstable ally to decolonization. Stalin's continued material support for Italy, even after its invasion of Ethiopia, was the dominant example. Indeed, Padmore's analysis of Italian (and German) fascist reach into Africa perceived it as an effort to cast off "surplus populations" from the metropole and an endeavor to maximize profits by exploiting indigenous black labor.

Padmore's analysis is thus significant in several ways: First, as an expression of growing tension between Communist Internationalism and the anticolonial movement. Second, as the articulation of an emerging Pan-African perspective on fascism. Third, as forerunner to Césaire's own 1950 analysis. Fourth, as a predictive example of a wider, emergent Third World discourse on fascism and colonialism. And fifth, as a reminder of the long-term role Ethiopia has played as touchstone in the anticolonial (and African American) freedom struggles. Padmore's fidelity to an African perspective on global events finally presaged his eventual move to Ghana and role as central advisor to then-president Kwame Nkrumah in the crucial years of that country's decolonization.

The Italo-Ethiopian War and the demand of Hitler for the return of the former German colonies in Africa has served to focus attention on the question of the "haves" and the "have nots" more than at any other time since the Versailles settlement. For as long as Germany was weak and disarmed, the Allied powers were able to ignore her colonial demands, which [Foreign Minister] Stresemann had raised as early as 1926 at the time of Germany's entry into the League of Nations. But with Hitler's repudiation of the Treaty of Versailles and the revival of Germany as a great military power, her colonial demands can no longer be ignored.

It is no exaggeration to say that there never was a period in the history of postwar Europe when the issue of peace or war has been so inseparably bound up with the scramble for colonies in Africa as at the present time.

Not without reason, Lord Salisbury once declared that "Africa has been created to plague ministers of foreign affairs." There is much truth in this, for in the epoch of imperialism the colonial question represents the most important problem for industrialized nations. And precisely for this reason, we find Germany, Italy and Japan, great powers with few or no colonies, demanding a redivision of the world at the expense of

England and France, the two powers with the most extensive colonial empires; as well as the Soviet Union, which covers one-sixth of the earth's surface.

The first-named states are sometimes referred to as the "have-nots," while the latter powers are considered the "haves."

With the reopening of the colonial question, Africa is once more being used as a pawn in the European diplomatic game and as such will undoubtedly influence the new alliances and alignments among the great powers, as she did during the decade prior to the World War. The African problem (Abyssinia) has already given rise to serious political repercussion, unleashing the forces of revolution and counterrevolution in Spain, which in turn has intensified class conflicts on the one hand and imperialist antagonisms on the other, all of which are accelerating the danger of another World War.

Colonies and War

These political events, especially the Abyssinian crisis, have forced large sections of public opinion in Europe and America to realize for the first time the close relationship which the colonial question bears to modern wars. Here is no international issue apart from the Versailles settlement which has such propaganda value as the colonial question, with its appeal to "national prestige" and "honor," and in this way everything is being done to arouse in the German and Italian peoples the most reactionary, chauvinistic and militaristic sentiments.

Commenting upon the question, "Colonies and Peace," the *Daily Herald*, the mouthpiece of the British Labour Party, writes: "What is the colonial problem? Is it economic, or *is it psychological*?" And goes on to say: "Primarily it is not a question of trade, it is a question of prestige, of status. The dangerous tensions are not economic, but psychological. The origin of impending trouble is a sense of inferiority." While there is much truth in this, the fact nevertheless remains that the chief reason for colonies is economic. Capitalists ceaselessly pursue profit and interest. They are more concerned with these concrete assets which colonies represent than with such abstract ideas as "prestige." Germany, Italy and Japan need markets, sources of raw materials and spheres for capital investment.

"Italy will not resign herself to the abused commonplace that she is poor in raw materials. It must be said instead that she does not possess certain raw materials. This is a fundamental reason for her colonial demands," thundered Mussolini to the Second National Assembly of Corporations on March 23, 1936. The satisfaction of these economic needs dictates the foreign policy of the fascist imperialists of these countries.

These needs, however, are nothing new. They existed before the World War and arise in the life of every capitalist nation at a particular stage of its industrial development—the stage of imperialism. "The desire to acquire markets and to possess new lands rich in natural resources . . . was also one of the compelling motives of national policy in the case of certain of the great powers of Europe in the closing quarter of the nineteenth century, and in fact, to the very eve of the World War itself."

Expanding Populations

The only new claim which the fascist dictators have put forward as an additional justification for colonial expansion is the need to find space for their "surplus" populations. And strange to say, it is precisely this question of "overpopulation" for which the dictators are themselves largely responsible.

Mussolini and Hitler have encouraged the increase of population by every possible means. They have taxed bachelors, offered premiums for large families, and organized mass marriages. The only thing they have not yet done is to nationalize the Italian and German women. This artificial stimulation of population has naturally intensified the problem of unemployment, which every capitalist nation, especially in its period of decline, is permanently confronted with. Therefore, it is sheer humbug to be exploiting the question of "overpopulation" as a means of furthering the economic-imperialist aims of the bourgeoisie. However, because of the dangers involved in this demand for suitable territories for colonization, the issue has to be faced. "For," says Mussolini, "we are hungry for land because we are prolific and intend to remain so." While Alfred Rosenberg, the Nazi racial theoretician and director of the foreign affairs bureau of the Nazi Party, declares: "Germany demands the right to expand in order to procure sufficient territory for its future 150 million inhabitants. In this great battle for existence of the future—the struggle for honor, freedom and bread ... people must be forced eastwards, in order to free the territory for German peasants to cultivate. Only thus can there be the possibility for the German people to breathe, again."

Italian Philosophy

Let us examine the so-called "overpopulation" problem as it is supposed to exist in Italy, before dealing with the economic aspects of the colonial question.

Italy is a country of 121,000 square miles, poor in mineral and agricultural resources, called upon to maintain a population of 42 million, which increases at the rate of about half a million a year.

Prior to the introduction of rigid immigration restrictions in 1924, about 400,000 Italian workers and peasants went to the United States annually. Since then, emigration has fallen off considerably, although France and her North African colonies—Tunis and Algeria—as well as Brazil, Argentina and other Latin American republics, absorbed several millions until the world economic blizzard burst over those countries.

Today, this safety valve of immigration is more or less definitely closed, and as the years go by unemployment and starvation will increase in Italy. Such a situation will naturally lead to social unrest, which might have the effect of endangering the Fascist regime. So Mussolini resorted to war against Abyssinia in order to distract the attention of the Italian workers from their misery. And now that the Abyssinians have been conquered, the dictator believes that he can solve "overpopulation," that is, unemployment, in that country, despite the fact that Italian colonization in Libya, Eritrea and Somaliland has been a complete failure. What are the facts?

Not more than 25,000 Italians, including some of the very poorest Sicilian peasants, have settled in Libya, which is three times the size of Italy. The truth is that there are six times more Italians living in the French territories of Tunis and Algeria than in all the Italian colonies in Africa. Why is this so? Because, unlike the French North African possessions, the Italian colonies are backward. They are backward precisely because Italy is poor and cannot afford the necessary capital to turn these desert areas into lands suitable for white colonization.

But apart from the poverty of Libya, tropical colonies as a rule offer very few economic opportunities to Europeans as settlers, except people with large amounts of capital, such as the Britons in Kenya, who are drawn from the upper classes—retired colonial officials and ex–army officers. And even they are largely subsidized by grants-in-aid from the British treasury and Kenyan government in the form of agricultural bank loans which are saddled upon the native taxpayers. Then there is another problem: that of climate. In this respect, Africa for all continents is the least suitable for white colonization, except in the extreme south (the Union [of South Africa]) and north (Tunis, Algeria, Morocco) and the highlands of Kenya and Kilimanjaro. But even in these areas fertile land is limited, and then, the whites are entirely dependent upon black labor.

Colonization Costly

Italian emigrants, unlike the British in Africa, would be drawn from among the poorest of the poor—unemployed workers and land-hungry peasants. Then, apart from this, the Italian government has not capital with which to subsidize them. Until recent years the Italian government gave an annual subsidy of 23 million lire to Eritrea, and 42 million lire to Somaliland, but has had to abandon colonization precisely because it was too costly. Even if Mussolini succeeded in borrowing money from bankers in Paris, London or New York to finance his colonization scheme in Abyssinia, he would have to guarantee these countries an "open door" policy in his East African "Empire." But this would deprive the Italian capitalists of monopoly. For the only way by which they can compete against their more powerful European, American and Japanese rivals is by pursuing a policy of economic nationalism carried out behind a protective tariff wall and currency manipulation. Mussolini has already instituted such a policy by expelling the well-known British-Indian firm of Mohammed Ali from Abyssinia.

History has shown that no people have ever voluntarily migrated from a country where they enjoyed a higher standard of living to one which offered not only less social and economic opportunities but greater hardship and misery. And this, by the way, has nothing to do with race; it is a question of cultural standards. The Japanese, for example, have had to face the same problem as many European peoples. For years, Japan has had control over large colonial possessions in close proximity to the motherland. Nevertheless, the Japanese workers and peasants, whose conditions of life are not very high, judged by Western standards, have not availed themselves in any large numbers of the possibilities of settling in these territories, for the very simple reason that as bad as their conditions are at home, they are still higher than those of the Koreans, Manchurians and Chinese, with whom they could never hope to compete. It is precisely for this reason that Europeans immigrants, including Italians, Poles and Balkan peoples, whose standards are among the lowest in Europe, have never gone to Africa and Asia. They have always migrated to the Americas—Brazil, Argentina and especially the United States—as well as the more industrialized European countries where they could hope to find employment and better their economic and social conditions. Even the British dominions offer few inducements to English workers, much less the African colonies.

Let Mussolini proceed. The Italian masses will soon discover that they have been duped. For regardless of the lip service which capitalists, be they fascist or non-fascist, give to racial solidarity and national patriotism, they are all after the same goal—superprofits. And this can only be obtained by exploiting the cheapest labor possible. In Abyssinia, the cheapest labor will be black and not white. This fact is so commonplace that it is hardly necessary to emphasize the point that Italian workers will be at a disadvantage in selling their labor power in Africa.

Competition with Native Labor

For example, take South Africa, where the proletariat is composed of two races: European and African. And what do we find? Things have gone so badly for the white workers that the government has had to resort to the Colour Bar Acts and other forms of discriminatory racial legislation in order to safeguard their interests. But even those measures have not solved the problem, for since the overwhelming majority of European workers are unable to find protection within the Colour Bar scheme, they are forced to compete with the natives, with the result that South Africa has one of the biggest social problems on its hands—the "poor white" class.

While it is true that the standard of life of Italian workers is among the lowest in Europe, nevertheless it is still much higher than that of the Abyssinian serfs, and when considered in relation to the climatic conditions under which they will have to live, theirs would be hopeless lot indeed. Furthermore, in a world of surplus stocks of raw materials, Abyssinian products would have to be produced by the lowest-paid labor in order to compete on the world market. Under such conditions what chances could Italian immigrants in Africa have against indigenous labor?

The same applies to the Germans to an even greater extent, since they are accustomed to a much-higher standard of living than the Italians. And precisely for this very reason, when Germany was a great colonial power, there were only 18,000 Germans, including civil and military officials, traders, and gentlemen farmers, in all her African possessions. The truth of the matter is that there were more Germans gainfully employed in Paris on the eve of the war than in all the overseas German territories.

Africa was, and still is, no place for German colonists, except the privileged few with sufficient capital to guarantee them the status of employers. Even Hitler seems to realize this, for while stressing the need of colonies as sources for raw materials, markets and outlets for capital, he has always emphasized the fact that when he talks of new lands as the future home for German peasants, he means the Soviet Ukraine.

Professor Sir Arthur Salter, of Oxford university, supports our contention that Africa is unsuitable for European colonization. He says:

I think it is well to say as emphatically as possible that as a contribution to the surplus population of the world by immigration, colonies offer just nothing at all ... Whatever Japan does in regard to Manchuria in ten years' time, there won't be as many Japanese in Manchuria as the increase of Japanese population over six months. If Italy conquered the whole of Abyssinia and planted settlers there as hard as ever she could in ten years' time she would not have dealt with the increase of population of Italy in two months. If you take central tropical Africa, all the Europeans in all the colonies established in the course of more than a quarter of a century, do not amount to as much as the increase of the Italian population in a year. There is no such thing as a surplus population anywhere except one that is relative to and caused by the economic system.

We wholeheartedly agree with the learned professor that "there is no such thing as a surplus population," for the USSR, a country with 175 million population and an even more rapidly increasing birth rate than that of Italy and Germany, is not only able to accommodate its population, but is continually raising the standard of life of the people; while that of the German and Italian workers goes from bad to worse. There is no mystery about this. It simply proves the superiority of the socialist economic system over capitalism. The Soviets have solved "overpopulation" to such an extent that they are fighting hard to give their people more bread; while the fascists want war because they cannot provide any bread for theirs.

Canada and Australia

Assuming for the sake of argument that there exists a legitimate demand on the part of Italy and Germany for territories on which to settle their "surplus" populations, it seems to us that Canada and Australia offer far more suitable conditions for European emigrants than Africa. Quite true, the dominions also have their unemployment problems, but so have the African colonies. None the less, these white men's lands, thanks to the tremendous areas which they cover, on the one hand, and their small populations on the other hand, should certainly be thrown open to Germans and Italians, especially since they debar non-Europeans. Would this not be a worthy gesture in the cause of world peace?

Charles Coughlin, "Not Anti-Semitism but Anti-Communism," Radio broadcast, December 4, 1938

Charles Coughlin (1891–1979) was arguably the most influential anti-Semite in US history and led the largest pro-fascist mobilization in the United States during the 1930s. A Roman Catholic priest born to Irish Catholic parents in Hamilton, Ontario, he moved to the Detroit area in 1923, where he began broadcasting sermons at the National Shrine of the Little Flower in 1926. His radio broadcasts became increasingly political: by the mid 1930s, they brought together Coughlin's notorious blend of virulent anti-Semitism, rabid anticommunism, anti–New Deal rhetoric, and nationalist populism. With an audience in the millions, he became the first major right-wing radio personality in the United States.

Coughlin also worked through a short-lived political party called the National Union for Social Justice (1934–1937), through the widely circulated newspaper Social Justice, *and through a movement he urged his followers to form in 1938 called the "Christian Front." The latter was based on Franco's call for a "Christian Front" to combat the Popular Front in Spain. Coughlin's most devoted followers tended to be Irish American men and were strongly concentrated in urban centers in the Northeast, particularly Boston.*

Coughlin's speeches are instructive because they allow us to see how even in the 1930s, American racists and anti-Semites often disavowed self-identifying as such. Here, Coughlin makes a half-hearted distinction between "good Jews" and "bad Jews" that enables him to appear fair-minded even as he blames Jews for what he sees as the world's major unfolding catastrophes.

Two weeks ago the minds of our American citizens were focused upon the latest outburst of Nazi persecution directed against the Jews of Germany. Every newspaper heralded abroad the news of a $400 million fine imposed upon 600,000 German Jews by a government which already had restricted the liberties of Catholic and Protestant and Jew[1]—a government which, thanks be to God, had not resorted officially to the guillotine, the machine gun or the kerosene-drenched pit.

This was the first time our apathetic generation was aroused to the cries of distress which were sounding upon heedless ears since 1917.

This magnificent publicity was regarded as a rainbow of hope which filtered through the dark clouds of despair. Recognizing it as such, I seized the opportunity to raise my voice not only in condemnation of this latest manifestation of persecution, but to amalgamate the forces of a sympathetic world against all persecution—be that of Catholic or Protestant, Jew or gentile.

Surely, thought I, these barbaric outbursts against race or creed must be traceable to some common origin. Surely a chastened world must be willing to sacrifice its selfish racial and nationalistic objectives to militate against the common cause of all the afflictions experienced by our fellow men resident abroad.

Without attempting to minimize the atrocities of Nazism, I drew to the attention of this audience the excesses of Communism. I insisted that Nazism was only a defense mechanism against Communism.

To an intelligent audience, composed of intelligent Christians and intelligent Jews, I appealed, "Let us distill our sympathies not only from the tears of the oppressed Jews but also from the lifeblood of 20 million Christians."[2]

---

1   Coughlin is referring to the aftermath of Kristallnacht ("The Night of Broken Glass"), a nationwide spasm of violence in which Nazis broke the windows of German Jewish businesses, burned synagogues, and beat and humiliated Jews in the streets. Following the pogrom, the Nazi government blamed the violence on the victims and forced the German Jewish community as a whole to pay a fine of 1 billion Reichsmarks (400 million US dollars). International media coverage of Kristallnacht solidified world opinion against the Nazi regime.

2   Coughlin frequently claimed that the Bolshevik Revolution was led by Jews and murdered 20 million Christians in a "Holocaust." His followers repeated this myth as well. Few doubt the horrifying nature of the Stalin regime, yet Coughlin grossly mischaracterizes the form of its terror to fit an anti-Semitic narrative. While the number of Stalin's victims is debated by scholars, it is now known that most of them were killed in a preventable

That was my prayer.

"Let us attack Communism and destroy it from the face of the earth, if we are scientific in our approach to the whole problem of persecution; for causes must be removed before effects can be destroyed."

That was my counsel.

For having made this appeal; for having suggested this counsel; for having pointed out that atheistic Jews were too prominent in furthering the cause of Lenin and Trotsky with its religion of atheism, its patriotism of internationalism and its security of confiscation, I was most unexpectedly assailed by those who characterized my address as a defense of Nazism and an expression of anti-Semitism. Of these misunderstandings I tried to dispose last Sunday when I produced the previous Sunday's broadcast by transcription. Unfortunately, however, those who seemingly reject both my pleas and my counsels and whose official, organized silence toward Communism manifests a most alarming situation—unfortunately they have not seen fit to meet my challenge of distilling their sympathy both from the tears of the Jews and the blood of the Christians. Instead they have intentionally dodged the issue by endeavoring to confuse the public mind, particularly through the use of managed editorials and mismanaged interviews. For emphasis, let me repeat that the controlled press has failed to face the issue which I presented.

Would not a dispassionate judge be inclined, then, to conclude that the effort on the part of my critics to assail my person and scoff at my presentation of facts—would he not conclude that this is related to their desire to protect Communism?

My friends, there would be no warrant for my continuing to occupy your attention with further argumentation on this subject had the press inaugurated an honest effort to arouse sympathy against the atrocities of Communism as well as against the injustices of Nazism.

But the press has failed.

Therefore, in loyalty to my fellow Christians, I, in turn, am challenged to pursue my course.

. . .

---

famine caused by the collectivization drives of the early 1930s. No scholar would make the fraudulent claim that at any point in Soviet history there was a Jewish-led campaign specifically against Christians resembling the Nazi Holocaust. For a post-Soviet account of the atrocities of the Stalin regime, see J. Arch Getty and Roberta T. Manning, eds., *Stalinist Terror: New Perspectives* (Cambridge, UK: Cambridge University Press, 1993).

As to the newspapers and their adverse editorials of the past week, do you recollect the complaint which I uttered two Sundays ago?

On that occasion I expressed the thought that when millions of Christians in Russia, Mexico, and Spain were made targets of the machine gun, little or no publicity was given by the public press to these persecutions which future generations will regard as the worst atrocities of all times. Then there was a silent press. Then there was a venal press that eulogized those responsible for establishing a policy of recognizing Russia. Then there was a calloused press that belittled the grief of Spain and Mexico.

Although many newspapers have not taken a position of "hands off the Communist question" and "hands off those whose silence supports it," a powerful group of papers practically have adopted that attitude. They gloss over our recognition of Russia. They applaud when congratulations are cabled to the haters of Christ. They vacillate between the Spanish loyalists and rebels. They praise the liberalism of Mexico.

And why? You ask me why?

. . .

In a spirit of truth and of courage to defend truth, I dare to unfold for you the following concrete story of a typical controlled newspaper—a story where those, or their representatives, who control the advertising dollar, control the freedom of the press.

Last week Rabbi Leo M. Franklin of Temple Beth El, Detroit, Michigan, sought an interview with Mr. Henry Ford to discuss with him, among other things, the possibility of the Ford organization's engaging the services of certain refugee Jews whom the rabbi expected to be expelled from Germany.

In the presence of Mr. Ford and his executives, this matter was discussed at some length. A résumé of Mr. Ford's conversation was written by the rabbi. Confessedly, it was the rabbi's composition—not Mr. Ford's. It was the rabbi's concept of not what Mr. Ford actually said, but what Rabbi Franklin would prefer he had said.

Following this meeting, the *Detroit Free Press* printed a purported first-person interview with Mr. Henry Ford. It was captioned by front-page headlines which read: "'Ford Assails Nazis' Persecutions and Welcomes Jewish Refugees as Valuable Addition to US Life.' In a statement severely critical of the Nazi persecution of the Jews, Henry Ford

Wednesday night declared that he favored the admission of persecuted Jews to this country under the selective quota system."

The purported interview quoting Mr. Ford [was] carried in all the newspapers at home and abroad—this purported interview quoting Mr. Ford, in the first-person singular throughout—was not given by Mr. Ford. The interview which the *Detroit Free Press* said was given out at Dearborn, Michigan, on Wednesday of last week was not given out by Mr. Ford or by any of his executives on Wednesday night or at any other time. Here, my friends, was a gigantic attempt to put into the mouth of America's foremost manufacturer words he did not say. To my mind, a new low in editorial responsibility—a mark seldom equaled in the history of American journalism—was attained.

Social Justice magazine, distrustful of the purported interview carried in the *Detroit Free Press* of December 1 relative to Nazi persecution, sent its investigators to ascertain the facts of the case.

Mr. Harry Bennett, speaking officially for the Ford Motor Company in the presence of Mr. Henry Ford—the same Harry Bennett who arranged the meeting between Rabbi Franklin and Mr. Ford—permits us to say the following in a signed statement:

1. The direct quotation carried in the paper is totally inaccurate and was not written by Mr. Ford but was composed by Rabbi Franklin.

2. Rabbi Franklin came to see Mr. Ford to ask him if his factory would assimilate Jewish refugees, the result of Nazi persecution. Mr. Ford said that he believed there was little or no persecution in Germany; if any, it was due not to the German government, but to the war-mongers, the international bankers.

Moreover, while Mr. Ford expressed his humanitarianism for all people, yet [*sic*] he believed that Jews wouldn't be content to work in factories.

That was the essence of the talk between Mr. Ford and Rabbi Franklin. But the story handed to "The Detroit Free Press" was written by Rabbi Franklin and handed to it by Rabbi Franklin and not by Mr. Ford.

Ladies and gentlemen, the above quotation, from an article which will appear in *Social Justice* magazine, on this travesty in journalism, is authentic.

There is a sample of inspired news which a controlled newspaper dispensed for public reading, as if it were, a direct statement composed by Mr. Ford himself. For what purpose, I ask?

Possibly for the same purpose and subject to the same influences as when some newspapers find it profitable to adopt the policy of silence on Christian persecution abroad, they are willing to headline the $400-million fine levied against 600,000 Jews day after day.

. . .

Next permit me to analyze and refute the statements publicized by Mr. Kerensky and Mr. Trotsky.

Alexander Kerensky—one of the chief witnesses whose testimony is supposed to stultify my plea to oppose Communism together with Nazism—a witness whose contribution was intended to confuse the public mind, is not well known to the younger generation.

Mr. Kerensky was prominent for a period of seven months in 1917. He was the leader of the first of the three Russian revolutions.

. . .

As a matter of record, Mr. Kerensky's revolution came in like a lion in the windy month of March 1917, and left the state of this troubled world like a lamb in October of that same year. Contrary to common opinion, Mr. Kerensky did not successfully annihilate tsarism. As a matter of fact, it was the guns and bayonets of the Trotskyites and Leninites that accomplished that in July 1918—they of the second revolution, which succeeded in overthrowing the Kerensky government.

The first revolution was devoid of atheistic Jewish domination and for that reason, possibly, was a failure. It lasted only seven months.

But the second Russian revolution, which for the sake of clarity we now refer to as the Trotsky Russian revolution,[3] not only drove Alexander Kerensky as a wanderer over the face of the earth; not only murdered the tsar and his family in 1918, but inaugurated the mass murder of 20,400,000 Christians. That was the real Russian revolution with its dictator; its subjugation of 160 million people; its pogroms against Christians; its professed atheism and its advertised internationalism.

Kerensky, the father of the first assault against the injustices of tsarism, practically vanished from the headlines in 1917. But on this,

---

3   By singling out the Jewish Trotsky, rather than non-Jewish Bolshevik leaders like Lenin and Stalin, Coughlin was able to make the false claim that the Bolshevik Revolution and Soviet state were "led" by Jews. Interestingly, the name "Stalin" rarely appears in Coughlin's rhetoric.

the occasion of his reappearance, I welcome the opportunity to agree with him heartily that the Jews had only an insignificant part in his failure. I agree with him that after he fled Russia ignominiously with the coming of the Lenins and Trotskys in October 1917—I agree with him wholeheartedly that the Jews who were successful in establishing Communism over the stillborn corpse of his socialistic effort—that these were apostate Jews, as he calls them, or atheistic Jews, as I term them.

. . .

Let us now turn our attention, momentarily, to the second Russian revolution, which began in the autumn of 1917.

Mr. Leon Trotsky was one of its prime movers. He was the successful revolutionary. Now an exile to neighboring Mexico, this witness was persuaded to enter the lists against me last week—a revolutionary who, after the death of Lenin and the advent of Stalin, was, in turn, forced to become a wanderer over the face of the earth.

I believe that history will support me when I state that Leon Trotsky has come to court with most unclean hands. He is the crystallization of Nero, Diocletian, Julian the Apostate, Ivan the Terrible, Cromwell and Napoleon Bonaparte—the outstanding mass murderer of time and eternity. This Leon Trotsky whose correct name is Bronstein; this most unfortunate of all possible witnesses whom my opponents could persuade to testify against me, said last week: "The name of Jacob Schiff means nothing to me—if Mr. Coughlin indicated an important sum, then it must be pure invention."[4]

I should not dignify such—shall I say—such an unreliable witness as is this Bronstein with a rebuttal lest the ghosts of his 20 million victims should rise from their resting places to assail me.

Ladies and gentlemen, permit me to discuss the widely read statement issued last week by the banking firm of Kuhn, Loeb & Company disavowing its connections with Russian revolutions in general, and Mr. Jacob Schiff's financial association with them in particular.

This statement appeared specifically in an early edition of the *New York Times* on Tuesday, November 29, 1938, and was withdrawn from the later editions of that paper on that same day. The statement, in part,

---

4   In a section of his address omitted in this volume, Coughlin claimed that a Jewish American banker named Jacob Schiff financed the "Kerensky Revolution."

reads as follows: "The firm of Kuhn, Loeb, & Co. has never had any financial relations, or other relations, with any government in Russia, whether Czarist, Kerensky, or Communist."

. . .

When considering the Kuhn, Loeb & Company we are considering a unit of the generic abstraction so often referred to as international bankers. In every nation throughout the world the various units of this fraternity operate, shuttling gold back and forth to balance exchanges; issuing credits from nation to nation, not only for productive commercial enterprises, but also for destructive and military ends.

From the sunset which marked the passing of the glories that characterized the thirteenth century, down through the welter of wars which besmirched the pages of each succeeding age, the shadow of the international banker hovered over every battlefield, cast gloom over every home and fastened the burden of debt upon every innocent babe.

Theirs is a fraternity which owes allegiance to no flag. Theirs is a patriotism which transcends the boundaries of every nation.

For them, empires and kingdoms, principalities and republics are chessboards.

With their shuttling of gold and credits, scepters fall; crowns roll in the dust and millions of pawns, victimized by purchased propaganda, are claimed by death.

Mammon is their god—the god of greedy gold. Internationalism is their religion—the religion of fettered slavery.

The Kuhn, Loeb & Company statement opens the avenues of thought which lead to such considerations; for the present members of this firm are anxious to deny any relationship to any revolution. First they should prove to a suspecting world that they have no relationship to the international bankers resident abroad.

Kuhn, Loeb & Company is an international banking firm. As such, then, I will refer to it when now considering the statement it issued as well as on future occasions if there be further need.

. . .

Last week I telephoned to Dr. Denis Fahey[5] at Blackrock Seminary, Dublin, Ireland, asking him to reinspect an original British "white

---

5   Denis Fahey (1883–1954) trained in France in the early years of the twentieth century, when he was a member of the then-protofascist Action Française.

paper" from which I quoted . . . he has records from which I am about to read now in connection with the assertions issued by Kuhn, Loeb & Company to the effect that "neither the firm of Kuhn, Loeb & Company nor any of its partners, past or present, assisted in any way to finance the Communist revolution in Russia or anywhere else."

Father Fahey quotes a document thus:

> If we bear in mind the fact that the Jewish Banking House of Kuhn, Loeb and Co. is in touch with the Westphalian-Rhineland Syndicate, German-Jewish House; and with the Brothers Lazare, Jewish House in Paris; and also with the Jewish House of Gunzbourg of Petrograd, Tokio and Paris; if, in addition, we remark that all the above-mentioned Jewish Houses are in close correspondence with the Jewish House of Speyer & Co., of London, New York, and Frankfort-on-the-Main, as well as with "Nya Banken," Judaeo-Bolshevik establishment at Stockholm, it will be manifest that the Bolshevik movement is in a certain measure the expression of a general Jewish movement, and that certain Jewish banking houses are interested in the organization of this movement.
>
> . . .

May I pause to repeat what the whole world knows—that these German financial institutions referred to in the Sisson Report[6] were dominated by international-minded Jews—warmongers—who, more than any other classification of citizens in all the world, were responsible for the holocaust of 1914 to 1918. One could add that they not only dominated the imperial government of Germany, but, it appears, they had tremendous influence in our own government . . .

Alas, my friends, history will not only attribute the financing of the Bolshevik Revolution to this type of internationalist. History will become more eloquent day by day in proclaiming to posterity the part they played in manipulating the press and propaganda, in controlling public opinion, in bestirring racial and national animosities, and in unleashing the four horsemen of the Apocalypse to run roughshod with their devastation over the face of civilization.

---

6   Coughlin refers here to a document published by the Committee on Public Information, the US government's propaganda agency during World War I, entitled *The German Bolshevik Conspiracy* (1918). It purported to show that the Bolshevik Revolution was in actuality a German plot to undermine the Allied war effort. Even the arch–Cold Warrior George Kennan argued in 1956 that the report was fraudulent.

Once before, we fell victims to their greed for power and lust for wealth.

An awakened civilization, throbbing to the experiences of the past twenty years, must not let history repeat itself!

In passing from this point of discussion—and in face of a plentitude of evidence submitted by eminent Jews that 65 to 75 percent of the officials of Soviet Russia are Jews who form only 2 percent of the population[7]—what, then, is the purpose or where is the substantiation for John. W. Stanton's article which is scheduled to appear in today's issue of the *Detroit News*—an article which says: "To say that the Russian revolution owes its origins to the activities of any group of foreign interests is to show only a superficial understanding of the facts underlying the forces that led to the downfall of the Romanovs and the advent of the Bolsheviks to power."

... Thanks be to God that the majority of Jews—poor, humble persons like the majority of Christians—played no part in this. They, as were we, were the pawns upon the checkerboard of death and persecution. These I invite to stand with us in our battle against Communism and Nazism.

My friends, by inviting the religious Jews and religious gentiles to join hands in assailing Nazism and Communism, together with the injustices which produced the latter, I shall be castigated as one who stirreth up the multitudes.

Most probably I shall be scourged at the pillar in the hall of some modern Pontius Pilate.

What of it?

I shall continue my crusade, with God's help, for the humble Jew who has been the victim of persecution down the ages, and for the humble Christian whose wails have remained inarticulate—cost what it may.

---

7   Jews certainly contributed disproportionately to the building of socialist and communist movements in Russia as elsewhere in Europe, and were overrepresented in left-wing parties, as many were drawn to the left's cosmopolitanism and modernity. Couglin, however, is no doubt exaggerating the Jewish communist role in order to feed the Judeo-Bolshevik myth. Yuri Slezkine's study found that Jews comprised 4 percent of the Russian Empire's population at the turn of the century, and that in 1922, non-Jewish ethnic Russians formed the vast majority of the Bolshevik Party (72 percent). The most overrepresented ethnicity in the party, including its security apparatus, were actually Latvians. See *The Jewish Century* (Princeton: Princeton University Press, 2004).

In my effort to arouse the decent elements of America to campaign against Communism as well as Nazism; in my effort to appeal to the Jewish gentlemen who have risen to such prominence in the fields of radio, press and cinema—the instruments which mold our public mind—I am characterized as being an anti-Semite—an anti-Semite because I decry atheistic Jews whom Jewry officially and consistently has not repudiated.

. . .

May I reiterate what I emphasized last Sunday: There is no anti-Semitic question in America. There is an anti-Communist question here, and there will continue to be an anti-Communist question, veil it how you will, until we conquer or until it conquers us.

From it there is no decent retreat on the part of decent Christians and decent Americans.

Toward it there is no respectable silence on the part of respectable, organized Jews.

Thus, once more I incorporate in the record of this day's speech a story told in the *New York Times* in reporting the meeting of the American Jewish Congress held in New York last October:

> The mention of Communism threw the convention into an uproar when delegates and visitors attempted to shout down Abraham Levin, a St. Louis, Mo., delegate, who demanded that a proposed declaration of the convention's principles be amended to include a denunciation of Communistic theories. After heated discussion Mr. Levin withdrew his demand.

This silence toward Communism; this refusal to condemn it officially on the part of this representative body of Jews is beyond explanation.

Official Jewry must condemn officially not only the theory but the practices of Communism—Communism whose policies have crimsoned the once-blue rivers of Europe with the blood of 20,400,000 martyrs and which is making charnel houses of the cathedrals of Spain.

Decent Jews—American Jews—must repudiate atheistic Jews and international Jews. By doing so they are hurling a challenge in the face of members of their own race who have disgraced their race—the Trotskys, the Zinovieffs, the Lunacharskys—men whose avowed purpose in life is to tear God from his heaven and tear patriotism from the hearts of nationalities.

To the highly intelligent Jews of America who recognize these truths, particularly, do I appeal. I humbly admit your influence in banking, press, and radio. And I humbly suggest, for your own sakes and the sakes of less informed members of your race, that you, too, will recognize that there is no anti-Semitic question which must be solved—a question which cannot be solved except your genius and your assets are thrown into the battle on the side of God and country.

In conclusion, I plead for impartiality in governmental decisions—an impartiality which will not only strike with all its might against the injustices of Nazism in regard to the Jew, but with equal strength will utilize its majesty in behalf of the persecuted Christians abroad—victims of Communism.

. . .

May the Holy Trinity infuse into the minds of our rulers a spirit of justice, of fairness both to Christian and Jew, and, if necessary, a spirit of militancy against the Communists both at home and abroad who, up to this present moment, this government has been protecting, aiding, and abetting both by its silence, its cooperation and its criminal "good neighborliness"!

American League for Peace and Democracy, *People's Program for Peace and Democracy,* 1938

Initially launched by the Communist Party USA (CPUSA) in 1933, the American League against War and Fascism, which changed its name to the American League for Peace and Democracy in 1937, was the largest American antifascist network in the 1930s and in many ways the quintessential US Popular Front organization. Most of its members were not in the CPUSA. It primarily served as a coordinating body for the antifascist activities of over 1,000 affiliate organizations representing 7 million people (at its peak), including the American Civil Liberties Union (ACLU), the National Association for the Advancement of Colored People (NAACP), the American Friends Service Committee (AFSC), union locals, and other civil rights organizations. Its activities mostly took the form of lobbying and political pressure campaigns at the local, state, and federal levels. It sought civil rights and labor reforms domestically, as it viewed racial violence and union busting as "steps leading to fascism," and pursued a shift in US foreign policy toward a clear rejection of fascist states. It was more successful in uniting liberals and communists than it was communists and socialists.

A key target of the League was the so-called Neutrality Acts of the US government, which prevented the sale of arms to all warring states. Instead, they promoted legislation that clearly favored antifascist forces in China and Spain while economically sanctioning Italy, Germany, and Japan. The League's injunctions against US military buildup illustrate that for the Popular Front, as for the American left in general, the goal was not to send

US troops to Europe and Asia. The famous argument pitting "isolationists" against "interventionists" in the 1930s was not over sending US combat troops abroad, which was beyond the pale of political debate in the 1930s. Rather, it was a fight between those who favored economic sanctions against Germany, Italy, and Japan, and those who saw even such limited moves as a step that could draw their country into war (the latter were mostly conservatives).

In its early days, the League was hostile to President Roosevelt, seeing him as an imperialist and even a protofascist. But the CPUSA's turn to the Popular Front line, and, more importantly, the president's "Quarantine the Aggressors" speech in October 1937, changed this relationship. In the late 1930s, the League saw Roosevelt as an ally and tried to lobby Congress behind his foreign policy vision vis-à-vis the fascist states.

In its later years, the League's rallies, congresses, and roundtables enjoyed the sponsorship of US members of Congress, state governors, city mayors, and even presidential cabinet members. Tragically, it fell victim to the Hitler-Stalin Pact of late 1939, after which the CPUSA withdrew its support and the organization folded. One of its last resolutions, in December 1939, was to call for economic sanctions against the USSR for its invasion of Finland.

The following program, adopted at the Fourth Congress of the American League, is not a creed. Those who do not agree with one or two of the points can work with the others, if they accept the general purpose of the American League. These nine points represent only an initial program. The rest has to be made as situations arise . . .

1. Organize emergency citizens' committees for labor's rights wherever those rights are attacked either by employers or by public officials.[1]

The reactionaries have used this tactic in fake "citizens' committees" for the purpose of thwarting and denying labor's democratic rights. It is to the interests of the people of the community to organize their own committees. To be effective they must be organized in advance—before

---

1   The editors have found no evidence of follow-up, at the national level, on this call for emergency citizens' committees. It seems the idea behind these committees was to build political coalitions among labor's allies, and not antifa-style "self-defense."

the people are deceived by the propaganda of the corporations, in time to provide adequate defense of labor's civil rights before the antidemocratic offensive begins. A part of the job is exposing the employers' hypocritical slogans of "law and order" and "the right to work." What do they mean by law and order when they take action into their own hands by means of hired thugs, subservient officials and company policy? . . .

2. Defeat legislative attempts to compel incorporation of unions and to control or inspect union finances by government or other outside agencies.
In Washington, reactionaries are trying to amend the Wagner Act for this very purpose. In several state legislatures anti-labor forces are seeking to destroy labor's recent gains by means of repressive and regulatory legislation. Compulsory incorporation is a limitation of the democratic rights of labor because there is no compulsory incorporation of business. Employers are free to incorporate or not as they choose. While business incorporates for the purpose of diminishing liability, incorporation of unions is proposed in order to increase liability . . . Labor unions are not profit organizations and should not be treated as such . . . All these proposals to regulate unions, making labor responsible, et cetera, point in one direction. They are steps toward the capitalist-controlled labor front of the Fascist state.

3. Press for anti-lynching law; and measures to guarantee full rights for the Negro people and the foreign-born.
For the third time the House has passed an anti-lynching bill. Again it has been opposed in the Senate by a combination of antidemocratic forces. Hotel discrimination against the Negro people is growing worse in many cities. Negroes on relief and in flood areas have suffered discrimination in securing the very necessities of life. Likewise the foreign-born—both those unemployed and those in unions—have been denied their rights on many occasions.

For every group that is denied the opportunities and privileges which democracy requires to be shared, the American League is both a service agency and an opportunity for expression in a common cause. It is a concrete expression of the old maxim of uniting all for the good of each, and joining each for the good of all. At Pittsburgh the League is now fighting in the courts the discrimination shown by hotels against Negro delegates to the People's Congress. It is insisting that the equal rights law adopted by the Pennsylvania legislature be fully observed in practice.

4. Oppose vigorously the propaganda of race prejudice and discrimination.

The Jewish people as well as the Negro people are now the objects of growing prejudice and discrimination. Anti-Semitic attitudes and activities pervade certain businesses, schools and committees. Persecution of racial and minority groups is a part of the pattern of developing Fascism. Opposition to this propaganda of hate and falsity is essential to the preserving of the democratic rights and welfare of all groups. With this Fascist propaganda of race hatred being circulated widely through our country—in violation of American tradition and even of some cases of law—it is the obligation of the supporters of democracy to expose its lies and counteract its influence. Such activities are of vital importance in thwarting the formation of Fascist forces in our nation.

5. Defeat the War Department plan to conscript labor and industry and to regiment press and radio.

Since 1921 our militarists have been working on this plan. Its essential principles, incorporated into the Sheppard-Hill Bill [HR 6704 / HR 9604],[2] are now being considered in Congress. This legislation is backed by both the War and Navy Departments and by the American Legion. The plan is designed to involve everybody, "from the soldier in the most forward line to the humblest citizen in the remotest hamlet in the rear." In operation this scheme would establish a military-industrial dictatorship and place Fascist controls upon American people.

Opposition of peace groups, labor bodies and other public-spirited organizations resulted in minor revisions of the Sheppard-Hill Bill during the 1937 session of Congress. But the principles and purposes of this piece of pro-Fascist legislation remain the same. Pressure by all types of national and community organizations that support democracy and oppose war is needed to defeat this bill when it comes up for vote in

---

2   This legislation was designed to give the president broad powers to carry out industrial mobilization planning in the event of a national emergency: that is, to enforce a coordinated system of industrial production goals and federal contract procurement for the purpose of building US armed forces.

Congress. The danger will continue as long as the industrial mobilization plan exists. Such plans to destroy democracy are the very nature of
modern war . . .

**6. Support the nationalization of the manufacture of arms, ammu-
nition and implements of war, forbidding export except when
ordered by Congress in cases of countries invaded by an aggressor.**
We must keep our materials and labor out of the aggressor's hands so he
cannot continue these conflicts. This country has not only helped
Germany and Italy to rearm in preparation for future war, but has
consistently sold them war supplies throughout the Spanish Civil War.
During 1937 American munitions companies sold Germany
$1,097,769.67 worth of war materials. The same has been true for Japan,
both before and since the beginning of her present invasion of China.
Last year Japan bought $1,896,514.09 worth of munitions from this
country. This trade of the "merchants of death" must be stopped.
Nationalization of the munitions industry is the only way that this
can be done. No other method can establish effective controls.
Nationalization of the manufacture of arms would also take the profit
out of human slaughter and thus remove one of the drives toward war.

Reserving to Congress this right to make exceptions to countries
invaded by an aggressor *is* the means of putting point no. 9b of this
program into effect. Under this method the people through Congress
will make the peace policy of the United States instead of leaving it in
the hands of the State Department or the president. This use of our
economic goods is the counterpart of withdrawing our economic
resources from aggressor nations both in time of peace and in time of
war . . .

National Defense Policy

Coupled with points number 5 and number 6 is the necessity of demanding a national defense policy consistent with keeping the United States
out of a foreign war and protecting our coasts and borders from invasion. Military and naval leaders of unquestioned reputation have testified that the present armed forces of the United States are amply
adequate.

Continual expansion of our military and naval forces can only be for the purpose of carrying on armed conflict far from the shores of this country. Annual budgets of over a billion dollars a year and $800 million appropriations for a big navy are utterly inconsistent with the needs of national defense. Battleships with 5,000 miles cruising radius are not for the protection of our coasts. A wartime army of 4 million men is not for the defense of our borders. *Reductions*, not increases, in military and naval appropriations are imperative in order to avoid entanglement in war outside the United States. Increases mean gravitation toward war. The American League's policy of economic action (through the people's boycott and embargo laws) does not require increased armaments. Such economic action is a realistic substitute for these huge expenditures.

At the beginning of the present Far Eastern conflict, the American League urged, in addition to the people's boycott and embargo on war supplies and raw materials to Japan, that our government announce that the time had come to make real the independence of China by withdrawing all foreign troops from her soil and warships from her waters, and by ending all national and international concessions which infringe upon the sovereignty of China.[3] We urged that our government—as evidence of its good faith—should immediately announce that its armed forces in China and in Chinese waters will be used only for the purpose of evacuating American citizens and providing some measure of safety for our diplomatic and consulate staff against methods of Japanese warfare properly characterized by Secretary Hull as "contrary to the principles of law and humanity." We pointed out that limitation of our naval forces in Chinese waters to those necessary for the above purpose is essential to reducing the risk of war-provoking incidents. The League further maintained that our government should inform the Japanese government that our commanders are instructed not to yield to any demands or requests to so dispose our ships as to make easier Japanese attack upon Chinese civilians or its unjustified aggression against China.

---

3   Japan launched its full-scale invasion of the Chinese mainland in July 1937, after which the war in China was in the headlines constantly. US antifascists in the late 1930s saw Spain and China as the two main battlegrounds in the global war against fascism.

7. Promote the people's boycott of Japanese goods.

This is a refusal to cooperate with Japanese militarists, not an attempt to punish the Japanese people. It is a method of helping to stop the Japanese war machine and of supporting the Japanese people who are opposed to the invasion of China. Japan's unfavorable trade balance makes her economy depend heavily on the continuous sale of her exports. Our refusal to buy Japanese goods withdraws economic support necessary to keep the war going. It is joining hands with people in Japan who refuse to support the war—labor leaders, workers, progressives and intellectuals, many of them now imprisoned by the Japanese militarists . . .

The American League also supports the boycott of German and Italian goods as an effective economic action against the Fascism and war policies of these governments.

8. Seek to remove and prevent restrictions on the access of the governments of China and Spain to our markets, applying regulations to purchases and shipments designed to remove the risk of our being involved in war.

By denying the recognized government of Spain the right to buy the means of its defense in our markets, the Neutrality Act of May 1937 has actually strengthened the war-making forces because it leaves Germany and Italy, the supporters of Franco, free to buy war supplies here, directly and through other nations. There has not been and there is not the slightest danger of our being drawn into the Spanish conflict, with or without the Neutrality Act. The experience of the Mexican government in continuously selling arms to the Spanish government proves the case.

The present Neutrality Act would cut off China from access to our markets. Under cash-and-carry procedure there would not be the slightest danger of our being involved in war over the sale of munitions to China for her defense against the Japanese aggressors. China and Spain are the concrete situations now to be met under the general policy laid down in point no. 9.

9. Demand a foreign policy based on:

a. The distinction between the aggressors and their victims.

b. The necessity of denying our economic resources to the war-making, treaty-breaking aggressors and opening them up to their victims under conditions designed to remove the risk of our being drawn into war.

c. The necessity of concerted action to quarantine aggressors.

(a) It is the failure to make this distinction between the aggressors and their victims that makes our present Neutrality Act un-neutral. When the Fascist allies found that the democratic states could be bullied and threatened into depriving the Spanish government of its international right to buy arms, they proceeded to pour in their own supplies and men to aid Franco. Japan applauded when President Roosevelt forbade the shipment of arms to China or Japan in federally owned ships. A foreign policy that does not distinguish between aggressors and victims is plainly helping to destroy justice, law and peace throughout the world.

(b) A foreign policy that makes the distinction between aggressors and victims in economic action is the alternative to one that leads to war. This means an embargo on all war supplies—arms, ammunition and implements of war, also such raw war materials as oil, scrap iron, cotton and copper—to Japan, Italy and Germany.[4] These powers are still loading war supplies at our docks while in Spain and China, American materials and labor are used to destroy peace-loving, democratic peoples and their lands. It is useless and hypocritical to talk about the sanctity of treaties while we are thus helping the treaty breakers.

Action by labor in refusing to handle war supplies for the invader is both a powerful pressure on our government and on the public of every nation. Already at Southampton, Middlesbrough, Glasgow and London, English workers have refused to load such materials for Japan. In Australia, the Waterside Workers' Federation has officially decided that its members shall not load war supplies to Japan and have so informed the government. Wherever labor takes such action, it requires the immediate support of the middle classes on the picket line, with legal defense in the courts and with relief funds.

. . .

(c) The type of concerted action called for here is defined in point b above. The "quarantine" refers to economic noncooperation with nations invading and attacking others. This noncooperation takes the threefold form of people's boycott, labor's refusal to handle goods and

---

4   A footnote in the original document listed the value, in millions of dollars, of all US arms and raw materials shipped from the United States to Germany, Italy, and Japan in 1937, based on US Department of Commerce data.

embargo legislation. To have the maximum effect such steps must be developed in concert by those nations which have the supplies the invading aggressors need to carry on their wars. Such concerted action does not necessarily require alliances. It can develop by the force of example or by treaties in some cases. In many countries at the present time the spontaneous people's boycott of Japanese goods is becoming so widespread and important that it is raising powerful pressures for the adoption of embargo laws.

An illustration of what the American League means by concerted action is the stand it took in September 1937, regarding our obligation under the Nine-Power Treaty to prevent Japanese conquest of North China. We urged the United States government to cut off supplies to Japan and to announce that there would be no recognition of any gains secured by violations of treaties. We also urged our government to invite the other signers of the Nine-Power Treaty and the Kellogg Pact to make similar declarations and take measures to prevent the use of their economic resources by the violator in carrying out his aggression.

Organizational Structure of the League

The American League is composed of national and local organizations and individual members. The basis of representation and the structure of the various bodies of the League are set forth in the constitution . . .

Individual members of the League are organized in branches which meet once or twice a month and carry on community or neighborhood programs of education and activity on the current issues and campaigns involving democracy and peace. In cities where more than one branch exists, a city council is formed, consisting of representatives from the branches and from local affiliated organizations. This council directs the League activities and campaigns for the whole community.

Local organizations affiliating to the League are entitled to two representatives on the city council. These representatives are responsible for carrying activities for peace and democracy into their organizations. Frequently a special peace committee is organized in the affiliated organization for the specific purpose of leading and stimulating antiwar and anti-Fascist activity on the part of the entire membership. Many locals or branches of National Affiliates of the League play a vital part in community activities for the protection of democracy and the achievement of peace. In addition many central and local labor bodies, fraternal, social and farm organizations are affiliated to the League.

National Officers and Executive Board

Dr. Harry F. Ward of New York City is national chair of the League, while Professor Robert Morss Lovett of Chicago and Mrs. Victor L. Berger of Milwaukee are vice-chairmen[5] . . . Additional members to make up the full board of eighteen will be selected as other national organizations become a part of the League.

The American League secures its financial support from membership fees, affiliates' dues, contributions from individuals and organizations and assessments upon its branches and city councils . . .

A Mass Movement

The composition of the American League as a combination of affiliated bodies and individual members makes it distinctly a people's organization. Its Fourth National Congress, where over 4 million American people were represented by elected and accredited delegates, indicates to some degree the scope of the organization. On occasions—such as opposition to the Sheppard-Hill Bill and other pieces of gag legislation—the League's campaigns have attained mass power and effectiveness. Through its publications and publicity the League reaches far beyond its membership and affiliated bodies, and influences organizations and individuals in many parts of the country. Its pressure power and prestige represent a mighty instrument of the people for the cause of peace and democracy.

---

5   In a long sentence redacted here, the pamphlet lists the eleven members of the national Executive Board, who were "responsible for the administration of the League."

What the League Has Done

Beginning in October, 1936, with the bringing of the first Spanish delegation to the United States, the League was cofounder and a moving force in the North American Committee to Aid Spanish Democracy. In addition to over $14,500 in cash, tons of clothing and thousands of cans of food were collected and contributed for the aid of the Spanish people. One American League home for forty children has already been established in Spain and several others are being developed. The League helped to bring about a reversal of the State Department's restrictions on passports to people going to Spain to perform humanitarian services. From the outset of the conflict in Spain, the League has urged application of embargoes on war supplies to Germany and Italy because of their alliance with Franco . . .

Aid to Labor

Aid to labor in its fight for democratic rights has been a continuous activity of the League. Members and affiliate bodies supported labor's rights in the auto and steel strikes of 1937, taking part in conferences, picket lines, issuing leaflets and press releases. A field organizer worked in Ohio on labor issues during the Little Steel strike and rendered valuable service. Members of the Chicago League supported the Citizens' Rights Committee in the campaign following the Memorial Day massacre. On October 8, 1937, the League organized an open hearing on vigilante activities at Pittsburgh. Before a panel of distinguished citizens, victims and witnesses of vigilante activities testified. A mass meeting followed wherein the community was rallied for a campaign to stop such illegal and antidemocratic practices. A forceful statement, issued by the League and signed by sixty-seven religious, educational and civic leaders, received wide publicity.

For China

Nationally the League was the first organization—so far as we can discover—to call for a boycott on Japanese-made goods. In addition to the holding of mass meetings and boycott conferences, collecting funds for relief and medical aid, the League serves as a clearing house for information and activities on behalf of the Chinese people. Its China aid council is responsible for the sending of the first American medical mission to China. In addition hundreds of thousands of boycott buttons, leaflets, stickers, posters and pamphlets on the China situation have been circulated.

A medical aid unit consisting of two physicians, a nurse, full operating implements for both physicians, [and] portable X-ray equipment has been sent to China and is now at work among the Chinese people. Over $15,000 had been sent to the Chinese people when this pamphlet went to press. This sum includes the support and monthly supplies for the medical unit.

In addition to its monthly magazine, the *Fight*, during 1937 the League published four pamphlets, a calendar and nine leaflets, totaling 209,000 pieces of literature on various subjects and issues.

Against the Sheppard-Hill Bill in the 1937 session of Congress the American League was one of the leaders in the fight to defeat this piece of pro-Fascist legislation. League representatives appeared before the Senate and House Military Affairs Committees in opposition to this measure. Support for the La Follette Civil Liberties Committee, passage of the anti-lynch bill, adoption of the Nye-Fish resolution to embargo war supplies in peacetime, revision of the Copeland Bill anti-labor clauses and support of the Celler Bill to remove section 213A of the Economy Act were other issues on the League's congressional program.

Local conferences, campaigns and meetings were held by League groups in many sections of the country, reaching a climax in the National Congress at Pittsburgh at the end of November 1937. In many cases the American League was the first organization in the community to swing into action when issues involving democracy and peace arose. Outstanding work was done by the Philadelphia League on the anti-Nazi issue and the Cleveland League in uncovering a local Fascist coalition called the Association of Leagues. San Francisco Leaguers took an active part in securing the repeal of an anti-picketing ordinance, while the New York City division helped rally the first big mass meeting for China, held in Madison Square Garden on October 1. The Washington, DC, League branch successfully picketed the Japanese consulate on several occasions and centered attention on the invasion of China.

Summary

It is now more than four years since the American League made its appearance on the American scene. This organization has done a pioneering job and a good deal more. Not only has its analysis of the intimate relation between Fascism and war, democracy and peace, been verified by a succession of tragic events, but the League has demonstrated the way to oppose and forestall these hideous pestilences. It has made significant progress in bringing together the forces that have the power and are under the necessity of ending war and stopping Fascism. It has put into practice the type of democratic coalition upon which the future of this country and other lands depends. Today, facing more pressing demands and more insistent problems, the American League has more actual power and greater potentialities than at any time in its history. It urges all organizations and individuals who desire peace and prize democracy to join the ranks of this people's movement and work on a constructive program to obtain these objectives.

Felix Morrow, "All Races, Creeds Join Picket Line," *Socialist Appeal*, February 24, 1939

New York City mounted policeman tries to take an American flag away from antifascist counterprotester outside Madison Square Garden during a German American Bund rally, February 20, 1939.

The February 1939 rally of the German American Bund in New York's Madison Square Garden was the largest pro-Nazi rally in US history. Twenty-two thousand packed the Garden under swastika-bearing Bund banners to hear speakers adorned in Nazi-inspired "Order Division" uniforms denounce "international Jewry" and pledge "1 million Bund members by 1940." Outside the Garden, 50,000 antifascists, with another 50,000 looking on, challenged the Bund and upward of 1,000 New York City cops. When the evening was over, the Socialist Workers Party, which organized the protest, declared victory, and the Bund's organizing momentum went into permanent decline.

The Bund rally was the brainchild of Fritz Kuhn, a Bavarian-born veteran of the German infantry during World War I who joined the Nazi Party while a student at the University of Munich. The Bund organized around 1935 in strict imitation of the German Nazi Party, bearing uniforms modeled on the SS, opening camps where trainees learned the German Nazi anthem, and circulating Nazi and anti-Semitic literature meant to "free America" of Jewish and communist influence.

Between 1936 and 1939, the Bund became the best-funded Nazi organization in the United States, its membership peaking at 25,000. In 1938, the Bund endorsed the Third Reich's Kristallnacht pogrom and cosponsored with the Silver Shirts—another fascist group—a Chicago rally that drew large protests. Kuhn decided to up the stakes, planning a "Pro-American Rally" for Madison Square Garden on George Washington's birthday—February 20. The Bund considered Washington "the first fascist."

The Socialist Workers Party had already challenged Silver Shirts in Minneapolis the previous fall, when the Garden rally was announced. Though smaller in number than the Communist Party USA, the SWP threw itself into organizing, printing 200,000 "Stop the Fascist" fliers. The CPUSA, meanwhile, abdicated protest, claiming that demonstrations would put the party in conflict with the city and the police. Meanwhile even the New York Times helped advertise organizing against the Bund.

The SWP's mass protest outside the Garden was notably echoed inside the halls that night by Isadore Greenbaum, a Jewish hotel worker who rushed the stage as Kuhn was delivering the event's final speech. Greenbaum was tackled and beaten by Bund security and the New York Police. Outside, as Felix Morrow reports here for Socialist Appeal, the SWP's newspaper, a coalition of diverse demonstrators, including Jewish war veterans, fought the police to at least a draw.

The Bund subsequently canceled two planned rallies in other cities. Later that year, Kuhn was sentenced to more than two years in prison for tax evasion. When Germany declared war on the United States, the state revoked his citizenship, and after he was released from prison in 1943, he was declared an enemy agent.

The fighting antifascists who answered the call of the Socialist Workers Party were of many types.

Among those who pressed against the horses, fighting for every inch of ground, were Spanish and Latin American workers, aching to strike the blow at fascism which had failed to strike down Franco; Negroes standing up against the racial myths of the Nazis and their 100 percent American allies; German American workers seeking to avenge their brothers under the heel of Hitler; Italian antifascists singing "Bandiera Rossa"; groups of Jewish boys and men, coming together from their neighborhoods to strike a blow against pogroms everywhere; Irish republicans conscious of the struggle for the freedom of all peoples if Ireland is to be free; veterans of the World War; office workers, girls and boys, joining the roughly clad workers in shouting and fighting; workers of every trade and neighborhood of the city.

Can't Stand Nazi Smell

They had come, the overwhelming majority of them, not because they were adherents of the Socialist Workers Party—to most of them indeed the name became etched on their consciousness for the first time—but because that party, alone among the working class and antifascist organizations of the city, had clearly and unambiguously called them to confront the hated fascists.

Some of them brought homemade signs, eloquent of their anxiety to speak out. "Give me a gas mask, I can't stand the smell of the Nazis," read one, perched on the end of an umbrella rib. "Hitlerism Is Political Gangsterism" read two others, identifying their bearers as "German-Americans of Yorkville." One group of Jewish American World War veterans from Brooklyn brought a large American flag.

Learn about Cops

Many of the demonstrators learned for the first time what the cops are. While the Socialist Workers Party spokesmen were addressing the huge crowd of Fifty-First Street, making clear to the demonstrators the role of the police as protectors of the Nazis, an impatient Jewish boy appealed to his friends: "Help me to get up to speak to the police for two minutes, they'll leave us through if we appeal to them and explain we just want to picket."

A few minutes later those he sought to appeal to were grinding him down under their horses' hooves.

As the main contingent of the demonstration pressed against the horses on Fifty-First Street, the veterans from Brooklyn sought a simpler solution. With their big flag at their head, they marched to Fifty-Third Street and Ninth Avenue to Fiftieth and attempted to turn east toward the Garden.

As they marched they sang "Hallelujah" with its original pious words, and shouted to onlookers: "All those who believe in democracy march behind the American flag." As they tried to turn toward the Garden, the police stopped them. "We're veterans," the front line shouted. "We're good American citizens." Then came the shambles.

The horses drove them onto the sidewalk, then followed them there—eight mounted cops driving them down on the street like so many hunted animals. At Fifty-First Street the cops wheeled and came back at full speed, driving those who had hidden in doorways out into the open where they could ride them down again. Veterans fought back wildly and hard, and gave the cops more than they took; at the end of the fight, their flag emerged with only tatters left on the flagstaff. The cops had torn it to ribbons. It was 9:15, two hours after the veterans had appeared. A lesson in democracy.

The Jolly Lieutenant

In the Forty-Seventh Street police station the lieutenant was laughing ruefully as the work piled up. A young student was brought in, picked out of the demonstration on one pretext or another. The lieutenant sought to question him. "Am I under arrest?" the boy asked. "If so I want to telephone for a lawyer." "Yah smart, young feller," grinned the lieutenant. "Well I ain't booking you, what do you know about that? Take him upstairs and make him talk!"

The Poor Horse

Almost tearfully, a cop reported that his horse's mouth had been injured when he had ridden him into the demonstration; he had arrested a demonstrator who had grabbed at the bridle when the horse came at him, and he blamed the bridle puller for the horse's injury.

"Is he hurt bad?," the lieutenant inquired solicitously. "Take him up to the veterinarian right away. Book your prisoner for disorderly conduct and separately for cruelty to animals. Where is he?" "We got him upstairs," the cop answered grimly.

. . .

Mood Changes

As the evening wore on, and incident piled upon incident, the mood of the crowd changed. "Curiosity seekers," as the press called them, who stood watching at 6 p.m., were shouting slogans at the direction of the party's squad marshals at 8 p.m. At 10:20 they fought back, blow for blow, as the cops rushed them on Eighth Avenue between Forty-Seventh and Forty-Eighth; they would not give way even when the mounted cops took to the sidewalk and drove them up against the plateglass store windows. Clear and musical came the sound of one window after another cracking under the weight, pressed against the windows by the horses, and determined not to retreat.

Cops in True Light

For hours thereafter, even when the Socialist Workers Party spokesmen had concluded the action and formal demonstration had ceased, the demonstrators walked up and down Broadway, and the appearance of a patrol wagon or a mounted or motorcycle cop was the signal for spontaneous boos. They had learned their lesson: the cops, whom they had been taught in public school were civil servants, they had found to be friends and protectors of the Nazis, and vicious, brutal, sadistic attackers of a peaceful antifascist demonstration.

Avedis Derounian, "Mobilizer and Queens Christian Front Street Meeting," ca. 1940

Outdoor meeting of the Christian Mobilizers, New York, NY, 1939.

Avedis Derounian (1909–1991) was a first-generation Armenian American writer and antifascist known for infiltrating right-wing extremist groups and reporting what he witnessed in hard-boiled, noir-styled exposés. His first book, Under Cover: My Four Years in the Nazi Underworld of America, *penned under the name John Roy Carlson, became the number-one bestseller in the category of nonfiction for 1943 and into 1944. His book* The Plotters, *on fascist groups in the United States and their appeal to veterans, also made the bestseller list in 1946. Derounian saw the Armenian genocide, the Holocaust, the politics of the American right, and US Cold War policy not as separate events, but as one unfolding catastrophe.*

Derounian reports here on a meeting of the Christian Mobilizers, a New York–based offshoot of the Christian Front that shared many of the same members as its parent organization. The membership of both the Coughlin-inspired Christian Front and the Mobilizers was heavily Irish American, some of them police officers. They were fascist, "anti-alien" organizations that formed their own militias while campaigning against the New Deal, "Jewish influence," and the admission of refugees into the United States. Their members also assaulted people they identified as Jews in public places, particularly in Boston and New York. Formed in 1939, the Christian Mobilizers were a more radical splinter of the Christian Front that worked closely with the German American Bund. The Front was effectively shut down in early 1940 after the FBI accused some of its Brooklyn-based members of a terror plot, yet it had a quasi-underground resurgence during World War II, particularly in Boston, when its followers again attacked Jews in the streets.

The following unpublished report was prepared for the Friends of Democracy, a liberal antifascist organization that tracked hate groups. Derounian worked closely with this organization, which was founded in 1937 by the Kansas-based Unitarian minister Leon Birkhead.

Springfield Blvd and Jamaica Ave—May 11—Queens Village

The night was fit for murder only, a chill rain beating down and going into your bones. The meeting was at the square beneath the Long Island Railroad station of Queens Village, next to a village park, and at the intersection of four busy corners. An [illegible] good place for a meeting. If it weren't for the weather you'd have had four times the crowd. You get them coming and going in all directions: they get off the train, and get on it; at least twenty-five buses pass the intersection every hour; it is a vital shopping center; the movie is right there; there's a park where people sit and can listen; the audibility is good except for the occasional rumble of the trains, and the honking of horns. I was under the impression we'd have seats and all, but it was merely a street meeting. A full dozen cops were around, two with gold badges. Their sympathies were with the leaders of the meeting, easy enough to see that. It did them no good to listen to two and a half hours of Christian and patriotic talk by Mack, Kurts and Lewis. It didn't do our side any good to have about 150 people listen to it. Many women around me came out with "Ain't he swell." "He is right." Quite a few participants in the audience. The cops kept the crowd moving, and the thing was highly orderly. At the very beginning of the meeting, a few hecklers in passing autos yelled out, and Mack took ten minutes to threaten them verbally. Mack had along his bodyguard, and I got a look at him for the first time, a good look. A tough six-foot bruiser, athletic and powerful, of probable Irish descent. A 200-pound beefer, with extremely alert eyes. Not a sleepy pug, but intelligent, apparently, at his work.

Mack[1] came in a closed car, license #3A–67–96. In the car were Helmond, the bodyguard, Mack, Philip, Daniel Horgan, and Reverend Lewis, and another fellow: the guy who owns the car, a Hungarian guy, dark and swarthy, who always loans his car out to Mack. They came about 9 p.m., and at just that time I got off the bus after having taken the wrong bus and being stranded out on a windswept highway, "with the wind and the rain in your hair"—it's the stanza of a song we used to sing in high school assembly: "There's a cottage small by the water-fall . . . at the closing of the day . . . with someone to wait by the garden gate . . . lalalala."

Kurts[2] was gassing on the speaker's platform, a convertible thing, with the American flag stuck on the right side. A powerfully built, pink-cheeked, keen-eyed, fanatically inclined brawler and rabble rouser of a speaker. He is nobody's fool, this guy, knows exactly what he is up to. As a speaker he is not bad, not as much personality as Mack, but capable at addressing those of a low mental level—lower than Mack's clientele.

---

1   "Mack" refers to Joe McWilliams (1904–1996), a notorious anti-Semite and leader of the Mobilizers. He was born in rural Oklahoma and moved to New York City in 1925. McWilliams was arrested in June 1940 for "disorderly conduct" on account of anti-Semitic remarks he had made in a street corner speech. In 1940, he ran for Congress as a Republican in the Yorkville district of Manhattan; after losing badly, he formed the American Destiny Party, modeled on the German Nazi Party.

2   Daniel Kurtz was leader of the Queens unit of the Christian Front.

"Are you," he asked the audience, "proud or ashamed of your Christianity?" The audience stood dumbly by. "If more than two of you are together," he quoted Christ as having said, "then I'm with you, but without me ye cannot do. Christ is here amongst us, though we can't see Him. He has to be here amongst us. This is a Christian meeting." It wasn't raining at the time, and he said that on two previous occasions it had rained continuously until he, Kurts, took the platform; then the rain stopped. It had resumed when [he] had finished speaking. It made me wonder which side Christ was on. I did not have long to wait, for even while he spoke it started to rain, and it kept raining, and the heavens kept on, kept on weeping, till I began to get chilly in my pants. I went over to [a] cop and asked if we could move under the railroad trestle. Good thing it was there, for the heavens wept bitterly in protest for Kurts's outlandish claims that God and Christ were with him. It almost seemed that God himself took a personal hand to convince the audience that He wasn't with Kurts.

Let me stop the rhetoric and quote directly from notes I made, full notes.

Kurts: "These are the kind of meetings that Father Coughlin and General Moseley have been telling us to hold, Christian meetings. We are preparing the earth for a better day to come, and the better you plant the earth, the better crops you can have. You know that. Last year it was no real Christian Front; their dues were too high and it was betrayed by the enemy. But this year we are going to have a real *united* Christian Front. I want to introduce to you the leading organization in New York of Christian Americans, the Christian Mobilizers." He went on in this vein for a while, and finally introduced Reverend Lewis.

The audience snickered when Lewis got up, pompously, his eyebrows coal black and shining out like a black cat in the dusk. His hair clipped short, and, presenting the appearance of anything but a cleric, he made an incongruous appearance. His gray suit was badly in need of a pressing; he had no dignity, no churchly front. He spoke guardedly, and did not mention any Jews by name. Spoke against communism. He claimed for himself to be a duly ordained minister . . . He said that communism led to dictatorship and nothing else. He characterized the Council of the Churches of Christ as being neither Christian nor representing the Protestant churches in America. "There is no such thing as Christian Socialism," he said. "We are fighting for our civil liberties, for freedom of press, speech and assembly. There are some in New York who are trying to take it away from us." He promised that under the Christian form of government he was advocating, all the poor would be taken care of, jobs would be given, and Americans would come *first*, and non-Americans last. He beefed around for fifteen minutes . . .

Mack got on the platform. Made a good appearance. I looked at him at close range. The strain he has been through the past year is telling on him. He was drawn, haggard. Maybe too much whatchamacallit. But anyway, he was going on nervous energy, drawing on his reserves. Most of us in the city are that way, but on Mack it can have a particularly injurious effect, because of his murmuring heart and other ailments.

But first, let me finish off Kurts—he made a second speech after Mack was finished. Said Kurts, taking courage from Mack's open[ly] anti-Jewish speech, "If the Jews want to conform to our Christian government, they are welcome. As a minority, with a minority voice in the affairs of the nation, the Jews are welcome to live with us." He had on a Christian Front button, was dressed in a light-brown suit. His wife was there, one of her front teeth missing. His wife seemed Irish, and Kurts, too, with possibly some German mixture. "Remember, friends, we are fighting communism—that same communism that destroyed 39 million Christians in Russia (wow!). We Christians will not let happen to this country what happened in Spain. We are not going to let happen to us what happened to the Christian Front in Brooklyn. We are not going to be framed. Maybe we are anti-Semitic. Maybe I myself am anti-Semitic, but we are telling you the truth, and that's our defense. We have to do it. If communism is Jewish, we are not anti-Jewish, but we are anticommunist, and above all, we are pro-Christian." He reached down to the floor of the platform and took something out of a paper bag. He swung it aloft like a baseball club. It was a cross, painted white. He dangled it high up above him, reaching up with his chubby legs. "In this sign we are fighting. For this cross we are fighting. Under the banner of Christ we are fighting the anti-Christ. In this sign we shall conquer. Goodnight, friends, and God bless you," he ended. "And God bless you," echoed a dope. I was too chilled to see who the guy was.

Now for Mack. Direct notes made on the spotsky: "I am glad, ladies and gentlemen, to speak for Dan Kurts to start him off on his political campaign. One of the things we need in this country is men with guts, who are not afraid to call a rat a rat and a Jew a Jew." Applause. "There's some of them here" (cries of "Get away you Hebs," "Shut up mockey" went up). "I have surrounded myself with ex-army men, men who served in the Irish Republican Army, and the Italian Army and the German Army. All last summer we spoke in the streets of New York. Hecklers suddenly found themselves lifted by the neck, and the next thing they knew they were in the gutter. I made up my mind last year to call a rat a rat, and a Jew a Jew." (He's good, he's swell, called out a woman to my right.) "It is our constitutional right to call them what we want. It was at meetings like this in 1775 that American patriots met and got rid the land of alien oppressors, and made this nation possible. We are merely fighting to preserve our flag, our freedom of speech. Our task is to put the fear of God in these people who have no belief in a God— except the god of money. We want to protect ourselves against those who take away our liberties."

He called over the fellow who was giving out copies of the *Voice*. He referred to his picture taken with Kuhn and said: "Last summer, I went out to see how my fellow white men were spending their summer Sundays, and they asked me to speak. I could not refuse, and I made many fine friends out there that day. If there were any Jews in New York as good as New York Germans, there would be no need for me to speak out in the streets of New York. If you are pro-British these days you're swell. If you're pro-Jewish, you can have anything you want. But if you are pro-American you are not welcome. They call you an anti-Semite. I'm not an anti-Semite, but I'm an anti-termite. Put two and two together and reach your own conclusion. To be pro-American is the crime of the crime."

"Why don't the Jewboys stay over there and fight for democracy, instead of coming here by the thousands and telling us to go there and fight Germany. No, they all come here" ([a] woman yelled out: "Let them all come, then we'll all get them together"). "There, now, there's a thought," said Mack. "Roosevelt is the greatest Jew since the time of Solomon. If you don't believe me, ask any Jew" (laughter). Mack brought up the Oppenheims and Joels who allegedly own the gold mines of South Africa, again said how gold which costs fourteen dollars an ounce and sold for twenty-two at a good profit, now sells for thirty-five dollars. The boys, meaning the Jewish owners, had determined to get a Jewish secretary of the Treasury, and had succeeded. Now we pay thirty-five dollars to take useless metal from one hole in Africa and put it in another hole in Kentucky. These are just a few of the tricks of the internationalist bankers that Father Coughlin writes about. Again the anti-Jewish cries. It would have been ruinous if the weather had been good.

Mack got a good round of applause. He quickly went to the car in which he was driving, and with his bodyguard and the other bums they all piled in. I had to wait for the bus. Fortunately it came within five minutes. The rains continued—and God demonstrated unmistakably that He was on our side.

You Belong In
THE CHRISTIAN FRONT
If You Believe, as We do, that:

1. Police should have as much right to belong to the Front, as Communists such as Gerson, have to be on the same (Municipal) payroll and remain members of the Communist party.

2. The place for refugees is certainly not our U.S.A., where unemployment is still our main problem, and where American citizens and world war veterans are actually being replaced in New York City business establishments by alien refugees.

3. The New Deal is not the United States of America. It is only a temporary tenant of the White House, and has been sponsoring the growth of Communism for seven years throughout government departments and very special so on WPA, where the New Deal has given its hearty endorsement to the Communistic Workers Alliance.

4. The campaign of lies, slander and misrepresentation carried on against us by the newspapers is motivated by a policy of editors pleasing their large advertisers rather than the reading public.

5. Such anti-Christian columnists as Winchell and Zeltner of the Mirror are actually engaged in stirring up anti-racial feeling which they pretend to be anxious to prevent. Winchell in his column referred to the ladies who attended mass meetings at Prospect Hall (held to raise legal defense funds) as B-U-M-S, bums, (the exact wording). We can show you this column on request.

6. Free speech belongs just as much to the Christian in the Christian Front as it belongs to Communists who have been causing disturbances outside Home Relief District offices ever since LaGuardia took office.

JOIN THE CHRISTIAN FRONT.
PROSPECT HALL
261 Prospect Avenue, Brooklyn, N. Y.
Any Friday Night

Nicholas DE MAURO PRESS · 482 Coney Island Ave. — WIndsor 6-9344

Leaflet of the Christian Front, 1940. Avedis Derounian Papers, drawer G2, National Association for Armenian Studies and Research, Belmont, MA.

Avedis Derounian, "America First Meeting—Manhattan Center," April 23, 1941

The following account of America First's 1941 assembly, also known as the "Lindbergh Rally," comes from the antifascist investigative reporter Avedis Derounian. Derounian was rightly concerned that the America First movement represented a mainstreaming of fascist politics in the United States.

The short-lived America First Committee (1940–1941) is often remembered as a fascist organization, though its history is more complex. It was formed as a nonpartisan, single-issue movement devoted to keeping the United States out of the growing wars in Europe and Asia, and it initially attracted individuals from a broad range of political persuasions, including pacifists and socialist leader Norman Thomas (a cofounder). Yet its membership tended on the conservative side, and most of its followers were not committed pacifists, but people unmoved—for a variety of reasons—by the idea of a war against fascism in particular.

Its spokesman, Charles Lindbergh, also raised legitimate fears that America First was a fascist front organization. In the 1930s, Lindbergh made a number of widely publicized trips to Nazi Germany, where he received a medal from Hermann Goering in October 1938. While Lindbergh generally avoided pro-Hitler statements as an America First spokesman, he had left a trail of openly racialist writings, such as his essay "Aviation, Geography, and Race" (1939). Lindbergh's April 23, 1941, speech, delivered in Manhattan Center auditorium, argued that Germany was on the verge of victory over Great Britain, and that rather than seek an American savior, the British should surrender and seek a negotiated peace.

Those wanting to find fascist politics in America First literature are likely to be disappointed. The organization consciously stuck to the narrow message of keeping the United States out of war. But this is where Derounian's unpublished on-the-ground report, once again prepared for the Friends of Democracy, proves very useful. It reveals the individuals and the overall climate at a Lindbergh rally, considerations often overlooked by America First's historians and largely invisible in the organization's literature.

I'm one guy who likes to give a commie or a fascist the benefit of a doubt. Name calling I don't like. So much of it has been done that I've personally become cautious about calling anybody anything without first getting something definite on 'em. Frankly, I had not as yet been convinced that America First was fascist. The leaflet prepared by Friends of Democracy was not conclusive. The meeting tonight made up my mind about them.

Flags were passed around, small flags, thousands of flags. The mob was asked to wave the flags as they sang. It waved them throughout the meeting. If you want to see if a man or woman has fascist potentialities, give him a flag. If he starts waving it, worshipping it, making a fetish of it, he's good fascist timber. If he just takes a quiet, respectable attitude toward it, he's apt to be a quiet, respectable citizen.

The details of the speeches made have been covered by newspapers. What the newspapers did not cover was the feeling of emotionalism which the speakers did their utmost to arouse in the mob. The distribution of thousands of flags was a clever stunt. The draping of the walls with flags, thickly studded halfway around the huge auditorium, too, was significant. The red-white-blue lettering of America First, too, was in line with the general scheme of things. America First Committee is fast approaching the line of superpatriotism generated by the out-and-out fascist organizations.

I would not be in the least surprised if it expressed anti-Semitic tendencies shortly. Promotional leaflets of *Scribner's Commentator*[1] were

---

1   The short-lived *Scribner's Commentator* (1939–1942) was formed from a merger of *Scribner's* and *Commentator* magazine. It was relentlessly isolationist and published the work of many individuals affiliated with America First.

given free inside the meeting. Many of the people who were there were violently anti-Jewish. Anti-Semitic cries frequently interrupted the speakers. An extensive anti-Semitic whispering campaign went on throughout the meeting. This I know. I heard it all around me. When Lindbergh said that America First was organized to give voice to those who had no access to the press, radio or movies, the guy next to me whispered: "He sure dug into the Jews that time."

On many occasions the mob yelled "sheenies"—which is a degree lower than "kike." When a speaker asked, "Who wants war?," the mob inevitably yelled, "Jews!" Now don't get the impression that the clamor was unanimous. It was individuals among the crowd who yelled out. But others laughed, and the sentiment was not looked down on by any of them. Some thought it to be in bad taste, and that, probably, was the reason why the mob did not take a louder share in anti-Semitism.

The indications are that America First is going to veer more and more to the right, more and more the way *Scribner's Commentator* is going. This will come about within five weeks. This morning an investigator friend of mine phoned John T. Flynn.[2] He gained his confidence and got Flynn to confess that Jews were at the bottom of the pro-war sentiment. Flynn also expressed subtle anti-Jewish sentiments. This information cannot be documented, of course, but my friend is wholly reliable, and I pass it on merely as a tip—something to be followed up.

Some big-shot fascists were present; a complete list is appended. August Klapprott was seated in a reserved seat, alongside Gustav Elmer. Around them were a bunch of storm troopers . . . John Snow, hiding under a big brown hat, came in the back way because the front entrance was blocked off . . . Van Nosdall waved his flag like a child. Edward James Smythe forced his way into the lobby of the hall, but had a difficult time getting inside.[3] One of the officials at the America First Committee tried to do something for him, which in itself would

---

2   One of the founders of America First, Flynn was anti–New Deal, but also opposed to fascism. He found himself increasingly isolated within the organization as he tried to distance it from the fascist elements drawn by Lindbergh.

3   In an appendix to his report, Derounian lists John Snow as "chairman of League for Constitutional Government, a white collar, pro-fascist group which sold the Protocols." In the same appendix, Van Nosdall is described as a "former Bund member, former president of Crusaders for Americanism, notoriously anti-Jewish and pro-Hitler." Derounian lists Smythe as a Klan leader who had led efforts to unite the KKK and the Bund, and Klapprott as a "Bund leader of long standing."

seem to indicate that Smythe was regarded with respect. Smythe finally found his way.

Sitting on the platform was Mrs. Leonora Schuyler. I have seen her at Mobilizer meetings, at meetings at which Fritz Kuhn was speaker, notably the one for the Crusaders for Americanism, Van Nosdall's group. I know the woman personally. She is violently anti-Jew; she is not "anti-British." Oh no. She loves the English people—she's part English, don't you know, but the ruling set is Jew controlled, et cetera . . .

Lawrence Dennis[4] was one of the last to leave the hall. I saw him quite by accident. He was accompanied by a tall, husky blond who might have been his bodyguard. Also accompanying Dennis was a youthful woman—which wasn't his wife. I've seen him with his wife.

The man who led the singing was Charles Albert McLain. Formerly he had advertised himself as director of the "Committee for the Preservation of Patriotic Songs." . . . Significant to note is that this man led the audience at the meetings of the Committee for the Preservation of America, a pro-Coughlin, high-tone fascist crowd which used to meet at Carnegie Hall, then at the "Brown House," Bund headquarters in the lower Bronx . . . This tie-up definitely established McLain in the category of the pro-fascists. In his introductions to speeches, he has frequently made subtle anti-Jewish remarks, and cracked down on "God Save America" as an un-American song, et cetera.

I think America First is now just about tops in the anti-war crusade. Note the additional role it is fulfilling. Many of the fascist groups are closed down. The membership is flocking to these peace meetings, morally, financially supporting America First. That the Committee is rapidly becoming an out-and-out Nazi transmission belt is obvious to any who have observed it at close range. I quote from the April 28, 1941, issue of *Social Justice*.[5] The editorial on the back page, "Britain's Power Unused."

Colonel Charles A. Lindbergh became a member of The America First Committee last week.

---

4   Lawrence Dennis (1893–1977) was a leading fascist intellectual in the United States and author of *The Coming American Fascism* (1936).

5   *Social Justice* was an anti-Semitic weekly newspaper of Charles Coughlin's National Union for Social Justice.

It is the same Committee under whose auspices Senator Burton K. Wheeler speaks.

It is the same Committee under whose auspices Father Charles E. Coughlin would be speaking did he enjoy one half as much liberty as a priest and as a citizen.

It is the same Committee which all non-interventionists should join in the hope of saving this country from the destructionists—the New Deal interventionists.

With active investigation of subversive groups under way,[6] they are now hiding under the cloak of America First and affiliate "peace" organizations. It is a blind. The attendance at the meetings attests to this. For example, at the Lindbergh meeting there were representatives of the following organizations, and I'm willing to sign affidavits to that effect:

Christian Front, Christian Mobilizers (American Destiny Party), Citizens Protective League, Allied Patriotic Society, Protestant War Veterans, American Nationalist Party, Committee for the Preservation of America, German American Bund, German American Business League, German American Vocational League, American Patriots, Inc., Flying Squadrons for Americanism, Paul Revere Sentinels, Crusaders for Americanism, Inc., No Foreign War, Women United, Molly Pitcher Brigade.

Social Justice was sold outside, and outside leaflets advertising the Mobilizer meeting in Astoria on April 24, too, were given out . . .

There is money, there is brains, there is tremendous strength behind this Committee. These are the facts. The rest is up to you.

---

6 In December 1939, the US Department of Justice began cracking down on organized anti-Semitism, which it saw as fomented by foreign agents. The House on Un-American Activities Committee, formed in 1938, also investigated far-right groups.

PART II

Antifascism and the State, 1941–1945

Franklin Roosevelt, "The Four Freedoms," from the State of the Union address delivered January 6, 1941

Excerpted here is the final and most famous section of Roosevelt's 1941 State of the Union address. It outlines the "Four Freedoms," which later became an official shorthand for the US mission in World War II. At the time of the speech, delivered almost a year before the bombing of Pearl Harbor, Roosevelt was still pushing for "all aid short of war" to the nations fighting the Axis powers. To this end, he achieved a major legislative victory with the passage of the Lend-Lease Act in March 1941. But as the year wore on, the president increasingly gave up his reservations about US military deployments; he even ordered a "shoot on sight" policy to protect US shipping against German U-boats, knowing it would likely trigger war.

Most of the original speech is devoted to combating isolationism and calling for a military buildup capable of responding to rising "dictatorship" abroad. Roosevelt only rarely used the word "fascism" in public speech, but it was certainly his subtext.

Three of his four freedoms are arguably within the realm of traditional liberalism. Yet "freedom from want" expanded conventional notions of liberty by adding economic equality to a list of established rights not generally understood to impinge upon the rights of property. As such, the "Four Freedoms" reveal the impact of labor and the left on wartime rhetoric. The degree to which US war aims in World War II prefigured US global politics during the Cold War is a source of debate among scholars.

The nation takes great satisfaction and much strength from the things which have been done to make its people conscious of their individual stake in the preservation of democratic life in America. Those things have toughened the fiber of our people, have renewed their faith and strengthened their devotion to the institutions we make ready to protect. Certainly this is no time for any of us to stop thinking about the social and economic problems which are the root cause of the social revolution which is today a supreme factor in the world. For there is nothing mysterious about the foundations of a healthy and strong democracy.

The basic things expected by our people of their political and economic systems are simple. They are:

Equality of opportunity for youth and for others.

Jobs for those who can work.

Security for those who need it.

The ending of special privilege for the few.

The preservation of civil liberties for all.

The enjoyment of the fruits of scientific progress in a wider and constantly rising standard of living.

These are the simple, the basic things that must never be lost sight of in the turmoil and unbelievable complexity of our modem world. The inner and abiding strength of our economic and political systems is dependent upon the degree to which they fulfill these expectations.

Many subjects connected with our social economy call for immediate improvement. As examples: We should bring more citizens under the coverage of old age pensions and unemployment insurance. We should widen the opportunities for adequate medical care.

We should plan a better system by which persons deserving or needing gainful employment may obtain it. I have called for personal sacrifice, and I am assured of the willingness of almost all Americans to respond to that call. A part of the sacrifice means the payment of more money in taxes. In my budget message I will recommend that a greater portion of this great defense program be paid for from taxation than we are paying for today. No person should try, or be allowed to get rich out of the program, and the principle of tax payments in accordance with ability to pay should be constantly before our eyes to guide our legislation.

If the congress maintains these principles, the voters, putting patriotism ahead of pocketbooks, will give you their applause. In the future days which we seek to make secure, we look forward to a world founded upon four essential human freedoms.

The first is freedom of speech and expression—everywhere in the world.

The second is freedom of every person to worship God in his own way—everywhere in the world.

The third is freedom from want, which, translated into world terms, means economic understandings which will secure to every nation a healthy peacetime life for its inhabitants—everywhere in the world.

The fourth is freedom from fear, which, translated into world terms, means a worldwide reduction of armaments to such a point and in such a thorough fashion that no nation will be in a position to commit an act of physical aggression against any neighbor—anywhere in the world. That is no vision of a distant millennium. It is a definite basis for a kind of world attainable in our own time and generation. That kind of world is the very antithesis of the so-called "new order" of tyranny which the dictators seek to create with the crash of a bomb.

To that new order we oppose the greater conception—the moral order. A good society is able to face schemes of world domination and foreign revolutions alike without fear. Since the beginning of our American history we have been engaged in change, in a perpetual, peaceful revolution, a revolution which goes on steadily, quietly, adjusting itself to changing conditions without the concentration camp or the quicklime in the ditch. The world order which we seek is the cooperation of free countries, working together in a friendly, civilized society.

This nation has placed its destiny in the hands, heads and hearts of its millions of free men and women, and its faith in freedom under the guidance of God. Freedom means the supremacy of human rights everywhere. Our support goes to those who struggle to gain those rights and keep them. Our strength is our unity of purpose.

To that high concept there can be no end save victory.

Franz Neumann, "The Theory of Racial Imperialism," from *Behemoth: The Structure and Practice of National Socialism*, 1942

Franz Neumann (1900–1954) was among the Frankfurt School intellectuals forced into exile in the United States in the 1930s. During World War II, the US government actively recruited members of the Frankfurt School, including Herbert Marcuse, Friedrich Pollock, Max Horkheimer, and Otto Kirchheimer, to serve as experts on Nazism. Among these individuals' writings, Neumann's work was the most widely read and respected in official circles, which is striking given that it maintained the essential left-wing position that fascism was a continuation of capitalism by authoritarian means. Neumann became a high-ranking figure in US intelligence, serving in the Office of Strategic Services (the precursor to the CIA), the intelligence division of the US Chief of Staff, and the Board of Economic Warfare. He also prepared analyses for the Nuremberg war crimes tribunal.

Behemoth *examines the German war machine both as an economy and as a domestic ideological project. It highlights the central place of expansionist war, ideologically and materially, within the fascist state. Its main theses also make the book noteworthy for students of empire more broadly: in particular, Neumann argues that fascism emerges from the contradictions between private property and political liberalism, and that modern empires, always grounded in racial logics, tend to erode true democracy.*

Neumann, as with many other antifascists in the 1940s, refused to place fascist imperialism in a separate moral universe from the colonialism of the Allied powers. Rather, for him, the German case formed a unique conjuncture within a continuum of Western imperialism. In the German example, fascist authoritarianism did not arise in opposition to liberalism, but as an outgrowth of it. His emphasis in this section is on how expansionist empires are inherently undemocratic. When the costs of empire are high, they must remove democratic rights; moreover, the consent that they are able to win comes only through racial, national, and pseudo-populist appeals that erode identification with genuinely egalitarian politics. Yet Neumann also rejects the "Luther to Hitler" thesis, common among US scholars and commenters during the war, that held German culture as a whole to be intrinsically militaristic.

Behemoth was published first in English. Neumann wrote it in 1941 while at the Institute of Social Research at Columbia University, the institutional home of the Frankfurt School in its American exile.

Up to this point we have simply accepted imperialism as the most significant trend in German politics. In fact, our whole analysis has centered on the problem of Germany's expansion.

The imperial period confined its preparations for expansion to establishing an army, navy, and a reliable bureaucracy, and to merging the interests of state, industrial, and agrarian leadership.[1] The working classes were excluded. For a time, their political and industrial organizations were suppressed, and when that experiment failed, their ideological isolation and their complete exclusion from public service kept them outside the state and the ruling groups.

1. Democracy and Imperialism

The World War of 1914–1918 saw the first attempt to incorporate the working classes into an imperialistic system. The Social Democrats and the trade unions actively cooperated. In doing so, they partly betrayed the principles of their party program, but some of them honestly believed that the war was defensive and that they would be able to carry out the socialist mission of overthrowing tsarist Russia, thereby setting free the forces of revolution. But despite an initial success, the attempt to incorporate the masses ultimately failed. The Independent Social

---

1 "Imperial period" here refers to Germany from the country's unification in 1871 to its entry into WorldWar I in 1914.

Democratic party and the Spartakus Bund [Spartacus League] grew at the expense of the Social Democrats and the trade unions. The imperialist goal of German industry became so clear that the problems of the peace aims could no longer be sidestepped. At the end, the terrific impact of the Wilsonian ideology completely shattered the ideological basis upon which German imperialism rested.

The Weimar democracy—that is, the Social Democrats, Democrats, and left-wing Catholics—attempted to build a society that was not imperialistic, but was concerned with the internal reconstruction of Germany and its participation in the concert of western European powers.[2] This attempt also failed, because the three partners could not destroy the monster that lay within the German economic system. In fact, instead of smashing the power of the industrial monopolists, they unwillingly strengthened it.

The imperialist sections of German society found in the National Socialist Party the ally needed to provide the mass basis for imperialism. This does not mean that National Socialism is merely a subservient tool of German industry, but it does mean that with regard to imperialistic expansion, industry and party have identical aims.

But how can an aggressive imperialistic policy be carried out today? Not within the framework of a political democracy. General Ludendorff and J. A. Hobson, the leading English authority on imperialism, are in complete agreement on this point.

> Peoples do not understand aggressive wars, but they have a very good understanding of a fight for the preservation of their own lives ... Neither a nation nor each individual within it will support the war to the utmost unless there is a sure conviction that the war is for the preservation of their lives.

For Hobson, the outstanding phenomenon of our period is that imperialism and democracy have become incompatible.

> A political democracy in which the interests and will of the whole people wield the powers of the whole state, will actively oppose the whole process of imperialism. Such a democracy has now learned the

---

2   The Weimer Republic was a liberal democratic period spanning 1918 to 1933.

lesson that substantial economic equality in income and ownership of property is essential to its operation. The defense of capitalism is, therefore, bound up in every country with the destruction of enfeeblement of the *public franchise* and representative government.

History amply proves the truth of Ludendorff's and Hobson's views. The First World War is an excellent illustration of this, as we have already indicated. What little democracy and few civil liberties still remained in the Germany of 1914–1918 were effective agents in promoting anti-imperialist propaganda, a propaganda that was not imposed from above but sprang from the innermost feelings of the masses. In Italy, the longing for peace and the hatred of war has increased by leaps and bounds since the Abyssinian war of 1896. The history of American foreign relations also provides ample material. The first attempt to annex Hawaii (February 16, 1893), undertaken by President Harrison, was a failure. Then President Grover Cleveland withdrew the annexation treaty. The second and successful attempt (April 16, 1897) was carried out under great difficulties, although no sacrifice in blood or money was required. Once again, the primary justification of the acquisition was the old slogan of the white man's burden. The acquisition of the Philippines in 1898 was similarly hazardous. Although "innumerable voices now called for an assumption of the armored imperial garb which European powers had just made the fashion," the opposition was so strong that it nearly prevailed.

The history of English imperialism shows similar developments. It may be admitted that popular feeling for imperialist acquisition can often be aroused. Skillful propaganda, such as invasion scares of the kind current during the Boer War in England, the coalescence of what Mr. [Albert] Weinberg calls humanitarianism and force, and concessions to the masses, such as the extension of the franchise or material benefits, can for a time succeed in securing mass support. But such a mass basis is never stable. Opposition may arise and has always arisen. Besides, the imperialistic wars of the nineteenth century did not require high sacrifices in blood and energy. The Spanish-American War is one example, and the Boer War another. No imperialistic war in the nineteenth and the beginning of the twentieth centuries required anything approaching the total mobilization of man power and productivity that have characterized the wars since 1914. None of them made it necessary to transform a nation into an armed camp; none completely changed social life; none revolutionized habits. Still, it is possible, even within a liberal democracy, so to intensify nationalism by skillful propaganda and the granting of material benefits to the lower classes that the war actually appears as the outcome of spontaneous demands by the masses and not as the deliberate policy of a single group.

2. The Proletarian Folk against Plutocracies

Throughout the history of modern imperialism, imperialistic propaganda always tried two different approaches: first, to present any war as a defensive one, as a fight for life; secondly, ideologically and organizationally to incorporate the masses into the war. The white man's burden, the mission of a people, manifest destiny are examples of the second kind of approach. This kind has never been able to produce support for a large-scale aggressive war. People will not voluntarily decide totally to organize themselves for imperialistic expansion when colossal sacrifices in blood and energy are required. They must be compelled to do so. They must be organized in such a way that they cannot resist. They must be submitted to such propaganda that they do not express open resistance. Their democratic convictions must be uprooted and other ideologies must be implanted.

Nor can such wars any longer be organized in the old framework of counterrevolution and absolutism, where only the war machine is centralized and where it relies simply upon the dictatorial powers of the military command. The war is a total one; no sphere of life remains untouched. Every activity must be subordinated to it; the individual must become completely immersed, must become part and parcel of it. Such incorporation is particularly necessary because a society that has passed through the phase of large-scale democracy can no longer exclude the masses. Organizational, ideological, and propagandistic patterns must be elaborated for this purpose. The new ideology must be democratic, at least in appearance. The rulers and the ruled must be represented as pursuing identical interests; the internal social antagonisms must be utilized and transformed into external aggression.

The new National Socialist doctrine of a racial proletarian imperialism is the culmination of this method. This doctrine fuses two basic elements: hatred of England and hatred of Marx.

The essence of the theory is simple. Germany and Italy are proletarian races, surrounded by a world of hostile plutocratic-capitalistic-Jewish democracies. The war is thus a war of proletarianism against capitalism. "This war is of the money power against labor and against the creative human being, the embodiment of labor." Creative human beings must combine. "For all awakening peoples who make labor the focus of their lives, the watchword must henceforth be: workers of all lands, unite to smash the rule of English capitalism." With these words, Dr. Robert Ley, head of the German Labor Front, initiated the new propaganda campaign that culminated in Hitler's speech of December 1940. This speech contrasted capitalistic liberty, namely the freedom "for everybody to grab for himself, free from state control," with "the power of work." "I built up my entire economy on the basis of work. Our German mark unbacked by gold is worth more than gold." The war is depicted as a war for a "world of cooperative labor" against "selfishness . . . capitalism . . . individual and family privileges," against "the accursed plutocracy, against those few dynastic families which administer the capitalistic market for the few hundred persons who, in the last analysis, direct those families."

According to National Socialism, capitalism is a Jewish invention; hence, the opponents of National Socialism must be Jews. The *Schwarze Korps*, the organ of the SS, repudiated the whole National Socialist racial theory and declared that the English are a nation of white Jews. Scholars were at once set to work to prove that English culture and civilization are predominantly Jewish. One such scholar has devoted two large books to show how the Jews have conquered and how they rule England. By completely perverting Max Weber's thesis, he presents the Puritan revolution and the rise of Puritanism generally as the victory of Judaism over Christianity. For the purpose of anti-English propaganda, a special periodical against plutocracy and the incitement of peoples, called *Die Aktion*, was launched in August 1940.

Racial proletarianism is the genuine theory of National Socialism and its most dangerous expression. It is its most fallacious and yet most attractive doctrine. Its fallaciousness is obvious. If gold constitutes wealth, then Germany is indeed poor. But National Socialism insists that gold is not wealth, that all wealth derives from the productivity of man. If that is so, then Germany is the richest country in the world. There is no doubt that the doctrine is attractive. It exploits the hatred of England, a powerful motive in Germany, in many parts of the British

Empire, and in many of the Latin American countries. It exploits hatred of the Jews, aversion to capitalism, and, finally, utilizes Marxist phraseology and symbolism to an ever-increasing extent. It is clear that the very purpose of the doctrine of racial proletarianism is to entice the working classes. This point requires further discussion.

The labor theory of value, the class struggle, and the classless society are the three categories basic to the development of Marxist theory in Germany. However much revisionists and orthodox Marxists may have transformed or even abandoned Marxism, there is no doubt that from these three concepts spring the fundamental impetus of the Social Democratic and Communist Parties. Marxist theory had spread through the masses. It formed the focus of a political discussion between and within the two parties. Every tactical measure was argued in terms of Marxist theory, and quotations from Marx and Engels were used in every discussion that touched fundamental problems. No leading socialist dared to throw out the theory of the class struggle; no one dared deny the ultima Thule of a classless society. Even collective bargaining was conceived as a form of the class struggle, and the participation of trade unionists in labor courts and arbitration bodies was hailed as the recognition of that principle. To a foreigner, such discussions may seem ridiculous, dogmatic, and the cause of the so-called "immaturity" of the German labor movement. We do not intend to argue this point. It is indisputable that Marxist theory and symbolism completely permeated the Social Democratic and Communist labor movements and molded their character, and it is in this setting that the theory of proletarian racism must be understood. This theory is an attempt to eradicate Marxism by a process of transmutation. The complete collapse of the German labor movement, resulting in the destruction of the Social Democratic and Communist organizations, has facilitated this difficult task. Whether the basic impetus has collapsed too is quite another question.

In the eyes of Social Democrats and Communists, the goal of a classless society and of a higher form of life is not achieved by the enslavement of foreign nations, but by the transformation of the capitalist system and the destruction of oppressive bureaucracy. To achieve such a goal requires supreme courage, willingness to make sacrifices, patience, and intelligence. The struggle against one's own ruling class is, as history shows, much more strenuous than foreign wars, and international proletarian solidarity is acquired only in a long, arduous political struggle.

But National Socialism offers the worker everything offered by Marxism, and without a class struggle. National Socialism offers him a higher form of life, the "people's community," and the rule of labor over money, without compelling him to fight against his own ruling class. On the contrary, he is invited to join the ruling classes, to share in their power, glory, and material benefits by being a part of a colossal machine. He need no longer be isolated or strive against the current. He is not asked to show more courage and make more sacrifice than anybody else. On the contrary, Germany's victory is his victory, the victory of labor over money, of the people's community over class rule, of true freedom over a liberty that was merely a cloak for exploitation. This doctrine has not been abandoned even after the attack on Russia.

Is the National Socialist ideology successful? Has the theory of proletarian racism really permeated the ranks of labor? Has it definitely destroyed the belief in a democratic socialism or in communism? This is the decisive question, for upon the answer to it depends the fate of Europe. Upon it also depend, to a great extent, the methods of psychological warfare that must be used against Germany. If every German, every German worker, is a potential Hitler, if the masses stand solidly behind the leader, if the people are united behind the doctrine of racial proletarian imperialism, then Germany's opponents can have but one war aim: to destroy Germany, divide her, and keep her enslaved. For if this is the case no attempt to drive a wedge between Hitler and the German people can be successful.

That, indeed, is a view held by many, in particular by those foreign statesmen who did most to destroy German democracy and to support National Socialism in every international crisis. It is these statesmen who wish to shift the responsibility for the victory of National Socialism from their own foreign policy exclusively to the German people.[3] It is true that this argument cannot be lightly dismissed. And it is much more difficult to substantiate the contrary view that the German people do not stand behind National Socialism. Germany's culture is now nothing but propaganda; public opinion in Germany is manipulated and controlled; and to

---

3   Neumann launches a jab here against the so-called "Luther to Hitler" thesis that was common among US academics and that formed one strand of US propaganda during the war. It viewed the German people as a whole to be intrinsically fascist due to deep-seated features of German philosophy and culture.

express oppositional views would mean death or a concentration camp. We have no direct means of ascertaining the real attitude of the German people, and we must develop indirect methods. We shall try to find out to what extent National Socialism has permeated the German people by analyzing the function of the new ideology in more detail, by discussing the origin of this type of social imperialism, by examining those social strata that are most responsible for German aggressive imperialism, and finally, by investigating the character of National Socialist social organization to see how far it is based on terror and how far on consent. Much of this discussion will be found in the final chapter.[4]

. . .

We may, by way of contrast, show the adaptation and the transformation of Marxist slogans to meet the needs of National Socialist policy.

Marxist Form	**National Socialist Form**
Class struggle	Proletarian war against capitalistic states
Labor theory of value	Money as the fetish of the nation's productive power
Classless society	People's community
The proletarian as the bearer of truth	The German race as a proletarian race is the incarnation of morality

The formulation of the new doctrine is thus in line with the adoption of Marxist symbols, such as the red flag (although adorned with the swastika), the elevation of the Marxist May Day to a national holiday, and the acceptance of many proletarian songs, though with new texts. All this serves the same purpose: to make the theory of racial imperialism the ideological basis of a war of the German people against the surrounding world, this war having as its object the attainment of a better life for the master race through reducing the vanquished states and their satellites to the level of colonial peoples.

. . .

---

4   In the section that follows in the original book, Neumann details the ways in which National Socialism strived to co-opt Marxism. We have retained only his final schematic here.

5. German Imperialism

German imperialism enjoys the benefits of a latecomer and a have-not state. It is this fact that gives German imperialism its efficiency and its brutality. In countries like England, Holland, or France, which have outgrown the state of mere investment and have passed on to colonial and protectorate imperialism, internal anti-imperialistic trends have inevitably arisen. Large-scale capital export creates a capitalistic stratum completely disinterested and even hostile to further expansion, the stratum of the rentier group. The rentier, whose income is not derived from productive work and from business activities but from stocks and bonds, is not an aggressor. On the contrary, he is an appeaser, who wants to keep what he possesses and who refuses to incur new risks. The antagonism between the rentier and the activistic imperialist has pervaded British foreign politics since the time of Joseph Chamberlain, and ended with the victory of the rentier under Balfour, Baldwin, and Neville Chamberlain. This antagonism is shown very clearly in Sir Austen Chamberlain's [letters: *Politics from Inside* [1906–1914]. It is expressed in the conflict between the Tory Democrats and the old Conservatives. Disraeli and Joseph Chamberlain may be called the forerunners of social imperialism. They were democratic imperialists, basing the expansion of the empire on the working classes, to whom the franchise and material benefits were granted; but ever since Balfour, the rentier class has pressed forward within the Conservative Party. It is no longer concerned with expansion; it detests risks. The conflict between [sic] the Conservative Party became an open one with the issue of free trade against protection. While Joseph Chamberlain clearly saw the impossibility of competing with expanding Germany on the basis of free trade and wanted to create a wall of tariffs around the empire, the rentier group refused to undertake an experiment that would have necessitated the complete reorganization of English industrial machinery involving full concentration and trustification. Balfour was finally overthrown in 1911, but Austen Chamberlain did not succeed him. Bonar Law became the leader of the party and the spokesman of the rentier group. Thus, the imperialistic group had lost the leadership within the Conservative Party as early as 1911; regained it only during the First World War under Lloyd George within a coalition government; and finally lost it again under Baldwin and Neville

Chamberlain. Germany was acutely aware of this conflict manifest in the English social structure and in English foreign policy. In all forms [that] the German hatred of England assumes . . . England is depicted as a decaying country, the country of a bourgeoisie no longer willing to expand which has violated the primary law of life in a competitive society: the law that one must expand or die.

Germany's rentier class was wiped out during the inflation. The war had already destroyed foreign investments; the inflation wiped out domestic savings. The annihilation of a prosperous middle class turned out to be the most powerful stimulus to aggressive imperialism, for it was the section of the middle class having but little to lose that wholeheartedly supported the drive by heavy industry for rearmament and for imperialism.

The problems faced by German imperialism were different from those of Great Britain in still another respect. British imperialism in the nineteenth and early twentieth centuries was directed against colonial, semicolonial, or weak powers; and Great Britain had its colonial wars fought primarily by native armies under British command. Germany was faced with the world already divided among states possessing large armies or navies. As no peaceful redistribution could be achieved, as international cartels and the carving out of economic spheres of interest were not sufficient, only war remained. The first attempt was 1914; 1939 the second. But Germany fully learned the lessons of 1914, that the preparation for war has to begin in peace, that war and peace are no longer two different categories, but two expressions of one and the same phenomenon, the phenomenon of expansion. The domestic structure of society must be transformed in order fully to utilize all the productive forces of society for war. In particular, labor must be incorporated, must become part and parcel of the totalitarian structure. Material benefits, terror, and propaganda must uproot any pacifist or socialist convictions.

There exist two basic types of imperialism, popularly known as "haves" and "have-nots." Each of these must be subdivided. Each is different in its ideology, technique, and aim. The following diagram will facilitate an understanding of these types, which, however, do not mean that a "have" state must eternally remain satiated. It can, under certain conditions, turn into an aggressor, but will then, today, inevitably become fascist.

Imperialism of the Satiated Powers

Pure Economic Imperialism:

Trade (Commercial) Imperialism—free trade—universal international law—competitive structure of economy—no changes in the domestic political system—retention of independence [by the dominated territory] . . . combined with certain rights for the imperialist power, trading zones, port privileges, etc.

Investment Imperialism—protective tariffs—beginnings of regionalism (spheres of interest)—monopolization and trustification—no changes in the domestic political system—independence of the desired territory economically undermined

---

Imperialism of the "Have-Nots"

"Social" Imperialism:

Continental Imperialism—ideological and organizational incorporation of the masses—autarky—the highest stage of monopolization and trustification—new Monroe Doctrine—transformation of subdued states (civilized) into colonies

World Imperialism—ideological and organizational incorporation of the masses—the continent as the kernel—proletarian racism as the ideology and the lever of world imperialism

---

Our contention is that Germany's imperialism is primarily the policy of its industrial leadership, fully supported by the National Socialist Party; that the other classes merely follow that leadership or even resist it. This contention must be proved. Such proof can only be given by showing the historical growth of imperialism in Germany by analyzing the attitudes of the various classes of society toward aggressive war. Such an analysis will in turn strengthen our contention that imperialistic war is the outcome of the internal antagonism of the German economy . . .

It is, indeed, the most striking phenomenon of Germany's history that the industrial bourgeoisie, unable or unwilling to fight for parliamentary democracy and submitting to the semi-absolutistic system of the empire, directed all their political energy toward an aggressive imperialism. German political liberalism was never mild and humanitarian; it was aggressive and brutal—even if the form seemed democratic. As early as the bourgeois revolution of 1848, Pan-German and annexationist programs and ideas become fully apparent. George Herwegh, a genuine democratic leader of 1848, and a poet of considerable distinction, wrote a poem in 1844 in which he expressed the dream of a Germany navy as the bearer of Germany's greatness: "Und in die Furchen die Kolumb gezogen, geht Deutschlands Zukunft auf" (Germany's future takes the course plotted by Columbus). The wide freedom won by this navy will, so he maintains, liberate Germany from England's "grocer spirit." . . .

Ever since its foundation in 1866, German National Liberalism has advocated an army and navy, expansion, and colonial acquisition. The fight that Eugen Richter, as the representative of the Left Liberals, undertook against army expansion was unsuccessful even within his own party, especially because Richter's hostility was primarily based on fiscal reasons. From 1893 on, German Liberalism has never actively fought against the expansion of the German military machine . . .

The National Liberal Party, as the party of the industrial bourgeoisie, gradually abandoned liberalism, which was still fully evident in the program of June 12, 1867, and concentrated primarily on military and naval rearmament. But perhaps even more characteristic are those men who were considered the true representatives of German liberalism: Theodor Barth, Max Weber, and Gerhart von Schulze-Gävernitz. They represented democratic liberalism in its hopes of breaking down the privileges of the conservative agrarians by supporting a navy and advocating an imperialistic foreign policy. Emil Rathenau, father of Walter Rathenau, founder of the General Electric Corporation,[5] as well as Georg von Siemens, his great competitor, both belonged to that group.

These trends merged or culminated in the Pan-German League, founded in 1890 (actually bearing that name since 1894). This league was the direct result of Germany's colonial policy and the direct ideological forerunner of the National Socialist Party. Of all the patriotic associations set up in Imperial Germany, the Pan-German League was undoubtedly the most aggressive and the most repulsive. Although never strong numerically, it had an extraordinary propaganda apparatus, continually agitating for land and sea rearmament, for colonial expansion, and for an aggressive anti-English policy. The league never hesitated to attack the monarchy when the foreign policy of Wilhelm II did not fit into its plans. It utilized anti-Semitism whenever and

---

5 Neumann is referring here to the German company Allgemeine Elektricitäts-Gesellschaft (AEG), a separate organization from the US-based General Electric Company.

wherever this appeared necessary. During the First World War it was, of course, the most radical annexationist group. The political affiliations of the members of the league are extraordinarily interesting:

47 percent of the members belonged to the National Liberal Party
15 percent to the Conservative Party
15 percent to the Deutsch Soziale and Reform Party (violently
    anti-Semitic)
14 percent to the Reichspartei
9 percent to the Wirtschaftliche Vereinigung (anti-Semitic agrarians)

Included among the members of the league were such illustrious German National Liberals as A. Bassermann, Heinze, and Gustav Stresemann. The two leaders of the league both came from the Liberal camp ... In 1914, 24 percent [of league members] belonged to the teaching profession, 31 percent were businessmen, 12 percent were officials, 8 percent were physicians, and the businessmen came primarily from small and medium-sized businesses.

. . .

7. Racial Imperialism and the Masses

So deep is the abyss between National Socialism and the old Social Democratic spirit that only a handful of Social Democratic labor leaders went over to National Socialism—a few in the central organization of the Social Democratic trade unions, here and there an editor of a socialist paper, here and there a party and a trade union secretary. But the great majority of all party and trade union functionaries remained either aloof or in opposition. This attitude is the really lasting merit of Social Democratic education. The defensive mentality that the party and trade unions had developed from 1914 to 1932, though it turned out to be catastrophic for the existence of the Weimar Republic, prevented the party officials from actually supporting the regime. Compared with the French trade unions and with the French Socialist Party, the German movement died a heroic death.

The latest phase of National Socialist theory, the doctrine of proletarian racism, of social imperialism, has failed to gain a complete hold over the masses. The old party and trade union bureaucracy does not collaborate with the regime. The large majority of trade unionists and Social Democrats are not National Socialists. Throughout their history they have resisted the seductive theory of social imperialism; there is no reason to believe that they support it today. The repressive social policy of the National Socialist regime gives additional substance to our contention. But we cannot, of course, say that Social Democrats and trade unionists are openly hostile to National Socialism. That would be asking too much of them. They are waiting. Their old organizations have been destroyed. Their belief in the usefulness of their organizations has gone. But even the younger genera-tion, which was not indoctrinated by the Social Democratic Party and by the trade unions, shows just as little National Socialist sympathy.

When we discuss the social structure of National Socialism, we shall draw attention to an outstanding phenomenon: thorough indoctrination of the masses is always accompanied by almost-complete terrorization. This is necessary because of the contradiction between the enormous capacity of the productive apparatus and the destructive uses to which it is actually put. Even the most unenlightened worker is forced to ask himself where it is possible to reconcile the flattery of the masses, the aping of Marxist ideology, high productivity, and terrorism. Even the most self-centered worker will, almost every day, come up against the question why so developed an industrial apparatus as the German has to be kept together by terror. Unlimited productive power, terror, and propa-ganda cannot create National Socialism among the workers. On the contrary, the workers are more likely to move along revolutionary syndi-calist lines, to evolve ideas of sabotage and of direct action, ideas that were frowned upon by Social Democrats and Communists alike, but which might be considered by them as the sole means of asserting man's dignity within a terroristic system.

The picture is not very different in regard to the communist worker. The Communist Party, as we have seen, has been prepared for social imperialism by the doctrine of National Bolshevism.[6] It is therefore

---

6   National Bolshevism was a current that first arose among fringe members (Heinrich Laufenberg and Fritz Wolffheim) of the German Communist Party (KPD) and in the Communist Workers' Party (KAPD), and then, later in the 1920s, around fringe elements of the radical nationalist and National Socialist movements (Karl Otto Paetel and Ernst Niekisch). Its devotees argued for a synthesis between nationalism and socialism, and even an alliance between a nationalist Germany and the Soviet Union. It is often associated with the "Strasserite" current and lives on today as a strand of neo-Nazism, particularly in Russia.

possible, and even likely, that some groups within the communist movement, especially the lowest-paid workers, were susceptible to social imperialist theories up to the outbreak of the German-Russian war. But the National Bolshevist slogan of the Communist Party was merely the formula of a corrupt leadership frantically searching for propaganda devices that would allow them to compete with nationalism, and National Bolshevism was never spontaneously accepted by the communist masses. It was accepted by the uprooted proletariat, by the lumpenproletariat, especially by many groups belonging to the Red Fighting League, which to a considerable extent, became absorbed by the Brown Shirts and the Black Shirts. Moreover, the National Bolshevist slogan was abandoned by the Communist Party when it became clear that the communist masses turned against nationalism and National Socialism in spite of the attempted collaboration by the Communist Party with the reactionary groups. The last remnants of National Bolshevism, especially among the lowest-paid strata of the communist workers, were finally driven out by the actual social policy of National Socialism, which was most terroristic against these very groups. It is the unskilled, untrained worker, especially the road builder, who has probably received the worst treatment and whose rights and interests are sacrificed almost daily.

The social imperialist ideology is, however, probably fully accepted by the uprooted middle classes, so far as they have been organized within the National Socialist Party. For these strata of the middle class are genuinely anti-capitalistic. For them, the new theory is really the formulation of a psychological demand for greater dignity. Under the Weimar Republic, to call a member of the middle class a proletarian was, in his view, to express contempt for him. But to call him a proletarian today is to invest his position with the highest-possible dignity: that is, to name him a fighter for a greater proletarian Germany against the surrounding capitalistic world. The SS man is anti-capitalistic and today he seems proud to be called a proletarian. The former retailer or handicraft man, the dispossessed peasant, the unemployed intellectual who never had time or money to finish his studies, the elementary school teacher; all these groups dislike capitalism as much as Communists and Social Democrats did. For them, the doctrine of social imperialism is an adequate expression of their longings and an adequate formulation of their claims for dignity and security. For them, socialism is an untenable doctrine—since they hate the very basis upon which the socialist doctrine rests: that is, the equality of men. In addition, the doctrine of social imperialism is, as it has always been, a device of the ruling classes, a device as old as imperialism itself. Social imperialism is the most dangerous formulation of National Socialist ideology. It appeals to all those groups throughout the world who are in danger of proletarianization: peasants, retailers, artisans, teachers and other intellectuals; it appeals to the unemployed, to all those who in the process of monopolization have lost security but do not want to be called proletarians. It becomes especially dangerous since it contains one element of truth: that the German economy is highly developed, is efficient, and contains many progressive elements. The amazing efficiency of Germany's technical apparatus, coupled with the social imperialist doctrine, is today Germany's greatest weapon.

Henry Wallace, "The Danger of American Fascism," *New York Times Magazine*, April 9, 1944

Henry Wallace (1888–1965) was vice president of the United States under Franklin Roosevelt from 1940 to 1944. Earlier, beginning in 1933, he had served in the Roosevelt administration as secretary of agriculture. Wallace came from a highly educated farm family in Iowa.

During the war, Roosevelt's public comments on the mission of the war were increasingly sparse: he mainly left this task to his surrogates, and chiefly to Wallace, whose essays and statements on the moral and political aims of the war were widely publicized and circulated. Wallace was seen at the time as representing the left wing of the New Deal, and conservative Democrats successfully forced him out of the vice presidency in 1944. Nonetheless, public opinion surveys ranked Wallace as one of the most admired men in the United States as late as 1946. He ran for president as a third-party candidate in 1948 on a platform of extending the New Deal, rapidly legislating civil rights, and continuing the wartime alliance with the Soviet Union.

Readers may find the following analysis of fascism to be limited and overly broad, yet its historical significance lies in the prominent position of Wallace and the way such narratives shaped the public image of fascism. This perspective on fascism was not rare within the US public sphere during the war, and it thus helps inform the debate as to whether or not the United States during World War II was a properly antifascist state, at least rhetorically. Wallace admired the work of anti-racist anthropologist Franz Boas, and he generally framed the war as a "people's war" that would

globally extend New Deal social democracy. His general view of fascism—
as racist, hyper-nationalist, and intimately connected to capitalism and to
Western imperialism—certainly places him within the antifascist left, of
which he was arguably the most visible representative in the 1940s.

On returning from my trip to the West in February, I received a request
from the *New York Times* to write a piece answering the following
questions:

1. What is a fascist?
2. How many fascists have we?
3. How dangerous are they?

A fascist is one whose lust for money or power is combined with such
an intensity of intolerance toward those of other races, parties, classes,
religions, cultures, regions or nations as to make him ruthless in his use
of deceit or violence to attain his ends. The supreme god of a fascist, to
which his ends are directed, may be money or power; may be a race or a
class; may be a military, clique or an economic group; or may be a
culture, religion, or a political party.

The perfect type of fascist throughout recent centuries has been the
Prussian Junker,[1] who developed such hatred for other races and such
allegiance to a military clique as to make him willing at all times to
engage in any degree of deceit and violence necessary to place his culture
and race astride the world. In every big nation of the world are at least a
few people who have the fascist temperament. Every Jew baiter, every
Catholic hater, is a fascist at heart. The hoodlums who have been dese-
crating churches, cathedrals and synagogues in some of our larger cities
are ripe material for fascist leadership.

The obvious types of American fascists are dealt with on the air and
in the press. These demagogues and stooges are fronts for others.
Dangerous as these people may be, they are not so significant as thousands of other people who have never been mentioned. The really
dangerous American fascists are not those who are hooked up directly

---

1   A Junker was a member of the German landed nobility, a class that had great
power within the German central government and the German military after unification
in 1871. The term was often associated with the Prussian nobility in particular.

or indirectly with the Axis. The FBI has its finger on those. The dangerous American fascist is the man who wants to do in the United States in an American way what Hitler did in Germany in a Prussian way. The American fascist would prefer not to use violence. His method is to poison the channels of public information. With a fascist the problem is never how best to present the truth to the public but how best to use the news to deceive the public into giving the fascist and his group more money or more power.

If we define an American fascist as one who in case of conflict puts money and power ahead of human beings, then there are undoubtedly several million fascists in the United States. There are probably several hundred thousand if we narrow the definition to include only those who in their search for money and power are ruthless and deceitful. Most American fascists are enthusiastically supporting the war effort. They are doing this even in those cases where they hope to have profitable connections with German chemical firms after the war ends. They are patriotic in time of war because it is to their interest to be so, but in time of peace they follow power and the dollar wherever they may lead.

American fascism will not be really dangerous until there is a purposeful coalition among the cartelists,[2] the deliberate poisoners of public information, and those who stand for the KKK type of demagoguery . . .

Fascism is a worldwide disease. Its greatest threat to the United States will come after the war, either via Latin America or within the United States itself . . .

The symptoms of fascist thinking are colored by environment and adapted to immediate circumstances. But always and everywhere they can be identified by their appeal to prejudice and by the desire to play upon the fears and vanities of different groups in order to gain power. It is no coincidence that the growth of modern tyrants has in every case been heralded by the growth of prejudice. It may be shocking to some people in this country to realize that, without meaning to do so, they hold views in common with Hitler when they preach discrimination

---

2   In the original draft, Wallace wrote that Wall Street may become "headquarters for one type of American fascism" after the war. In this sentence, he had originally written "the Wall Street brand" instead of "cartelists," which would have placed his thinking closer to Dimitrov's communist definition of fascism (fascism as an extension of finance capital).

against other religious, racial or economic groups. Likewise, many people whose patriotism is their proudest boast play Hitler's game by retailing distrust of our Allies and by giving currency to snide suspicions without foundation in fact.

The American fascists are most easily recognized by their deliberate perversion of truth and fact. Their newspapers and propaganda carefully cultivate every fissure of disunity, every crack in the common front against fascism. They use every opportunity to impugn democracy. They use isolationism as a slogan to conceal their own selfish imperialism. They cultivate hate and distrust of both Britain and Russia. They claim to be superpatriots, but they would destroy every liberty guaranteed by the Constitution. They demand free enterprise, but are the spokesmen for monopoly and vested interest. Their final objective toward which all their deceit is directed is to capture political power so that, using the power of the state and the power of the market simultaneously, they may keep the common man in eternal subjection.

Several leaders of industry in this country who have gained a new vision of the meaning of opportunity through cooperation with government have warned the public openly that there are some selfish groups in industry who are willing to jeopardize the structure of American liberty to gain some temporary advantage. We all know the part that the cartels played in bringing Hitler to power, and the role the giant German trusts have played in Nazi conquests. Monopolists who fear competition and who distrust democracy because it stands for equal opportunity would like to secure their position against small and energetic enterprise. In an effort to eliminate the possibility of any rival growing up, some monopolists would sacrifice democracy itself.

The worldwide, agelong struggle between fascism and democracy will not stop when the fighting ends in Germany and Japan. Democracy can win the peace only if it does two things:

1. Speeds up the rate of political and economic inventions so that both production and, especially, distribution can match in their power and practical effect on the daily life of the common man the immense and growing volume of scientific research, mechanical invention and management technique.
2. Vivifies with the greatest intensity the spiritual processes which are both the foundation and the very essence of democracy.

The moral and spiritual aspects of both personal and international relationships have a practical bearing which so-called practical men deny. This dullness of vision regarding the importance of the general welfare to the individual is the measure of the failure of our schools and churches to teach the spiritual significance of genuine democracy. Until democracy in effective enthusiastic action fills the vacuum created by the power of modern inventions, we may expect the fascists to increase in power after the war, both in the United States and in the world.

Fascism in the postwar inevitably will push steadily for Anglo-Saxon imperialism and eventually for war with Russia. Already American fascists are talking and writing about this conflict and using it as an excuse for their internal hatreds and intolerances toward certain races, creeds and classes.

It should also be evident that exhibitions of the native brand of fascism are not confined to any single section, class or religion. Happily, it can be said that as yet fascism has not captured a predominant place in the outlook of any American section, class or religion. It may be encountered in Wall Street, Main Street or Tobacco Road. Some even suspect that they can detect incipient traces of it along the Potomac. It is an infectious disease, and we must all be on our guard against intolerance, bigotry and the pretension of invidious distinction. But if we put our trust in the common sense of common men and "with malice toward none and charity for all" go forward on the great adventure of making political, economic and social democracy a practical reality, we shall not fail.

W. E. B. Du Bois, "Negro's War Gains and Losses," *Chicago Defender*, September 15, 1945

In this essay, W. E. B. Du Bois (1868–1963) accesses the meaning of World War II for African Americans and nonwhite peoples globally. Du Bois's tepid enthusiasm for the defeat of European fascism as a stay against destruction of racial minorities was mediated by his continued protest against racist conditions for African Americans in the United States. World War II was famous for its "Double Victory" campaign by African American newspapers—that is, defeat fascism abroad, defeat racism at home. Indeed, Du Bois presciently cautions against the war's advance of "military regimentation" in the United States, a regimentation with costs borne mainly by the oppressed. The essay's protest against the "marriage between science and destruction" is an overt nod to the US atomic bombings of Nagasaki and Hiroshima just one month earlier. Its political focus is on the war's potential to unleash new anticolonial movements in Asia, Africa, the Caribbean and the United States. Fascism's defeat, Du Bois hopes, might signal new confidence and new victories for those Frantz Fanon called "the wretched of the earth."

Du Bois wrote several earlier essays on Nazi anti-Semitism, comparing it to the Spanish Inquisition and the African slave trade. The Holocaust deepened Du Bois's loyalty to Jewish nationalism and Zionism, expressed in ardent support for the formation of the state of Israel in 1948. The creation of Israel was for Du Bois the victory of an oppressed minority's goal of statehood; only after Israel's collaboration with French and British imperialists in the attempted Suez Canal seizure of 1956 did he ameliorate his support. Du Bois's analogy of the Holocaust to the slave trade would also inform his role in crafting We Charge Genocide, *the Civil Rights Congress petition to the United Nations in 1950 for crimes against African American people. In his late writings, including his* Autobiography, *Du Bois increasingly used fascism as a metaphor for racial conditions in the United States, anticipating this same characterization by the Black Power movement.*

Now that the Second World War has ended, what have we Americans of Negro descent lost and gained? We may record five groups of losses:

1. War itself is always a loss which bears hardest among the segregated and the oppressed, leaving a legacy of death and destruction which is almost incalculable.
2. We have suffered the tremendous disadvantage of a "Jim Crow" army and of segregation in army circles, which will form and have formed a basis of similar segregation in civil life. This segregation is not simply separation of human beings in their ordinary life: in order to make segregation effective it has been found necessary to suppress ability and deny opportunity.
3. The defeat and humiliation of Japan marks the tragedy of the greatest colored nation which has risen to leadership in modern times. No matter how we explain and assess the damage, the result of thinking along the lines of race and color will affect human relations for many years and will excuse contempt and injustice toward colored skins. It will set back the time of the emancipation of the majority of people in the world.
4. If the military regimentation of living will retard civilization, it means the training of men through long and costly years for murder and destruction and then afterward to use these same men and the same methods for cultural uplift. The whole proposal is impossible.
5. And finally, we have seen in this war, to our amazement and distress, a marriage between science and destruction; a marriage such as we had never dreamed of before. We have always thought of science as the emancipator. We see it now as the enslaver of mankind.

Six Gains Listed

We turn from this sad picture to six gains which have come out of war, not necessarily because of it, but in most cases despite the organized destruction:

1. The world of culture has been compelled to make a restatement of democracy at a time in our development when we are beginning to distrust and ignore democracy. We have been compelled to come back to the basic idea that the government and direction of human beings must in the long run rest upon the wishes and the will of those who are governed and guided.

2. We have been compelled to admit Asia into the picture of future political and democratic power. We can no longer regard Europe as the sole center of the world. The development of human beings in the future is going to depend largely upon what happens in Asia.

3. We have been compelled to admit China as a great power. When China was first attacked it was because of attack by Europe. When the attack continued it was through the acquiescence of Europe and America; and when finally, against the will of the white world, we were dragged into the great center of Asiatic war, we took up and espoused the cause of Chinese freedom and independence because we knew well that the Japanese cry of "Asia for the Asiatics" would be turned against us unless we helped China maintain her independence.

Russian Recognition

4. We have been compelled to recognize Russia as an equal country in spite of the fact that her economic organization is directly and categorically opposed to the profit-making industrial organization of the Western world. And moreover, because of the prominence given Russia today in this war, her backing of China and alliance with China means that China will not be at the sole direction of Western Europe. The dream of Europe as the profiteer of China, and the controller of her destiny through its efforts, falls before the menace of Russia.

5. More specifically there can be no doubt but [that] India and the Dutch Netherlands and French Indochina are going in our day to achieve something approaching autonomy in government.

6. And last there is upheaval in Pan Africa among the people in
   Africa itself, north, west and south; but also, and just as significantly among the people of African descent in the Caribbean area,
   in South and Central America and in the United States of America.

It cannot be said that, balancing these losses and gains, the war has
been either a vast success or a terrible failure. It can be said that civilization after this year has a chance to go forward, and no group of civilized
people have better opportunity to forward the advance of human culture
than American Negroes.

PART III

Antifascism, Anticolonialism, and the Cold War, 1946–1962

Theodor Adorno, Else Frenkel-Brunswik, Daniel Levinson, and Nevitt Sanford, from *The Authoritarian Personality*, 1950

In the late 1940s and early 1950s, US antifascism's most intricate intersectional analysis of power came from a highly influential work within the academic social sciences: The Authoritarian Personality (1950), by Theodor Adorno and University of California–Berkeley psychologists Else Frenkel-Brunswik, Daniel Levinson, and Nevitt Sanford. They sought to discover individual susceptibility to fascism at the level of personality. Their introduction argued that personality was "an agency through which sociological influences on ideology are mediated." Formed mainly in childhood, personality was deeply stamped by both familial and social forces. They originally wanted to call the study "The Fascist Personality" but deemed this title too risky in the early Cold War context, in which visibly antifascist politics could trigger McCarthyite attacks.

The empirical base of the study was an extensive set of interviews, mainly conducted between 1944 and 1946 in California and Washington, DC, with college students, prisoners, veterans, and men and women from a range of working- and middle-class occupations. The book is most remembered for its development of an "F scale," a quantifiable measure of an individual's amenability to fascism, gleaned from survey questions and interviews. Its contributors tried to find the link between fascism and broader social attitudes by correlating the F scale with other quantified indexes, such as the "A-S scale" for anti-Semitism, a "PEC scale" for politico-economic conservatism, and the "E scale" for ethnocentrism (the latter had a number of subscales: the "N scale" for attitudes toward "Negroes," an "M scale" for attitudes toward all racial

minority groups, and a "P scale" for patriotism). These related scales under-
score the intersectional nature of the study, namely, its seamless linkage of race,
class, gender, sexuality and nationalism.

The book was quite well received by reviewers from both academic and
popular presses, its success inspiring a flood of academic studies of the
political right. This wave culminated in the collection The New American
Right *in 1955 (expanded and republished as* The Radical Right *in 1963),*
in which Daniel Bell, Nathan Glazer, and David Riesman also drew upon
the experience of fascism as a way of explaining the American right, albeit
within Cold War frames.

The Authoritarian Personality was part of the Studies in Prejudice
series, sponsored by the American Jewish Committee and edited by Max
Horkheimer and Samuel Flowerman. Its release came shortly after
Horkheimer and Adorno returned to West Germany to reconstitute the
Institute of Social Research in Frankfurt. Like many Frankfurt School
works of the 1940s and '50s, it combined European critical theory with
empiricist methods culled from US social sciences.

In their conclusion, the authors were certain that they had found a close
correlation between anti-Semitism, ethnocentrism, and nationalism (the
A-S and E scales), but were uncertain as to whether they had found a solid
instrument for measuring fascist potential at the level of personality.

Chapter 7: "The Measurement of Implicit Antidemocratic Trends"

At a certain stage of the study, after considerable work with the A-S and E
scales had been done,[1] there gradually evolved a plan for constructing a
scale that would measure prejudice without appearing to have this aim
and without mentioning the name of any minority group. It appeared that
such an instrument, if it correlated highly enough with the A-S and E
scales, might prove to be a very useful substitute for them. It might be
used to survey opinion in groups where "racial questions" were too "tick-
lish" a matter to permit the introduction of an A-S or E scale, e.g., a group
which included many members of one or another ethnic minority. It
might be used for measuring prejudice among minority group members

---

1   The A-S scale was for anti-Semitism, and the E scale for ethnocentrism.

themselves. Most important, by circumventing some of the defenses which people employ when asked to express themselves with respect to "race issues," it might provide a more valid measure of prejudice.

The PEC scale[2] might have commended itself as an index of prejudice, but its correlations with the A-S and E scales did not approach being high enough. Moreover, the items of this scale were too explicitly ideological, that is, they might be too readily associated with prejudice in some logical or automatic way. What was needed was a collection of items each of which was correlated with A-S and E but which did not come from an area ordinarily covered in discussions of political, economic, and social matters. The natural place to turn was to the clinical material already collected, where, particularly in the subjects' discussions of such topics as the self, family, sex, interpersonal relations, moral and personal values, there had appeared numerous trends which, it appeared, might be connected with prejudice.

At this point the second—and major—purpose of the new scale began to take shape. Might not such a scale yield a valid estimate of antidemocratic tendencies at the personality level? It was clear, at the time the new scale was being planned, that anti-Semitism and ethnocentrism were not merely matters of surface opinion, but general tendencies with sources, in part at least, deep within the structure of the person. Would it not be possible to construct a scale that would approach more directly these deeper, often unconscious, forces? . . .

This second purpose—the quantification of antidemocratic trends at the level of personality—did not supersede the first, that of measuring anti-Semitism and ethnocentrism without mentioning minority groups or current politico-economic issues. Rather, it seemed that the two might be realized together . . . Indeed, if such a correlation [between the A-S, E, and F scales] could be obtained it could be taken as evidence that anti-Semitism and ethnocentrism were not isolated or specific or entirely superficial attitudes, but expressions of persistent tendencies in the person . . . The new instrument was termed the F scale, to signify its concern with implicit prefascist tendencies.

. . . Given emotionally determined antidemocratic trends in the person, we should expect that *in general* they would be evoked by the A-S and E items, which were designed for just this purpose, as well as by

---

2 The "politico-economic conservatism" scale.

the F scale and other indirect methods. The person who was high on F but not on A-S or E would be the exception, whose inhibitions upon the expression of prejudice against minorities would require special explanation . . .

A number of . . . variables were derived and defined, and they, taken together, made up the basic content of the F scale. Each was regarded as a more or less central trend in the person which, in accordance with some dynamic process, expressed itself on the surface in ethnocentrism as well as in diverse psychologically related opinions and attitudes. These variables are listed below, together with a brief definition of each.

a. *Conventionalism.* Rigid adherence to conventional, middle-class values.

b. *Authoritarian submission.* Submissive, uncritical attitude toward idealized moral authorities of the in-group.

c. *Authoritarian aggression.* Tendency to be on the lookout for, and to condemn, reject, and punish people who violate conventional values.

d. *Anti-intraception.* Opposition to the subjective, the imaginative, the tender minded.

e. *Superstition and stereotypy.* The belief in mystical determinants of the individual's fate; the disposition to think in rigid categories.

f. *Power and "toughness."* Preoccupation with the dominance/submission, strong/weak, leader/follower dimension; identification with power figures; overemphasis upon the conventionalized attributes of the ego; exaggerated assertion of strength and toughness.

g. *Destructiveness and cynicism.* Generalized hostility, vilification of the human.

h. *Projectivity.* The disposition to believe that wild and dangerous things go on in the world; the projection outward of unconscious emotional impulses.

i. *Sex.* Exaggerated concern with sexual "goings-on."

These variables were thought of as going together to form a single syndrome, a more or less enduring structure in the person that renders him receptive to antidemocratic propaganda. One might say, therefore, that the F scale attempts to measure the potentially antidemocratic personality. This does not imply that *all* the features of this personality pattern are touched upon in the scale, but only that the scale embraces a fair sample of the ways in which this pattern characteristically expresses itself. Indeed, as the study went on, numerous additional features of the pattern, as well as variations within the overall pattern, suggested themselves—and it was regretted that a second F scale could not have been constructed in order to carry these explorations further. It is to be emphasized that one can speak of personality here only to the extent that the coherence of the scale items can be better explained on the ground of an inner structure than on the ground of external association.

The variables of the scale may be discussed in more detail, with emphasis on their organization and the nature of their relations to ethnocentrism. As each variable is introduced, the scale items deemed to be expressive of it are presented. It will be noted, as the variables are taken up in turn, that the same item sometimes appears under more than one heading. This follows from our approach to scale construction. In order efficiently to cover a wide area it was necessary to formulate items that were maximally rich, that is, pertinent to as much as possible of the underlying theory—hence a single item was sometimes used to represent two, and sometimes more, different ideas . . .

a. Conventionalism[3]

12. The modern church, with its many rules and hypocrisies, does not appeal to the deeply religious person; it appeals mainly to the childish, the insecure, and the uncritical.[4]

19. One should avoid doing things in public which appear wrong to others, even though one knows that these things are really all right.

---

3   Later iterations of the F scale form added the following item to test for "conventionalism": "Obedience and respect for authority are the most important virtues children should learn."

4   This was one of the few items in which agreement with the statement indicated a democratic sensibility. The authors later deemed it an overly ambiguous and unproductive entry.

38. There is too much emphasis in colleges on intellectual and theoretical topics, not enough emphasis on practical matters and on the homely virtues of living.

55. Although leisure is a fine thing, it is good hard work that makes life interesting and worthwhile.

58. *What* a man does is not so important so long as he does it well.

60. Which of the following are the most important for a person to have or to be? *Mark X the three most important.*

> artistic and sensuous
> popular, good personality
> drive, determination, willpower
> broad, humanitarian social outlook
> neatness and good manners
> sensitivity and understanding
> efficiency, practicality, thrift
> intellectual and serious
> emotional expressiveness, warmth, intimacy
> kindness and charity

It is a well-known hypothesis that susceptibility to fascism is most characteristically a middle-class phenomenon, that it is "in the culture" and, hence, that those who conform the most to this culture will be the most prejudiced. Items referring to the holding of conventional values were included in order to gather data bearing on this hypothesis. Many of the early findings of the present study, however, gave evidence that the matter was not quite so simple. The correlation between conventional values and prejudice seemed to be positive but not very high; whereas unconventional people tended to be free of prejudice, it was clear that some conventional people were prejudiced while others were not. It seemed that, among the conventional group, what might make the difference was the deeper source of the conventionality, or rather the type of broader personality structure within which it had a functional role. If the adherence to conventional values was an expression of a fully established individual conscience, then we should expect no necessary connection between these values and antidemocratic potential. The same standards which render the individual easily offended by what he conceives to be the morally loose behavior of unassimilated minority group members or of "lower-class" people, would—if they are well internalized—cause him to resist the violence and delinquency which characterize the advanced stages of fascism. If, on the other hand, adherence to conventional values is determined by contemporary external social pressure, if it is based upon the individual's adherence to the standards of the collective powers with which he, for the time being, is identified, then we should expect a close association with antidemocratic receptivity. It is this latter state of affairs that we wish to call conventionalism—and to distinguish from mere acceptance of conventional values. The conventionalistic individual could in good conscience follow the dictates of the external agency wherever they might lead him and, moreover, he would be capable of totally exchanging one set of standards for another quite-different one—as in a conversion from official Communism to Catholicism.

The scale items listed under "Conventionalism" afford the subject an opportunity to reveal whether or not his adherence to conventional values is of the rigid, absolutist character just described. For example, this would seem to be indicated by a mark of +3 on the item "Obedience and respect for authority are the most important virtues children should learn." However, a sound decision on this matter would depend on the individual's responses to items in the other categories. For example, extreme conventionalism going with a strong inclination to punish those who violate conventional values is a different thing from conventional values associated with a philosophy of live and let live. In other words, the meaning of a high score on this variable, as on any of the others, is to be known from the broader context within which it occurs.

b. Authoritarian Submission[5]

20. One of the main values of progressive education is that it gives the child great freedom in expressing those natural impulses and desires so often frowned upon by conventional middle-class society.[6]

---

5   A later version of the form added to this list: "Nobody ever learned anything really important except through suffering."

6   Again, one of the few exceptions in which agreement indicates a democratic personality. The authors later regarded it as an unfruitful question.

23. He is indeed contemptible who does not feel an undying love, gratitude, and respect for his parents.

32. It is essential for learning or effective work that our teachers or bosses outline in detail what is to be done and exactly how to go about it.

39. Every person should have a deep faith in some supernatural force higher than himself to which he gives total allegiance and whose decisions he does not question.

43. Sciences like chemistry, physics, and medicine have carried men very far, but there are many important things that can never possibly be understood by the human mind.

50. Obedience and respect for authority are the most important virtues children should learn.

74. What this country needs is fewer laws and agencies, and more courageous, tireless, devoted leaders whom the people can put their faith in.

77. No sane, normal, decent person could ever think of hurting a close friend or relative.

Submission to authority, desire for a strong leader, subservience of the individual to the state, and so forth, have so frequently and, as it seems to us, correctly, been set forth as important aspects of the Nazi creed that a search for correlates of prejudice had naturally to take these attitudes into account. These attitudes have indeed been so regularly mentioned in association with anti-Semitism that it was particularly difficult to formulate items that would express the underlying trend and still be sufficiently free of logical or direct relations to prejudice—and we cannot claim to have been entirely successful. Direct references to dictatorship and political figures were avoided for the most part, and the main emphasis was on obedience, respect, rebellion, and relations to authority in general. Authoritarian submission was conceived of as a very general attitude that would be evoked in relation to a variety of authority figures—parents, older people, leaders, supernatural power, and so forth.

The attempt was made to formulate the items in such a way that agreement with them would indicate not merely a realistic, balanced respect for valid authority but an exaggerated, all-out, emotional need to submit. This would be indicated, it seemed, by agreement that obedience and respect for authority were the *most important* virtues that children should learn, that a person should *obey without question* the decisions of a supernatural power, and so forth. It was considered that here, as in the case of conventionalism, the subservience to external agencies was probably due to some failure in the development of an inner authority, i.e., conscience. Another hypothesis was that authoritarian submission was commonly a way of handling ambivalent feelings toward authority figures: underlying hostile and rebellious impulses, held in check by fear, lead the subject to overdo in the direction of respect, obedience, gratitude, and the like.

It seems clear that authoritarian submission by itself contributes largely to the antidemocratic potential by rendering the individual particularly receptive to manipulation by the strongest external powers. The immediate connection of this attitude with ethnocentrism has been suggested in earlier chapters: hostility against in-group authorities, originally the parents, has had to be repressed; the "bad" aspects of these figures—that they are unfair, self-seeking, dominating—are then seen as existing in out-groups, who are charged with dictatorship, plutocracy, desire to control, and so forth. And this displacement of negative imagery is not the only way in which the repressed hostility is handled; it seems often to find expression in authoritarian aggression.

c. Authoritarian Aggression[7]

6. It is only natural and right that women be restricted in certain ways in which men have more freedom.

---

7 A later version of the F scale form added the following item to this list: "The trouble with letting everybody have a say in running the government is that so many people are just naturally stupid or full of wild ideas."

23. He is indeed contemptible who does not feel an undying love, gratitude, and respect for his parents.

31. Homosexuality is a particularly rotten form of delinquency and ought to be severely punished.

47. No insult to our honor should ever go unpunished.

75. Sex crimes, such as rape and attacks on children, deserve more than mere imprisonment; such criminals ought to be publicly whipped.

The individual who has been forced to give up basic pleasures and to live under a system of rigid restraints, and who therefore feels put upon, is likely not only to seek an object upon which he can "take it out" but also to be particularly annoyed at the idea that another person is "getting away with something." Thus, it may be said that the present variable represents the sadistic component of authoritarianism just as the immediately foregoing one represents its masochistic component. It is to be expected, therefore, that the conventionalist who cannot bring himself to utter any real criticism of accepted authority will have a desire to condemn, reject, and punish those who violate these values. As the emotional life which this person regards as proper and a part of himself is likely to be very limited, so the impulses, especially sexual and aggressive ones, which remain unconscious and ego alien are likely to be strong and turbulent. Since in this circumstance a wide variety of stimuli can tempt the individual and so arouse his anxiety (fear of punishment), the list of traits, behavior patterns, individuals, and groups that he must condemn grows very long indeed. It has been suggested before that this mechanism might lie behind the ethnocentric rejection of such groups as zoot-suiters, foreigners, other nations; it is here hypothesized that this feature of ethnocentrism is but a part of a more general tendency to punish violators of conventional values: homosexuals, sex offenders, people with bad manners, et cetera. Once the individual has convinced himself that there are people who ought to be punished, he is provided with a channel through which his deepest aggressive impulses may be expressed, even while he thinks of himself as thoroughly moral. If his external authorities, or the crowd, lend their approval to this form of aggression, then it may take the most violent forms, and it may persist after the conventional values in the name of which it was undertaken have been lost from sight.

One might say that in authoritarian aggression, hostility that was originally aroused by and directed toward in-group authorities is *displaced* onto out-groups. This mechanism is superficially similar to but essentially different from a process that has often been referred to as "scapegoating." According to the latter conception, the individual's aggression is aroused by frustration, usually of his economic needs; and then, being unable due to intellectual confusion to tell the real causes of his difficulty, he lashes out about him, as it were, venting his fury upon whatever object is available and not too likely to strike back. While it is granted that this process has a role in hostility against minority groups, it must be emphasized that according to the present theory of displacement, the authoritarian *must*, out of an inner necessity, turn his aggression against out-groups. He must do so because he is psychologically unable to attack in-group authorities, rather than because of intellectual confusion regarding the source of his frustration. If this theory is correct, then authoritarian aggression and authoritarian submission should turn out to be highly correlated. Furthermore, this theory helps to explain why the aggression is so regularly justified in moralistic terms, why it can become so violent and lose all connection with the stimulus which originally set it off.

. . .

d. Anti-intraception[8]

28. Novels or stories that tell about what people think and feel are more interesting than those which contain mainly action, romance, and adventure.[9]

38. There is too much emphasis in colleges on intellectual and theoretical topics, not enough emphasis on practical matters and on the homely virtues of living.

---

8   In a later version of the F scale form, the following items were added to this list: "When a person has a problem or worry, it is best for him not to think about it, but to keep busy with more cheerful things"; "One main trouble today is that people talk too much and work too little"; and "The businessman and the manufacturer are much more important to society than the artist and the professor."

9   Again, agreement here indicated a democratic sensibility.

53. There are some things too intimate or personal to talk about even with one's closest friends.

58. *What* a man does is not so important so long as he does it well.

66. Books and movies ought not to deal so much with the sordid and seamy side of life; they ought to concentrate on themes that are entertaining and uplifting.

Intraception is a term introduced by [Henry A.] Murray to stand for "the dominance of feelings, fantasies, speculations, aspirations—an imaginative, subjective human outlook." The opposite of intraception is *extraception*, "a term that describes the tendency to be determined by concrete, clearly observable, physical conditions (tangible, objective facts)." The relations of intraception/extraception to ego weakness and to prejudice are probably highly complex, and this is not the place to consider them in detail. It seems fairly clear, however, that anti-intraception, an attitude of impatience with and opposition to the subjective and tender-minded, might well be a mark of the weak ego. The extremely anti-intraceptive individual is afraid of thinking about human phenomena because he might, as it were, think the wrong thoughts; he is afraid of genuine feeling because his emotions might get out of control. Out of touch with large areas of his own inner life, he is afraid of what might be revealed if he, or others, should look closely at himself. He is therefore against "prying," against concern with what people think and feel, against unnecessary "talk"; instead he would keep busy, devote himself to practical pursuits, and instead of examining an inner conflict, turn his thoughts to something cheerful. An important feature of the Nazi program, it will be recalled, was the defamation of everything that tended to make the individual aware of himself and his problems; not only was "Jewish" psychoanalysis quickly eliminated, but every kind of psychology except aptitude testing came under attack. This general attitude easily leads to a devaluation of the human and an overvaluation of the physical object; when it is most extreme, human beings are looked upon as if they were physical objects to be coldly manipulated—even while physical objects, now vested with emotional appeal, are treated with loving care.

e. Superstition and Stereotypy[10]

2. Although many people may scoff, it may yet be shown that astrology can explain a lot of things.

10. It is more than a remarkable coincidence that Japan had an earthquake on Pearl Harbor Day, December 7, 1944.

39. Every person should have a deep faith in some supernatural force higher than himself to which he gives total allegiance and whose decisions he does not question.

43. Sciences like chemistry, physics and medicine have carried men very far, but there are many important things that can never possibly be understood by the human mind.

65. It is entirely possible that this series of wars and conflicts will be ended once and for all by a world-destroying earthquake, flood, or other catastrophe.

Superstitiousness, the belief in mystical or fantastic external determinants of the individual's fate, and stereotypy, the disposition to think in rigid categories, have been mentioned so frequently in the foregoing chapters and are so obviously related to ethnocentrism that they need little discussion here. A question that must be raised concerns the relations of these trends to general intelligence—and the relations of intelligence to ethnocentrism. Probably superstition and stereotypy tend to go with low intelligence, but low intelligence appears to be correlated with ethnocentrism to only a slight degree. It appears likely that superstition and stereotypy embrace, over and above the mere lack of intelligence in the ordinary sense, certain dispositions in thinking which are closely akin to prejudice, even though they might not hamper intelligent performance in the extraceptive sphere. These dispositions can be understood, in part at least, as expressions of ego weakness. Stereotypy

---

10 The revised and expanded F scale questionnaire added the following items to this list: "People can be divided into two distinct classes: the weak and the strong"; and "Some people are born with an urge to jump from high places."

is a form of obtuseness particularly in psychological and social matters. It might be hypothesized that one reason why people in modern society—even those who are otherwise "intelligent" or "informed"— resort to primitive, oversimplified explanations of human events is that so many of the ideas and observations needed for an adequate account are not allowed to enter into the calculations: because they are affect laden and potentially anxiety producing, the weak ego cannot include them within its scheme of things. More than this, those deeper forces within the personality which the ego cannot integrate with itself are likely to be projected onto the outer world; this is a source of bizarre ideas concerning other people's behavior and concerning the causation of events in nature.

Superstitiousness indicates a tendency to shift responsibility from within the individual onto outside forces beyond one's control; it indicates that the ego might already have "given up," that is to say, renounced the idea that it might determine the individual's fate by overcoming external forces. It must, of course, be recognized that in modern industrial society the capacity of the individual to determine what happens to himself has *actually* decreased, so that items referring to external causation might easily be realistic and hence of no significance for personality. It seemed necessary, therefore, to select items that would express ego weakness in a nonrealistic way by making the individual's fate dependent on more or less fantastic factors.

f. Power and "Toughness"[11]

9. Too many people today are living in an unnatural, soft way; we should return to the fundamentals, to a more red-blooded, active way of life.

35. There are some activities so flagrantly un-American that, when responsible officials won't take the proper steps, the wide-awake citizen should take the law into his own hands.

---

11   These items were later added to determine (f): "No weakness or difficulty can hold us back if we have enough will power"; "Any red-blooded American will fight to defend his property"; and "What the youth needs most is strict discipline, rugged determination, and the will to work and fight for family and country."

47. No insult to our honor should ever go unpunished.

70. To a greater extent than most people realize, our lives are governed by plots hatched in secret by politicians.

74. What this country needs is fewer laws and agencies, and more courageous, tireless, devoted leaders whom the people can put their faith in.

This variable refers, in the first place, to overemphasis upon the conventionalized attributes of the ego. The underlying hypothesis is that overdisplay of toughness may reflect not only the weakness of the ego but also the magnitude of the task it has to perform, that is to say, the strength of certain kinds of needs which are proscribed in the subject's culture . . .

Closely related to the phenomenon of exaggerated toughness is something which might be described as a "power complex." Most apparent in its manifestations is overemphasis on the power motif in human relationships; there is a disposition to view all relations among people in terms of such categories as strong/weak, dominant/submissive, leader/follower, "hammer/anvil." And it is difficult to say with which of these roles the subject is the more fully identified. It appears that he wants to get power, to have it and not to lose it, and at the same time is afraid to seize and wield it. It appears that he also admires power in others and is inclined to submit to it—and at the same time is afraid of the weakness thus implied. The individual whom we expected to score high on this cluster readily identifies himself with the "little people," or "the average," but he does so, it seems, with little or no humility, and he seems actually to think of himself as strong or to believe that he can somehow become so. In short, the power complex contains elements that are essentially contradictory, and we should expect that sometimes one feature and sometimes another will predominate at the surface level. We should expect that both leaders and followers will score high on this variable, for the reason that the actual role of the individual seems to be less important than his concern that leader-follower relations shall obtain. One solution which such an individual often achieves is that of alignment with power figures, an arrangement by which he is able to gratify both his need for power and his need to submit. He hopes that by submitting to power he can participate in it. For example, a man who reports that the most awe-inspiring experience for him would be "to shake hands with the president" probably finds his gratification not in submission alone but in the idea that some of the big man's power has, as it were, rubbed off onto him, so that he is a more important person for having "shook his hand" or "known him" or "been there." The same pattern of gratification can be obtained by acting in the role of "the lieutenant" or by functioning in a middle position in some clearly structured hierarchy where there is always somebody above and somebody below.

The power complex has immediate relations with certain aspects of ethnocentrism. An individual who thinks of most human relations in such terms as strong versus weak is likely to apply these categories in his thinking about in-groups and out-groups, e.g., to conceive of "superior" and "inferior races." And one of the psychologically least costly devices for attaining a sense of superiority is to claim it on the basis of membership in a particular "race."

g. Destructiveness and Cynicism[12]

3. America is getting so far from the true American way of life that force may be necessary to restore it.

9. Too many people today are living in an unnatural, soft way; we should return to the fundamentals, to a more red-blooded, active way of life.

14. After we finish off the Germans and Japs, we ought to concentrate on other enemies of the human race such as rats, snakes, and germs.

17. Familiarity breeds contempt.

24. Today everything is unstable; we should be prepared for a period of constant change, conflict, and upheaval.

---

12 To determine (g), the following item was added in a later version of the questionnaire: "Human nature being what it is, there will always be war and conflict."

30. Reports of atrocities in Europe have been greatly exaggerated for propaganda purposes.

35. There are some activities so flagrantly un-American that, when responsible officials won't take the proper steps, the wide-awake citizen should take the law into his own hands.

42. No matter how they act on the surface, men are interested in women for only one reason.

56. After the war, we may expect a crime wave; the control of gangsters and ruffians will become a major social problem.

59. Human nature being what it is, there will always be war and conflict.

67. When you come right down to it, it's human nature never to do anything without an eye to one's own profit.

According to the present theory, the antidemocratic individual, because he has had to accept numerous externally imposed restrictions upon the satisfaction of his needs, harbors strong underlying aggressive impulses. As we have seen, one outlet for this aggression is through displacement onto out-groups leading to moral indignation and authoritarian aggression. Undoubtedly this is a very serviceable device for the individual; yet, the strong underlying aggression seems at the same time to express itself in some other way—in a nonmoralized way. It was assumed, of course, that primitive aggressive impulses are rarely expressed with complete directness by adults, but must instead be sufficiently modified, or at least justified, so that they are acceptable to the ego.

The present variable, then, refers to rationalized, ego-accepted, nonmoralized aggression. The supposition was that a subject could express this tendency by agreeing with statements which though thoroughly aggressive were couched in such terms as to avoid his moral censorship. Thus, some items offered justifications for aggression, and were formulated in such a way that strong agreement would indicate that the subject needed only slight justification in order to be ready for all-out aggression. Other items dealt with contempt for mankind, the theory being that here the hostility is so generalized, so free of direction against any particular object, that the individual need not feel account-able for it. Still another guiding conception was that a person can most freely express aggression when he believes that everybody is doing it; and hence, if he wants to be aggressive, he is disposed to believe that everybody *is* doing it, e.g., that it is "human nature" to exploit and to make war upon one's neighbors. It goes without saying that such undif-ferentiated aggressiveness could easily, by means of propaganda, be directed against minority groups, or against any group the persecution of which was politically profitable.

h. Projectivity

46. The sexual orgies of the old Greeks and Romans are nursery school stuff compared to some of the goings-on in this country today, even in circles where people might least expect it.

56. After the war, we may expect a crime wave; the control of gangsters and ruffians will become a major social problem.

65. It is entirely possible that this series of wars and conflicts will be ended once and for all by a world-destroying earthquake, flood, or other catastrophe.

70. To a greater extent than most people realize, our lives are governed by plots hatched in secret by politicians.

73. Nowadays, when so many different kinds of people move around so much and mix together so freely, a person has to be especially careful to protect himself against infection and disease.

The mechanism of projection was mentioned in connection with authoritarian aggression: the suppressed impulses of the authoritarian character tend to be projected onto other people who are then blamed out of hand . . . The subject's tendency to project is utilized, in the present group of items, in an attempt to gain access to some of the deeper trends in his personality. If the antidemocratic individual is disposed to see in the outer world impulses which are suppressed in himself, and we wish to know what these impulses are, then something may be learned by noting what attributes he most readily, but unrealistically, ascribes to the world around him. If an individual insists that someone has hostile designs on him, and we can find no evidence that this is true, we have good reason to suspect that our subject himself has aggressive intentions and is seeking by means of projection to justify them. A notorious example is Father Coughlin's referring to anti-Semitism as a "defense mechanism," i.e., a protection of Gentiles against the supposed aggressive designs of the Jews. Similarly, it seemed that the greater a subject's preoccupation with "evil forces" in the world, as shown by his readiness to think about and to believe in the existence of such phenomena as wild erotic excesses, plots and conspiracies, and danger from natural catastrophes, the stronger would be his own unconscious urges of both sexuality and destructiveness.

i. Sex

31. Homosexuality is a particularly rotten form of delinquency and ought to be severely punished.

42. No matter how they act on the surface, men are interested in women for only one reason.

46. The sexual orgies of the old Greeks and Romans are nursery school stuff compared to some of the goings-on in this country today, even in circles where people might least expect it.

75. Sex crimes, such as rape and attacks on children, deserve more than mere imprisonment; such criminals ought to be publicly whipped.

Concern with overt sexuality is represented in the F scale by four items, two of which have appeared in connection with authoritarian aggression and one other as an expression of projectivity. This is an example of the close interaction of all the present variables; since taken together they constitute a totality, it follows that a single question may pertain to two or more aspects of the whole. For purposes of analysis, sex may be abstracted from the totality as well as any of the other variables. Which of these variables are most basic must be determined by clinical study. In any case, it seemed that countercathexis (repression, reaction formation, projection) of sexual wishes was well qualified for special study.

The present variable is conceived of as ego-alien sexuality. A strong inclination to punish violators of sex mores (homosexuals, sex offenders) may be an expression of a general punitive attitude based on identification with in-group authorities, but it also suggests that the subject's own sexual desires are suppressed and in danger of getting out of hand. A readiness to believe in "sex orgies" may be an indication of a general tendency to distort reality through projection, but sexual content would hardly be projected unless the subject had impulses of this same kind that were unconscious and strongly active. The three items pertaining to the punishment of homosexuals and of sex criminals and to the existence of sex orgies may, therefore, give some indication of the strength of the subject's unconscious sexual drives.

Aimé Césaire, from *Discourse on Colonialism*, originally published as *Discours sur le colonialisme*, 1950, translated by Joan Pinkham

Aimé Césaire's Discourse on Colonialism *(1950) is the most important single document on fascism produced by an anticolonial revolutionary. The essay's argument that fascism is simply the technique of
colonialism applied by Europeans to their own populations, including
the Jews, is a provocative landmark in antifascist thought. It culminated mid-century criticism of Western Europe as perpetrator of ideological violence against the nonwhite world. Césaire's piece served as
fighting words for a nascent anticolonial movement propelled forward
by the costs of fascism on Europe's colonial powers. Moreover, the text
anticipated major works of anticolonial critique, like Fanon's* Wretched
of the Earth, *which analyzed fascism as symptomatic of the lie of civi-
lizationist discourses Europe had used to crush the "savage" under the
heel of colonial rule. Shortly after its publication, Hannah Arendt's*
Origins of Totalitarianism *(1951) also argued that modern anti-Semitism in Europe developed as a blowback from its application of colonial
racist discourses abroad.*

*Césaire (1913–2008) was born in Bass-Pointe, Martinique, then under
French rule. His mother was a dressmaker and his father a tax collector.
After leaving home and attending the École Normale Supérieure in Paris,
he returned to Martinique, became a leader of the Communist Party, and
immersed himself in the study of poetry and négritude—a term he coined
in 1935 to define the totalizing historical experience, culture and knowledge of black people from antiquity to the present.*

To Césaire, fascism's threats were personal and multiple. It sought to erase the historical contributions of nonwhite peoples to human history. Its racism dehumanized not only the victims of its violence, but its perpetrators. Fascism was also a form of instrumental reason that, left unchallenged, would destroy not only black beauty, culture and thought, but the very idea of humanity as purported by European intellectual history. In this respect, his analysis shares something with the Frankfurt School critique of Enlightenment rationality.

The essay's timing is also significant. It was first published five years after the Holocaust, one year after China's successful Communist Revolution, and in a year of anticolonial fervor across Asia, Africa, and the southern United States. Its appeal for both decolonization and proletarian revolution was Césaire's interpretive revision of a Marxism suitable to revolutions across the global South—one that anticipated the Bandung Conference in Indonesia, five years later. Césaire's synthesis of anticolonialism and Marxism helped give birth to an independent "Third World" discourse against Europe, North America, and eventually the Soviet Union. The Black Panthers' later designation of the US state as "fascist" in its treatment of African Americans also owes a theoretical debt to Césaire's essay.

A civilization that proves incapable of solving the problems it creates is a decadent civilization.

A civilization that chooses to close its eyes to its most crucial problems is a stricken civilization.

A civilization that uses its principles for trickery and deceit is a dying civilization.

The fact is that the so-called European civilization—"Western" civilization—as it has been shaped by two centuries of bourgeois rule, is incapable of solving the two major problems to which its existence has given rise: the problem of the proletariat and the colonial problem; that Europe is unable to justify itself either before the bar of "reason" or before the bar of "conscience"; and that, increasingly, it takes refuge in a hypocrisy which is all the more odious because it is less and less likely to deceive.

Europe is indefensible.

Apparently that is what the American strategists are whispering to each other.

That in itself is not serious.

What is serious is that "Europe" is morally, spiritually indefensible.

And today the indictment is brought against it not by the European masses alone, but on a world scale, by tens and tens of millions of men who, from the depths of slavery, set themselves up as judges.

The colonialists may kill in Indochina, torture in Madagascar, imprison in Black Africa, crack down in the West Indies. Henceforth, the colonized know that they have an advantage over them. They know that their temporary "masters" are lying.

Therefore, that their masters are weak.

And since I have been asked to speak about colonization and civilization, let us go straight to the principal lie which is the source of all the others.

Colonization and civilization?

In dealing with this subject, the commonest curse is to be the dupe in good faith of a collective hypocrisy that cleverly misrepresents problems, the better to legitimize the hateful solutions provided for them.

In other words, the essential thing here is to see clearly, to think clearly—that is, dangerously—and to answer clearly the innocent first question: What, fundamentally, is colonization? To agree on what it is not: neither evangelization, nor a philanthropic enterprise, nor a desire to push back the frontiers of ignorance, disease, and tyranny, nor a project undertaken for the greater glory of God, nor an attempt to extend the rule of law. To admit once for all, without flinching at the consequences, that the decisive actors here are the adventurer and the pirate, the wholesale grocer and the shipowner, the gold digger and the merchant, appetite and force, and behind them, the baleful projected shadow of a form of civilization which, at a certain point in its history, finds itself obliged, for internal reasons, to extend to a world scale the competition of its antagonistic economies.

Pursuing my analysis, I find that hypocrisy is of recent date; that neither Cortés discovering Mexico from the top of the great teocalli, nor Pizarro before Cuzco (much less Marco Polo before Cambaluc), claims that he is the harbinger of a superior order; that they kill; that they plunder; that they have helmets, lances, cupidities; that the slavering apologists came later; that the chief culprit in this domain is Christian pedantry, which laid down the dishonest equations *Christianity = civilization, paganism = savagery*, from which there could not but ensue abominable colonialist and racist consequences, whose victims were to be the Indians, the yellow peoples, and the Negroes.

That being settled, I admit that it is a good thing to place different civilizations in contact with each other; that it is an excellent thing to blend different worlds; that whatever its own particular genius may be, a civilization that withdraws into itself atrophies; that for civilizations, exchange is oxygen; that the great good fortune of Europe is to have been a crossroads, and that because it was the locus of all ideas, the receptacle of all philosophies, the meeting place of all sentiments, it was the best center for the redistribution of energy.

But then I ask the following question: Has colonization really *placed civilizations in contact*? Or, if you prefer, of all the ways of *establishing contact*, was it the best?

I answer no.

And I say that between *colonization* and *civilization* there is an infinite distance; that out of all the colonial expeditions that have been undertaken, out of all the colonial statutes that have been drawn up, out of all the memoranda that have been dispatched by all the ministries, there could not come a single human value.

First we must study how colonization works to *decivilize* the colonizer, to *brutalize* him in the true sense of the word, to degrade him, to awaken him to buried instincts, to covetousness, violence, race hatred, and moral relativism; and we must show that each time a head is cut off or an eye put out in Vietnam and in France they accept the fact, each time a little girl is raped and in France they accept the fact, each time a Madagascan is tortured and in France they accept the fact, civilization acquires another dead weight, a universal regression takes place, a gangrene sets in, a center of infection begins to spread; and that at the end of all these treaties that have been violated, all these lies that have been propagated, all these punitive expeditions that have been tolerated, all these prisoners who have been tied up and "interrogated," all these patriots who have been tortured, at the end of all the racial pride that has been encouraged, all the boastfulness that has been displayed, a poison has been instilled into the veins of Europe and, slowly but surely, the continent proceeds toward *savagery*.

And then one fine day the bourgeoisie is awakened by a terrific reverse shock: the gestapos are busy, the prisons fill up, the torturers around the racks invent, refine, discuss.

People are surprised, they become indignant. They say: "How strange! But never mind—it's Nazism, it will pass!" And they wait, and they hope;

and they hide the truth from themselves, that it is barbarism, but the supreme barbarism, the crowning barbarism that sums up all the daily barbarisms; that it is Nazism, yes, but that before they were its victims, they were its accomplices; that they tolerated that Nazism before it was inflicted on them, that they absolved it, shut their eyes to it, legitimized it, because, until then, it had been applied only to non-European peoples; that they have cultivated that Nazism, that they are responsible for it, and that before engulfing the whole of Western, Christian civilization in its reddened waters, it oozes, seeps, and trickles from every crack.

Yes, it would be worthwhile to study clinically, in detail, the steps taken by Hitler and Hitlerism and to reveal to the very distinguished, very humanistic, very Christian bourgeois of the twentieth century that without his being aware of it, he has a Hitler inside him, that Hitler *inhabits* him, that Hitler is his *demon*, that if he rails against him, he is being inconsistent and that, at bottom, what he cannot forgive Hitler for is not *crime* in itself, *the crime against man*, it is not *the humiliation of man as such*, it is the crime against the white man, the humiliation of the white man, and the fact that he applied to Europe colonialist procedures which until then had been reserved exclusively for the Arabs of Algeria, the coolies of India, and the blacks of Africa.

And that is the great thing I hold against pseudo-humanism: that for too long it has diminished the rights of man, that its concept of those rights has been—and still is—narrow and fragmentary, incomplete and biased and, all things considered, sordidly racist.

I have talked a good deal about Hitler. Because he deserves it: he makes it possible to see things on a large scale and to grasp the fact that capitalist society, at its present stage, is incapable of establishing a concept of the rights of all men, just as it has proved incapable of establishing a system of individual ethics. Whether one likes it or not, at the end of the blind alley that is Europe, I mean the Europe of Adenauer, Schuman, Bidault, and a few others, there is Hitler. At the end of capitalism, which is eager to outlive its day, there is Hitler. At the end of formal humanism and philosophic renunciation, there is Hitler.

And this being so, I cannot help thinking of one of his statements: "We aspire not to equality but to domination. The country of a foreign race must become once again a country of serfs, of agricultural laborers, or industrial workers. It is not a question of eliminating the inequalities among men but of widening them and making them into a law."

That rings clear, haughty and brutal, and plants us squarely in the middle of howling savagery. But let us come down a step.

Who is speaking? I am ashamed to say it: it is the Western *humanist*, the "idealist" philosopher. That his name is Renan is an accident.[1] That the passage is taken from a book entitled *La Réforme intellectuelle et morale*, that it was written in France just after a war which France had represented as a war of right against might, tells us a great deal about bourgeois morals.

The regeneration of the inferior or degenerate races by the superior races is part of the providential order of things for humanity. With us, the common man is nearly always a déclassé nobleman, his heavy hand is better suited to handling the sword than the menial tool. Rather than work, he chooses to fight, that is, he returns to his first estate. *Regere imperio populos*, that is our vocation. Pour forth this all-consuming activity onto countries which, like China, are crying aloud for foreign conquest. Turn the adventurers who disturb European society into a *ver sacrum*, a horde like those of the Franks, the Lombards, or the Normans, and every man will be in his right role. Nature has made a race of workers, the Chinese race, who have wonderful manual dexterity and almost no sense of honor; govern them with justice, levying from them, in return for the blessing of such a government, an ample allowance for the conquering race, and they will be satisfied; a race of tillers of the soil, the Negro; treat him with kindness and humanity, and all will be as it should; a race of masters and soldiers, the European race. Reduce this noble race to working in the ergastulum like Negroes and Chinese, and they rebel. In Europe, every rebel is, more or less, a soldier who has missed his calling, a creature made for the heroic life, before whom you are setting *a task that is contrary to his race*—a poor worker, too good a soldier. But the life at which our workers rebel would make a Chinese or a fellah happy, as they are not military creatures in the least. *Let each one do what he is made for, and all will be well.*

*   *   *

1   Ernest Renan (1823–1892) was a highly respected French philosopher and scholar most known for his theories on nationalism, which rejected the idea that a nation was bound together by race or language.

Hitler? Rosenberg? No, Renan.

But let us come down one step further. And it is the long-winded politician. Who protests? No one, so far as I know, when Monsieur Albert Sarraut, the former governor-general of Indochina, holding forth to the students at the École Coloniale, teaches them that it would be puerile to object to the European colonial enterprises in the name of "an alleged right to possess the land one occupies, and some sort of right to remain in fierce isolation, which would leave unutilized resources to lie forever idle in the hands of incompetents."

And who is roused to indignation when a certain Reverend Barde assures us that if the goods of this world "remained divided up indefinitely, as they would be without colonization, they would answer neither the purposes of God nor the just demands of the human collectivity"?

Since, as his fellow Christian, the Reverend Muller, declares: "Humanity must not, cannot allow the incompetence, negligence, and laziness of the uncivilized peoples to leave idle indefinitely the wealth which God has confided to them, charging them to make it serve the good of all."

No one.

I mean not one established writer, not one academician, not one preacher, not one crusader for the right and for religion, not one "defender of the human person."

And yet, through the mouths of the Sarrauts and the Bardes, the Mullers and the Renans, through the mouths of all those who considered—and consider—it lawful to apply to non-European peoples "a kind of expropriation for public purposes" for the benefit of nations that were stronger and better equipped, it was already Hitler speaking!

What am I driving at? At this idea: that no one colonizes innocently, that no one colonizes with impunity either; that a nation which colonizes, that a civilization which justifies colonization—and therefore force—is already a sick civilization, a civilization that is morally diseased, that irresistibly, progressing from one consequence to another, one repudiation to another, calls for its Hitler, I mean its punishment.

Colonization: bridgehead in a campaign to civilize barbarism, from which there may emerge at any moment the negation of civilization, pure and simple.

Elsewhere I have cited at length a few incidents culled from the history of colonial expeditions.

Unfortunately, this did not find favor with everyone. It seems that I was pulling old skeletons out of the closet.

Indeed!

Was there no point in quoting Colonel de Montagnac, one of the conquerors of Algeria: "In order to banish the thoughts that sometimes besiege me, I have some heads cut off, not the heads of artichokes but the heads of men."

Would it have been more advisable to refuse the floor to Count d'Hérisson: "It is true that we are bringing back a whole barrelful of ears collected, pair by pair, from prisoners, friendly or enemy."

Should I have refused Saint-Arnaud the right to profess his barbarous faith: "We lay waste, we burn, we plunder, we destroy the houses and the trees." Should I have prevented Marshal Bugeaud from systematizing all that in a daring theory and invoking the precedent of famous ancestors: "We must have a great invasion of Africa, like the invasions of the Franks and the Goths."

Lastly, should I have cast back into the shadows of oblivion the memorable feat of arms of General Gérard and kept silent about the capture of Ambike, a city which, to tell the truth, had never dreamed of defending itself: "The native riflemen had orders to kill only the men, but no-one restrained them; intoxicated by the smell of blood, they spared not one woman, not one child . . . At the end of the afternoon, the heat caused a light mist to arise: it was the blood of the five thousand victims, the ghost of the city, evaporating in the setting sun."

Yes or no, are these things true? And the sadistic pleasures, the nameless delights that send voluptuous shivers and quivers through Loti's carcass when he focuses his field glasses on a good massacre of the Annamese? True or not true? And if these things are true, as no one can deny, will it be said, in order to minimize them, that these corpses don't prove anything?

For my part, if I have recalled a few details of these hideous butcheries, it is by no means because I take a morbid delight in them, but because I think that these heads of men, these collections of ears, these burned houses, these Gothic invasions, this steaming blood, these cities that evaporate at the edge of the sword, are not to be so easily disposed of. They prove that colonization, I repeat, dehumanizes even the most civilized man; that colonial activity, colonial enterprise, colonial conquest, which is based on contempt for the native and justified by that contempt, inevitably tends to change him who undertakes it; that the colonizer, who in order to ease his conscience gets into the habit of seeing the other man as an animal, accustoms himself to treating him like an animal, and tends objectively to transform *himself* into an animal. It is this result, this boomerang effect of colonization that I wanted to point out.

Civil Rights Congress,
We Charge Genocide,
1951

Civil Rights Congress publicity for *We Charge Genocide* petition in Harlem. *The Daily Worker* and *Daily World* Photographs Collection, box 114, folder 2, Tamiment Library, New York University.

Beginning almost immediately after its foundation, African Americans saw the United Nations as a site to protest domestic racism. Fueled by the "Double Victory" campaign during World War II—"Defeat racism at home, defeat fascism abroad"—by the tragic examples of anti-Semitism and the Holocaust, and by the influence of left political organizations like the Communist Party, the National Negro Congress and the National Association for the Advancement of Colored People (NAACP) both petitioned the UN to act against American racial discrimination.

In 1951 these efforts coalesced when the Communist-influenced Civil Rights Congress presented separate petitions titled "We Charge Genocide" to the UN headquarters in New York City (authored by Paul Robeson) and in Paris (written by William Patterson, CRC director and Communist Party member). The originality of the petition's argument lay in the use of the UN's charter against genocide as the basis of its appeal, inverting the history of the Holocaust itself; they contended that rather than fascism leading to genocide, genocide—the mass killings of African Americans— would lead to fascism.

The legal argument of We Charge Genocide *was not baseless. Article II of the United Nations' Convention on the Prevention and Punishment of the Crime of Genocide (1948) defined genocide as the "intent to destroy, in whole or in part, a national, ethnical, racial or religious group." This broad definition included the slow violence of economic misery. The US refused to sign the Convention on Genocide in 1948 because of a fear that it would allow the UN to prosecute Southern lynchers who had been acquitted in US courts: the very thing the CRC was now attempting get the United Nations to do.*

We Charge Genocide *is a significant document to the history of US fascism and anti-racism in several ways. It signaled a high point of African American coalitions with the Communist Party that began in the 1920s and would soon recede under McCarthyist attack. It was also virtually coterminous with Aimé Césaire's* Discourse on Colonialism *and attempted to put the argument of that piece—that fascism represented only the most demonic expression of Western racial logic—to legal use.*

After 1951, the phrase "We Charge Genocide" recurrently appeared in black radical activism and reportage; these words, repeated time and again, became a means through which African Americans and other racialized groups used the memory of fascism to articulate their own oppression. In 2012 after African American teenager Trayvon Martin was murdered, a black youth group calling itself We Charge Genocide emerged

in Chicago to document police violence against African Americans. The
group sent eight members on a delegation to Geneva, Switzerland, to offer
its findings to the UN Committee against Torture.

To the General Assembly of the United Nations:

The responsibility of being the first in history to charge the government of the United States of America with the crime of genocide is not
one your petitioners take lightly. The responsibility is particularly grave
when citizens must charge their own government with mass murder of
its own nationals, with institutionalized oppression and persistent
slaughter of the Negro people in the United States on a basis of "race," a
crime expressed in the Convention on the Prevention and Punishment
of the Crime of Genocide adopted by the General Assembly of the
United Nations on December 9, 1949.

Genocide Leads to Fascism and to War

If our duty is unpleasant, it is historically necessary both for the welfare
of the American people and for the peace of the world. We petition as
American patriots, sufficiently anxious to save our countrymen and all
mankind from the horrors of war to shoulder a task as painful as it is
important. We cannot forget Hitler's demonstration that genocide at
home can become wider massacre abroad, that domestic genocide develops into the larger genocide that is predatory war. The wrongs of which
we complain are so much the expression of predatory American reaction
and its government that civilization cannot ignore them nor risk their
continuance without courting its own destruction. We agree with these
members of our General Assembly who declared that genocide is a
matter of world concern because its practice imperils world safety.

But if the responsibility of your petitioners is great, it is dwarfed by
the responsibility of those guilty of the crime we charge. Seldom in
human annals has so iniquitous a conspiracy been so gilded with the
trappings of respectability. Seldom has mass murder on the score of
"race" been so sanctified by law, so justified by those who demand free
elections abroad even as they kill their fellow citizens who demand free
elections at home. Never have so many individuals been so ruthlessly
destroyed amid so many tributes to the sacredness of the individual. The

distinctive trait of this genocide is a cant that mouths aphorisms of Anglo-Saxon jurisprudence as it kills.

The genocide of which we complain is as much a fact as gravity. The whole world knows of it. The proof is in every day's newspaper, in everyone's sight and hearing in these United States. In one form or another it has been practiced for more than 300 years, although never with such sinister implications for the welfare and peace of the world as at present. Its very familiarity disguises its horror. It is a crime so embedded in law, so explained away by specious rationale, so hidden by dull talk of liberty, that even the conscience of the tender minded is sometimes dulled. Yet the conscience of mankind cannot be beguiled from its duty by the pious phrases and the deadly legal euphemisms with which its perpetrators seek to transform their guilt into high moral purpose.

Killing Members of the Group

Your petitioners will prove that the crime of which we complain is in fact genocide within the terms and meaning of the United Nations Convention providing for the prevention and punishment of this crime. We shall submit evidence, tragically voluminous, of "acts committed with intent to destroy, in whole or in part, a national, ethical, racial, or religious groups as such"—in this case the 15 million Negro people of the United States.

We shall submit evidence proving "killing members of the group," in violation of Article II of the Convention. We cite killings by police, killings by incited gangs, killings at night by masked men, killings on the basis of "race," killings by the Ku Klux Klan, that organization which is chartered by the several states as a semiofficial arm of government and even granted the tax exemptions of a benevolent society.

Our evidence concerns the thousands of Negroes who over the years have been beaten to death on chain gangs and in the back rooms of sheriff's offices, in the cells of country jails, in precinct police stations and on city streets, who have been framed and murdered by sham legal forms and by a legal bureaucracy. It concerns those Negroes who have been killed, allegedly for failure to say "sir" or tip their hats or move aside quickly enough, or, more often, on trumped-up charges of "rape," but in reality for trying to vote or otherwise demanding the legal and inalienable rights and privileges of United States citizenship formally guaranteed them by the Constitution of the United States, the United Nations Charter and the Genocide Convention.

Economic Genocide

We shall offer proof of economic genocide, or in the words of the Convention, proof of "deliberately inflicting on the group conditions of life calculated to bring about its destruction in whole or in part." We shall prove that such conditions so swell the infant and maternal death rate and the death rate from disease, that the American Negro is deprived, when compared with the remainder of the population of the United States, of eight years of life on the average.

Further we shall show a deliberate national oppression of these 15 million Negro Americans on the basis of "race," to perpetuate these "conditions of life." Negroes are the last hired and the first fired. They are forced into city ghettoes or their rural equivalents. They are segregated legally or through sanctioned violence into filthy, disease-bearing housing, and deprived by law of adequate medical care and education. From birth to death, Negro Americans are humiliated and persecuted, in violation of the Charter and the Convention. They are forced by threat of violence and imprisonment into inferior, segregated accommodations, into Jim Crow buses, Jim Crow trains, Jim Crow hospitals, Jim Crow schools, Jim Crow theaters, Jim Crow restaurants, Jim Crow housing, and finally into Jim Crow cemeteries.

We shall prove that the object of this genocide, as of all genocide, is the perpetuation of economic and political power by the few through the destruction of political protest by the many. Its method is to demoralize and divide an entire nation; its end is to increase the profits and unchallenged control by a reactionary clique. We shall show that those responsible for this crime are not the humble but the so-called great, not the American people but their misleaders, not the convict but the robed judge, not the criminal but the police, not the spontaneous mob but organized terrorists licensed and approved by the state to incite to a Roman holiday.

We shall offer evidence that this genocide is not plotted in the dark but incited over the radio into the ears of millions, urged in the glare of public forums by senators and governors. It is offered as an article of faith by powerful political organizations, such as the Dixiecrats, and defended by influential newspapers, all in violation of the United Nations Charter and the Convention forbidding genocide.

This proof does not come from the enemies of the white supremacists but from their own mouths, their own writings, their political resolutions, their racist laws, and from photographs of their handiwork. Neither Hitler nor Goebbels wrote obscurantist racial incitements more voluminously than do their American counterparts, nor did such incitements circulate in Nazi mails any more freely than they do in the mails of the United States.

Through this and other evidence we shall prove this crime of genocide is the result of a massive conspiracy, more deadly in that it is sometimes "understood" rather than expressed, a part of the mores of the ruling class often concealed by euphemisms, but always directed to oppressing the Negro people. Its members are so well drilled, so rehearsed over the generations, that they can carry out their parts automatically and with a minimum of spoken direction. They have inherited their plot, and their business is but to implement it daily so that it works daily. This implementation is sufficiently expressed in decision and statute, in depressed wages, in robbing millions of the vote and millions more of the land, and in countless other political and economic facts, as to reveal definitively the existence of a conspiracy backed by reactionary interests in which are meshed all the organs of the executive, legislative and judicial branches of government. It is manifest that a people cannot be consistently killed over the years on the basis of "race"—and more than 10,000 Negroes have so suffered death—cannot be uniformly segregated, despoiled, impoverished and denied equal protection before the law, unless it is the result of the deliberate, all-pervasive policy of government and those who control it.

Emasculation of Democracy

We shall show, more particularly, how terror, how "killing members of the group," in violation of Article II of the Genocide Convention, has been used to prevent the Negro people from voting in huge and decisive areas of the United States in which they are the preponderant population, thus dividing the whole American people, emasculating mass movements for democracy and securing the grip of predatory reaction on the federal, state, county and city governments. We shall prove that the crimes of genocide offered for your action and the world's attention have in fact been incited, a punishable crime under Article II of the Convention, often by such officials as governors, senators, judges and peace officers whose phrases about white supremacy and the necessity of maintaining inviolate a white electorate resulted in the bloodshed as surely as more direct incitement.

We shall submit evidence showing that the existence of a mass of American law, written as was Hitler's law solely on the basis of "race," providing for segregation and otherwise penalizing the Negro people, [is] in violation not only of Articles II and III of the Convention but also in violation of the Charter of the United Nations. Finally we shall offer proof that a conspiracy exists in which the government of the United States, its Supreme Court, its Congress, its executive branch, as well as the various state, county, and municipal governments, consciously effectuate policies which result in the crime of the genocide being consistently and constantly practiced against the Negro people of the United States.

The Negro Petitioners

Many of your petitioners are Negro citizens to whom the charges herein described are no mere words. They are facts felt on our bodies, crimes inflicted on our dignity. We struggle for deliverance, not without pride in our valor, but we warn mankind that our fate is theirs. We solemnly declare that continuance of this American crime against the Negro people of the United States will strengthen those reactionary American forces driving toward World War III as certainly as the unrebuked Nazi genocide against the Jewish people strengthened Hitler in this successful drive to World War II.

We, Negro petitioners whose communities have been laid waste, whose homes have been burned and looted, whose children have been killed, whose women have been raped, have noted with peculiar horror that the genocidal doctrines and actions of the American white supremacists have already been exported to the colored peoples of Asia. We solemnly warn that a nation which practices genocide against its own nationals may not be long deterred, if it has the power, from genocides elsewhere. White supremacy at home makes for colored massacres abroad. Both reveal contempt for human life in a colored skin. Jellied gasoline in Korea and the lyncher's faggot at home are connected in more ways than that both result in death by fire. The lyncher and the atom bomb are related. The first cannot murder unpunished and unrebuked without so encouraging the latter that the peace of the world and the lives of millions are endangered. Nor is this metaphysics. The tie binding both is economic profit and political control. It was not without significance that it was President Truman who spoke of the possibility of using the atom bomb on the colored peoples of Asia, that [it] is American statesmen who prate constantly of "Asiatic hordes."

"Our Humanity Denied and Mocked"

We Negro petitioners protest this genocide as Negroes and we protest it as Americans, as patriots. We know that no American can be truly free while 15 million other Americans are persecuted on the grounds of "race," that few Americans can be prosperous while 15 million are deliberately pauperized. Our country can never know true democracy while millions of its citizens are denied the vote on the basis of their color.

But above all we protest this genocide as human beings whose very humanity is denied and mocked. We cannot forget that after Congressman Henderson Lovelace Lanham, of Rome, Georgia, speaking in the halls of Congress, called William L. Patterson, one of the leaders of the Negro people, "a God-damned black son-of-bitch," he added, "We gotta keep the black apes down." We cannot forget it because this is the animating sentiment of the white supremacists, of a powerful segment of American life. We cannot forget that in many American states it is a crime for a white person to marry a Negro on the racist theory that that Negroes are "inherently inferior as an immutable fact of Nature." The whole institution of segregation, which is training for killing, education for genocide, is based on the Hitler-like theory of the "inherent inferiority of the Negro." The tragic fact of segregation is the basis of the statement, too often heard after murder, particularly in the South, "Why I think no more of killing a n----r, than of killing a dog."

We petition in the first instance because we are compelled to speak by the unending slaughter of Negroes. The fact of our ethnic origin, of which we are proud—our ancestors were building the world's first civilizations 3,000 years before our oppressors emerged from barbarism in the forests of western Europe—is daily made the signal for segregation and murder. There is infinite variety in the cruelty we will catalog, but each case has the common denominator of racism. This opening statement is not the place to present our evidence in detail. Still, in this summary of what is to be proved, we believe it necessary to show something of the crux of our case, something of the pattern of genocidal murder, the technique of incitement to genocide, and the methods of mass terror.

Our evidence begins with 1945 and continues to the present. It gains in deadliness and in number of cases almost in direct ratio to the surge toward war. We are compelled to hold to this six year span if this document is to be brought into manageable proportions.

The Evidence

There was a time when racist violence had its center in the South. But as the Negro people spread to the north, east and west seeking to escape the southern hell, the violence impelled in the first instance by economic motives, followed them, its cause also economic. Once most of the violence against Negroes occurred in the countryside, but that was before the Negro emigrations of the twenties and thirties. Now there is not a great American city from New York to Cleveland or Detroit, from Washington, the nation's capital, to Chicago, from Memphis to Atlanta to Birmingham, from New Orleans to Los Angeles, that is not disgraced by the wanton killing of innocent Negroes. It is no longer a sectional phenomenon.

Once the class method of lynching was the rope. Now it is the policeman's bullet. To many an American the police are the government, certainly its most visible representative. We submit that the evidence suggests that the killing of Negroes has become police policy in the United States and that police policy is the most practical expression of government policy.

Our evidence is admittedly incomplete. It is our hope that the United Nations will complete it. Much of the evidence, particularly of violence, was gained from the files of Negro newspapers, from the labor press, from the annual reports of Negro societies and established Negro year-books. A list is appended.

But by far the majority of Negro murders are never recorded, never known except to the perpetrators and the bereaved survivors of the victim. Negro men and women leave their homes and are never seen alive again. Sometimes weeks later their bodies, or bodies thought to be theirs and often horribly mutilated, are found in the woods or washed up on the shore of a river of lake. This is a well-known pattern of American culture. In many sections of the country police do not even bother to record the murder of Negroes. Most white newspapers have a policy of not publishing anything concerning murders of Negroes or assaults upon them. These unrecorded deaths are the rule rather than the exception—thus our evidence, though voluminous, is scanty when compared to the actuality.

Causes Célèbres

We Negro petitioners are anxious that the General Assembly know of our tragic causes célèbres, ignored by the American white press but known nevertheless the world over, but we also wish to inform it of the virtually unknown killed almost casually, as an almost-incidental aspect of institutionalized murder.

We want the General Assembly to know of Willie McGee, framed on perjured testimony and murdered in Mississippi because the Supreme Court of the United States refused even to examine vital new evidence proving his innocence. But we also want it to know of the two Negro children, James Lewis Jr., fourteen years old, and Charles Trudell, fifteen, of Natchez, Mississippi, who were electrocuted in 1947, after the Supreme Court of the United States refused to intervene.

We want the General Assembly to know of the martyred Martinsville

Seven, who died in Virginia's electric chair for a rape they never committed, in a state that has never executed a white man for that offense. But we want it to know, too, of the eight Negro prisoners who were shot down and murdered on July 11, 1947, at Brunswick, Georgia, because they refused to work in a snake-infested swamp without boots.

We shall inform the assembly of the Trenton Six, of Paul Washington, the Daniels cousins, Jerry Newsom, Wesley Robert Wells, of Rosa Lee Ingram, of John Derrick, of Lieutenant Gilbert, of the Columbia, Tennessee, destruction, the Freeport slaughter, the Monroe killings—all important cases in which Negroes have been framed on capital charges or have actually been killed. But we want it also to know of the typical and less known—of William Brown, Louisiana farmer, shot in the back and killed when he was out hunting on July 19, 1947, by a white game warden who casually announced his unprovoked crime by saying, "I just shot a n----r. Let his folks know." The game warden, one Charles Ventrill, was not even charged with the crime.

. . .

Klan Terror

With statesmen justifying genocide, it remains for others in the scores of vigilante organizations that dot the South, chartered and encouraged, as we shall show, by the various states, to carry out the crime more specifically. Great inflammatory anti-Negro meetings in which thousands of robed members participate are common throughout the South, particularly during election years. A Reverend Harrison, known as the "Railroad Evangelist," told a meeting of the Atlanta Ku Klux Klan, for example, on November 1, 1948, "In God's sight it is no sin to kill a n----r, for a n----r is no more than a dog." At the same meeting, according to witnesses, one "Itchy Trigger Finger" Nash, an Atlanta patrolman to whom the Klan had given an award for killing more Negroes than any of his colleagues, expressed the hope that he would "not have to kill the Negroes in the South by myself. I want some help from my brother Klansmen."

Typical of the membership oaths of these vigilante organizations is that of the United Sons of Dixie, which was incorporated in Tennessee on December 28, 1943, and operated as a wartime front organization for the Ku Klux Klan. The oath included: ". . . The United States of America must, and shall be, a white man's country for white people, the master race. We must keep it that way." At one point in a ceremony for new members, according to a report filed with the Federal Bureau of Investigation, the president of the United Sons of Dixie said, "We want 15,000,000 members in the United States, and every one of them with a good gun and plenty of ammunition. Eventually we must eliminate the Negroes from this country."

Typical, too, of speeches heard on many street corners in Southern cities, was that of Homer Loomis Jr., leader of the Columbians, a racist vigilante organization chartered by the state of Georgia, on the corner of Stovall Street and Flatshoals Avenue, Atlanta, Georgia, on October 1, 1946. "We don't want anybody to join," he said, "who's not ready to get out and kill n----rs and Jews." Two days later at a meeting of the Columbians at 198 ½ Whitehall Street, Atlanta, Loomis said: "There is no end to what we can do through the ballot. If we want to bury all n----rs in the sand, if we will organize white Gentiles politically to combat the Jews and n----r blocs, we can pass laws enabling us to bury all n----rs in the sand." During the same year, Loomis told the Imperial Kloncilium of the Ku Klux Klan, East Point Klavern, Georgia, "We propose that all n----rs in America be shipped back to Africa with time-bombs on board the ship as an economy measure."

Other racist terrorist organizations include, as we shall show, the American Gentile Army, sometimes called the Commoner Party, and J. B. Stoner's Anti-Jewish Party. But by far the largest is the Ku Klux Klan, chartered in most of the Southern states as well as elsewhere. Its philosophy, so reminiscent of Hitler's, is exemplified by the statement of its Imperial Wizard, Hiram W. Evans, writing in "Negro Suffrage—Its False Theory":

The first essential to the success of any nation, and particularly of any democracy, is a national unity of mind. Its citizens must be One People (Ein Volk). They must have common instincts and racial and national purpose . . . we should see in the negro race a race even more diverse from ourselves than are the Chinese, with inferior intellect, inferior honesty, and greatly inferior industry . . . His racial inferiority . . . applies equally to all alien races and justifies our attitude toward Chinese, Japanese, and Hindus . . . No amount of education can ever make a white man out of a man of any other color. It is a law on this earth that races can never exist together in complete peace and friendship and certainly never in a state of equality.

Operating on this principle thousands of hooded, masked Klansmen, robed in white, ride through the countryside, killing, flogging, shooting, wrecking, pillaging. Their activities are winked at by what passes for democratically elected legal authority, when not initiated by it. Police officers themselves often participate in their activities. The target of their organized terror is almost always the Negro people—although with increasing frequency members of this Klan are hired to prevent the unionization of workers to keep wages down. The terror organized by the Klan, with the cooperation as we shall prove, of the various states, is a powerful mechanism in preventing almost two-thirds of those eligible to vote under the law and the Constitution in seven Southern states from actually voting. It is the major instrument of terror in preventing political democracy in Southern United States, thus perpetuating in power, as we shall show, a minority clique and the corporate interests that represent, not only locally but also nationally in the Federal Congress.

. . .

Genocide for Profit

Thus the foundation of this genocide of which we complain is economic.[1] It is genocide for profit. The intricate superstructure of "law and order" and extralegal terror enforces an oppression that guarantees profit. This was true of that genocide, perhaps the most bloody ever perpetrated, which for 250 years enforced chattel slavery upon the American Negro. Then as now it increased in bloodiness with the militancy of the Negro people as they struggled to achieve democracy for themselves. It was particularly bloody under slavery because the Negro people never ceased fighting for their freedom. There were some 250 years of chattel slavery in the United States.

---

1   In a preceding section, redacted here, the petitioners explained in detail the profitability of cotton and the South's agricultural commodities in the world market and their roles in US economic development.

That genocide that was American slavery, the killing of part of the group so that the remainder could more readily be exploited for profit, resulted in two wars. The first was the aggression against Mexico in 1846 seeking more territory for the expansion of slavery. The second was the nineteenth century's deadliest war—the Civil War of the states. The American Civil War (1861–1865) was a revolutionary war in which the American people destroyed the slavocracy, that minority of slaveholders who had controlled the country and its government for generations. In the wake of this conflict, a rising industrialism, then the dominant and most revolutionary current in American life, joined with 4 million liberated slaves and the poor whites of the South to impose its democracy on the former slavocracy, giving the Negro the right to vote and to participate in the South's political life.[2]

. . .

The Negro people fought back [against the abandonment of Reconstruction and consolidation of economic power] chiefly through the populist parties that opposed the Wall Street trusts through the eighties and nineties of the last century. But their fight became more hopeless against the increased power of American monopoly. Terror was unleashed against them at home—there were 1,955 *recorded* lynchings from 1889 through 1901, according to the minimal count of the Tuskegee Institute. Side by side went terror unleashed abroad, as American imperialism entered the international arena by subjugating the Filipino, Puerto Rican and Cuban peoples and reduced many Latin American countries to economic and political vassalage.

The Growth of Terror

It was during this period of American imperialist adventure abroad that most of the state laws segregating Negroes and illegally denying them the vote were enacted in the Southern states. Disfranchisement laws were passed in Louisiana in 1898, in North Carolina and Alabama in 1901, Virginia, 1902, Georgia, 1908, Oklahoma, 1910. They but codified what was taking place in life. They disfranchised poor whites as well as

---

2 The petitioners go on to the explain, in a section redacted here, how this democratic ferment was betrayed by the failure of federal commitment to Reconstruction, and later by the destruction of the multiracial Populist farmers movement.

Negroes, thus breaking the populist movement. It was during this period, too, in which Negroes still had a remnant of political power, that the spurious charge of rape was elevated into an institution, an extralegal instrument for terrorizing all Negroes, particularly those demanding their rights under the Constitution. With the charge of rape, reaction sought to justify its bestiality and to divorce from the Negroes those white allies who had helped to carry out the democratic practices of Reconstruction . . .

Genocide and War

Thus there is ample historical precedent for genocidal crime increasing against the Negro people in time of war or threat of war as it is now increasing and has been since 1945. As Senator Edwin C. Johnson remarked on May 17, 1951, in the United States Senate, calling for an end to the Korean War, that conflict is "a breeder of bitter racial hatred." Murder on the basis of race by police and courts, as in the typical cases of the innocent Willie McGee in Mississippi and the Martinsville Seven in Virginia, has long since become so frequent and widespread as to constitute an American phenomenon. Now it is increasing.

It is increasing partly because unpopular war requires a silencing of the people, a breaking of their will for resistance. Increasing violence against the Negro people goes hand in hand with increased repression throughout American life . . . Reaction knows that liberty is indivisible; that a victory for the Negro people in their fight for freedom may well presage a victory for labor and the forces of peace. Moreover, it feels that clamor against this baleful American crime, against genocide by the government of the United States, is unendurable when all iniquity is supposed to rest with the enemy . . .

The End of Genocide Means Peace

This genocide of which your petitioners complain serves now, as it has in previous forms in the past, specific political and economic aims. Once its goal was the subjugation of American Negroes for the profits of chattel slavery. Now its aim is the splitting and emasculation of mass movements for peace and democracy, so that reaction may perpetuate its control and continue receiving the highest profits in the entire history of man. That purpose menaces the peace of the world as well as the life and welfare of the Negro people whose condition violates every aspect of the United Nations' stated goal—the preservation of "peaceful and friendly relations among nations" by the promotion of "respect for human rights and fundamental freedoms for all without distinction as to race."

. . .

The end of genocide against the Negro people of the United States will mean returning this country to its people. It will mean a new growth of popular democracy and the forces of peace. It will mean an end to the threat of atomic war. It will mean peace for the world and all mankind.

Political Committee of the Socialist Workers Party, "Fascist Menace Grave, SWP Warns: Urges All-Out Labor Offensive to Smash McCarthyism," *Militant*, vol. 17, no. 49, December 7, 1953

Not all leftists and liberals saw McCarthyism as fascism, but the equation was common, and the article below, published in the December 1953 issue of the Militant, *reflects such fears. As we outlined in the introduction to this volume, while a number of cultural and political developments in the 1950s alarmed veterans of earlier antifascist struggles, most notable among them was the rise of Joseph McCarthy and investigative bodies like the House Un-American Activities Committee.*

The Militant *was the newspaper of the Socialist Workers Party (SWP), a Trotskyist organization. The membership of the SWP shrank during the 1950s, a victim of McCarthyism, and suffered splits within the organization, but many of the views expressed below were common among leftists and even liberals. It should be noted that despite the SWP's horror at the targeting of communists, as a Trotskyist organization it was stridently opposed to the Soviet Union and to Communist parties. It correctly saw such targeting as an attack on the entire left.*

McCarthy's attack on Truman and Eisenhower reveals that McCarthy is now bidding for leadership of the Republican Party, for an electoral victory on the issue of "McCarthyism" in 1954, and for nomination to the presidency in 1956.

The victory of McCarthyism would signal the crushing of the labor movement, the conversion of the labor movement, the conversion of the United States, into a land of concentration camps, and a reign of terror against political dissenters and minority groupings that would make the horrors of Hitlerism seem like amateur beginnings.

For it must be clearly understood: *McCarthyism is the new American form of fascism.*

This new native fascist movement is developing by leaps and bounds within the Republican Party. It has strong backing from the most reactionary wing of the Democrats. It is the reappearance of the fascist movement that brought Mayor ("I Am the Law") Hague and Father Coughlin to the fore in 1939.

McCarthyism is the evil spawn of the witch hunt that has raged in America unchecked for six years. The witch hunt was deliberately fostered and set in motion by Big Business and its political representatives as part of the preparations for atomic war. The aim of the witch hunt was to gag all opposition to the war drive and to help prepare the ground for major blows against labor.

In the foul witch-hunt atmosphere, McCarthyism feeds on the feeling of insecurity that is widespread, especially in the middle class, despite the prosperity accompanying war preparations. Resentment at rising living costs and high taxes, bitterness over the Korean conflict, alarm over the signs of possible depression, dread of atomic war, worry over continual international crises, emotional upsets caused by the war propaganda, spy scares, and the witch hunt, frustration over perspectives— these are the feelings McCarthy appeals to.

Just as Hitler tried to mobilize such sentiments against "the Jews," so McCarthy is trying to direct them against a national scapegoat prepared by the Democrats and Republicans—"the communists" and those "associated" with them.

The fascist danger is grave.

It is graver than in 1939 when Big Business plunged America into World War II and put its fascist club on the shelf for the time being.

The world position of US capitalism today is much worse than in 1939. Consequently, to meet these foreign difficulties, Big Business is readier than in 1939 to resort to fascist rule.

Compared with the fascist movement of 1939, McCarthyism is more powerful, having a bigger, more united following, stronger financial backing and far more influential political positions. It rides the momentum of a witch hunt that has blighted free thought in America and spread fear everywhere.

At the first major signs of depression, the fascist movement gathered around the Wisconsin demagogue can grow at phenomenal speed.

If the labor movement fails to stand up in time and fight McCarthyism, this fascist movement can come to power in America. That is the cold, brutal truth.

It is necessary right now to recognize the danger for what it is: *McCarthyism is American fascism on the march.*

Labor must immediately work out a program to meet this menace. We propose:

1. An abrupt break of all ties with capitalist politicians. An end to the witch hunt in the unions. A decision to swing labor's power and influence against the witch hunt in every walk of life.
2. Immediate steps to form an independent Labor Party. A national Congress of Labor should be called at once to consider the problem of fighting McCarthyism. This congress should work out practical plans for an all-out campaign to put labor's own candidate in 1954 and a Workers and Farmers government in power in Washington in 1956.

Smash McCarthyism before McCarthyism smashes us!

Julius Jacobson, "McCarthy and McCarthyism: The New Look at America's Post War Reaction," *New International*, January/February 1954

In the 1950s, there was a lively debate on the left as to whether or not McCarthyism was an American fascism. This essay argues that it was not fascist in its present form, but that it was paving the way for authoritarianism by hollowing out a democratic culture. Jacobson's reflections on the relationship between fascist parties, fascist states, and fascist personalities demonstrates how antifascist analysis can be just as illuminating when it rules out the fascist label as when it applies it.

Joe McCarthy is known in US political history as one of the first major right-wing populists of the twentieth century. His public persona was that of a hard-drinking, poker-loving everyman who showed no respect for parliamentary protocol—something he dismissed as a smug restraint thrown in his way by Ivy League snobs who lacked the stomach to do what needed to be done. Jacobson, like McCarthy's other left and liberal critics, comments here on the undemocratic nature of the anti-intellectual culture he fostered.

Julius Jacobson (1922–2003), who wrote under the pen name "Julius Falk" during the 1950s, grew up in a working-class, Jewish American family in the Bronx and worked as a machinist for most of his life. He saw combat in France during World War II, and after the war, he founded his own machine shop with fellow Trotskyist Herman Benson. He was a Trotskyist or "third camp" socialist for most of his life, critical of both the capitalist and Soviet blocs. With his wife Phyllis Jacobson, he cofounded the journal New Politics *in 1961.*

McCarthyism has become the political issue of the day in America. Even the most cynical sophisticate who reflects for a moment on such a grotesque fact cannot fail to be amazed at this degradation of political life in the United States. The newspaper accounts of the present conflict of McCarthy-Cohn versus the US Army have the quality of parody. An alleged Communist dentist drafted into the army, who, at most, could have kept the Kremlin well informed on the national state of GI cavities, becomes a cause célèbre, the basis for McCarthy's usual accusation, this time directed at the army, of "coddling Communists." The senator's wild accusation is then "substantiated" by the sensational exposure of another allegedly dangerous and coddled Communist in the Pentagon, this time a sixty-dollar-a-week "code clerk," who, it is now apparent, knew as little about codes as she does of communism, the Communist Party or why she was subpoenaed.

The skit-like quality of McCarthyism is by no means monopolized by McCarthy. The former conservative president of Harvard, Dr. James Conant, upon his appointment as American high commissioner to Germany, was opposed by Senator [Karl] Mundt because, "he is too bookish a fellow." As Stuart Chase sardonically noted in a recent letter to the *New York Times*, "Anyone who can read" can be made an object of suspicion. These McCarthyist techniques and accusations are not limited to the political arena. McCarthyism has spread from Washington like a plague of insects carrying a noxious disease, penetrating every area of social and cultural life. Recently two teachers were fired for having the audacity to read in class belle-lettristic essays by D. H. Lawrence. The principal remarked that it was a disgrace and that Lawrence was probably a Communist.

These, of course, are but a minute sampling of atrocities committed in this flowering age of McCarthyism. What removes them from the stage of pure burlesque is not only the criminal injustices perpetrated against personal victims and artistic sensibilities, but that they are symptomatic of substantial changes taking place in the American political system. They are the indices of a falling barometer.

How is it possible for the shift in American politics to assume such unprecedentedly crude, clumsy and universal manifestations? This is the question which disturbs American liberals and confounds Europeans.

McCarthyism is a peculiarly American phenomenon. It is the warped product of the growing disproportion between the capacities of American capitalism and the momentous problems which confront it. It is not the inevitably begotten fruit of capitalism in the abstract but is revealed by its specific features as the natural product of American capitalism. We doubt that any European bourgeois class would emulate the methods and techniques of McCarthyism under similar circumstances. It is not a matter of the superior morality or virtue of European capitalism; its history is bloody; the actions of French imperialism in Indochina and North Africa, the brutality of British imperialism in Kenya, the memory of Nazism embraced by the German bourgeoisie and fascism in Italy unmasks their affected moral indignation. The European bourgeoisie is perturbed by the fact that they, too, are being victimized by American McCarthyism; and they are confounded by what appears to them as its needless elements of irrationality, grossness and stupidity.

The perplexity of European critics of McCarthyism stems from their failure to understand that every reaction assumes specific forms reflecting the character, background and psychology of its ruling class. The fascist reactions in Germany and Italy for example, while fundamentally identical, assumed different forms in each country. The racism and anti-Semitism most peculiar to German fascism were, in a sense, not an essential part of fascism but a reflection of the training, history and temperament of German capitalism. We cannot compare McCarthyism with fascism as parallel reactions; our comparison with fascism is merely designed to illustrate that while a reaction in postwar America would have been propelled by any type of bourgeoisie, the level on which this reaction manifests itself reflects the special development of American capitalism.

In the United States capitalism came into its own relatively recently; its Industrial Revolution is less than a century old. America has no pre-capitalist history as is the case with Europe. It had no Old Order to combat, not only physically but intellectually. Feudalism was already a thing of the past when capitalism was consolidated here. It didn't have to depend as much on its wits; it did not need to develop trained diplomats and felt no compelling need for men of learning to represent it in struggle against competing capitalisms or the Old Order. In short what America developed were many politicians but few statesmen. Capitalism here grew rich on its native resources, relatively independent of European capitalism and divorced from the refinements of European culture. It became a hard-headed class of practical men, preoccupied with compounding their wealth, distrustful of "bookish fellows" or anything smacking of intellectuality.

The European bourgeoisie, given its heritage, achieved varying degrees of sophistication, unknown to modern American capitalism. Europe developed a certain tradition of literate statesmen, while the United States has specialized in the manufacture of a special breed of web-footed politicians. Whatever fine traditions existed in the early period of postcolonial American capitalism have long since been lost.

The current administration is a clinical example of the backwardness of American politics; McCarthyism is its sick offspring. In what other age could one find an administration so totally lacking in subtlety and sophistication? In what other period have the forces of pedestrianism and philistinism established such a tight stranglehold on official political life? In what other administration can we fail to find an interesting personality?

In the president's chair sits a smiling, bumbling trout fisherman and golfer whose favorite reading material, he genially informs us, are cowboy stories. In the vice presidency is a miserable huckster, a cheap publicity salesman whose pose as a modern Clay is marred only by the fact that he can neither think, write nor speak with the intelligence of the great compromiser.[1] His recent speech, supposedly a rebuke to McCarthy, but more like a gentle pat, is required reading for any person willing to inflict upon himself a study of platitudes in American political life. Note the following passage from the speech by this "anti"-McCarthy McCarthyist, the vice president of a nation of 160 millions and the international troubleshooter of the most powerful nation in the world. It is the only passage that resembles a rebuke to McCarthy, and should be read for its typical richness of thought, imagery and prose style:

> Now I can imagine that some of you who are listening will say "well, why all of this hullabaloo about being fair when you're dealing with a gang of traitors?" As a matter of fact I've heard people say, "After all, they're a bunch of rats. What we ought to do is to go out and shoot 'em." Well, I'll agree they're a bunch of rats, but just remember this. When you go out to shoot rats, you have to shoot straight, because

---

1   Jacobson refers here to Dwight Eisenhower, US president from 1952 to 1960, and to his vice president, Richard Nixon.

when you shoot wildly it not only means that the rat may get away more easily, you make it easier on the rat. But you might hit someone else who's trying to shoot rats too. And so we've got to be fair.

. . .

This primitivism of a type which has no parallel in European politics provides the necessary bacteriological culture in which McCarthyism can fester.

Whether the Ides of March have cast their baleful spell upon McCarthy or not, McCarthyism will remain firmly implanted in American bourgeois life. In this fact lies the weakness of the term. For *McCarthyism* represents no thought-out social philosophy of a particular senator from Wisconsin, but can best be understood in its broadest sense as the excesses of the postwar reaction. This reaction preceded McCarthy and will continue should he be eclipsed; it was induced by the fear, panic and paralysis of the bourgeoisie in the face of Stalinist expansionism, already assuming dangerous proportions under the Truman administration. It was during the Fair Deal reign that the foundation of what is popularly known today as McCarthyism was solidly established. The loyalty oaths, the subversive lists, congressional inquisitions, Executive Order Number 9835, all familiar activities of the Truman administration, planted the seeds of the now-lush political jungle in America in which McCarthyite cavemen conduct their barbarous, and sometimes cannibalistic, rites. It was under the Truman administration that the character of the present Supreme Court was finally shaped with the selection of four political backwoodsmen to the nation's highest judicial body; men who have used every shabby argument to keep the offensive against democratic liberties free of legal and constitutional booby traps. It was under the Truman administration that the whole political atmosphere in this country became poisonous and intellectually asphyxiating with but the feeblest protest from left-wing Democrats and the approval of the Democratic Party as a whole. It was Truman who suggested, personally and publicly, that neighbor spy on neighbor, reporting suspicions to the FBI. It was under the Truman administration that the denial of the right of a member of the Communist Party to teach became an accepted doctrine of Democrat and Republican alike. These activities of the Fair Dealers were carried out with hesitation and even with reluctance. Let us give the devil his due, even when it is so little. But conscience could not compete with what seemed in their eyes political expediency; with what liberals thought was a necessary liberal compromise with their abstract democratic values. However, our analysis, while taking their conscience into account, gives prime importance to the cold fact that their concessions and capitulations mark the first phase of McCarthyism in America.

This first phase provided McCarthy with the political tenor and precedent from which he could proceed with the wisdom, cunning and logic of a shrewd and brutal politician. This poisoned atmosphere was to the arch-reactionaries as oxygen to life. It gave hope and courage to elements in the antediluvian political spectrum ranging from the American Legion and the Grant Wood Ladies to the professional race-baiters and fascists; the semi-repressed xenophobes of the Midwest were revived by the foul air, America Firsters and ex-Bundists felt their oats once again, the Texas oil millionaires[2] whose wealth is in direct proportion to their ignorance became the social and financial benefactors of the scum of American society. These are the cadres of the current phase of McCarthyism, carrying through with inexorable logic the aforementioned policies of Truman, and, tragically, winning wide popular support through demagogic passion and vigor.

McCarthyism as it now exists cannot be defined with a single phrase. It has no organization which it can call its own, but is a force which operates within and outside of both major parties. It has nothing which can properly be called an ideology. McCarthyism is a reaction which is more easily recognized by its specific acts and techniques. Nevertheless, for all its lack of formal organization and programmatic detail, McCarthyism is a social reaction with sufficiently visible characteristics and effects to mark it as something unique in American politics.

We have already mentioned in passing one fundamentally different characteristic of McCarthyism as compared to previous reactions: its durability. Its impact has been made on every phase of political and social life in America, and those conditions, primarily international,

---

2   The reference here could be to a number of far-right leaders of the US oil industry: Torkild Rieber, founder of Texaco, a Hitler admirer who helped finance Franco's fascists during the Spanish Civil War while starving the Spanish Republic of oil; Fred Koch, father of the Koch brothers, a far-right John Birch Society member who built one of the Third Reich's largest oil refineries; or H. L. Hunt, an antidemocratic Texas oil baron who funneled money into McCarthyite causes.

which facilitated the growth of McCarthyism show no signs of soon disappearing or even receding. McCarthyism is fated to remain as a symmetrical political parallel to the permanent war economy.

The beginning of the Cold War signified the beginning of the end of the traditional bourgeois democratic values *as we knew them in the thirties*. This does not mean by any stretch of the imagination that we are on the brink of fascism or that totalitarianism is imminent or that McCarthyism has no limits beyond which it cannot successfully trespass in this period. It is simply a recognition of the more-than-quantitative difference between the era of hard-won rights the American people enjoyed in the thirties and the wretched state of political freedoms today. It is the American form of retrogression, a reflex to the last imperialist war and its aftermath—the Cold War and the sweep of Stalinism over half of Europe and Asia. In Europe retrogression was manifested in the loss of national dignity, increasingly enforced dependence on the United States and political stagnation. McCarthyism's corrupting impact on democratic rights is America's throwback and no less revealing of the futility of bourgeois opposition to Stalinism.

A victory of the Democratic Party in the coming congressional elections would, at best, tend to level off the present McCarthyite reaction, but reasonable people, above all, among the Democrats, cannot foresee in a Democratic victory a return to anything resembling the bourgeois liberalism of the thirties ...

More recently, the behavior of the liberals in the McCarthy-Cohn-Schine-Army fracas[3] reveals the fragility of their liberal values. Again, in the interests of political expediency they have resorted to an absolutely shameless defense of the military as a virtually untouchable caste, whose inviolability is not to be trespassed upon by popularly elected legislators, thus diluting their liberal appeal and at the same time weakening the struggle against McCarthy ...

That the best that can be hoped for today under either a Democratic or Republican administration is a relaxation of the reaction, and possibly an attempt to restrain McCarthy is related to another distinctive feature of

---

3   By 1954, McCarthy met fierce opposition from the US Army after he accused its leadership of communism. The public conflict between McCarthy and the Army in the "Army-McCarthy hearings" (April–June 1954) would mark the beginning of his downfall. Historians of the period tend to agree with Jacobson (below) that McCarthy's attack on the Army was a classic case of overreach.

McCarthyism. Reactionary movements and moods in the United States in the past have been, for the most part, a product of internal conflict. Economic crises and acute class struggles provided their impulse. These elements are totally absent as causal factors in the rise of McCarthy and McCarthyism. McCarthyism was already flourishing when family income and employment were at the highest level in history, and the labor movement was not engaged in any militant class struggle activities which would sound the alarm for industrialists or politicians. It would be futile to seek primary reasons for the growth of McCarthyism strictly in internal political problems. McCarthyism was essentially generated by the fear of international Stalinism and thrived upon revelations of espionage. With or without McCarthy, this movement has become the pathetic answer of the American bourgeoisie to Stalinism. Every victory of Stalinism has been accompanied by a McCarthyite advance, and every advance of McCarthyism facilitates further victories of Stalinism . . .

The unique features of McCarthyism can be summed up in a comparison with the reaction following World War I. At that time the Palmer Raids, the activities of the Lusk Committee in New York, and the wholesale arrests, prosecutions and deportations carried out by local and federal agencies were a hysterical outburst by a bourgeoisie made newly aware of its role as a world power and terrified by the very real prospect of a European socialist revolution. This fear of international socialism—similar in effect to the present fear of international Stalinism—was aggravated by the rapid decline in living standards and the growing militancy of the labor movement. The bourgeoisie reacted with a violence then much greater than is the case today, but one which did not outlast the decline of the European revolution, the disembowelment of the Industrial Workers of the World and the Communist Party and the economic upswing of the early twenties. McCarthyism is different in that it is fed by an increasingly powerful world-Stalinist force which shows no signs of abating its drive for world supremacy. It developed at a time when there was neither depression nor general strikes, and it victimizes more than Wobblies or Communists—it attacks the institutions of bourgeois democracy.[4]

---

4   "Wobblies" is the nickname for members of the Industrial Workers of the World (IWW), which was founded in Chicago in 1905 and peaked in the 1910s. The IWW was a radical, syndicalist labor union most active in isolated mines, mills, and factories in the Western states. They worked toward a general strike that would end capitalism and bring a direct democracy of workers' councils in its wake.

In discussing McCarthyism one must be careful to avoid the pitfall of characterizing this movement in the same terms which might be applied to a few of its more notorious spokesmen and supporters. Most pointedly, a distinction must be made between the man, McCarthy, and the movement named in his dubious honor. McCarthy may with justice be referred to as America's totalitarian personality. He is brutal, ruthless, intolerant, demagogic, a conscientious liar, ego driven, power hungry, vigorous and a cunning political barbarian. He has, in more moderate words, all the pathological and political equipment of a totalitarian fascist type. This does not concern us at the moment. Of paramount importance is to recognize that McCarthyism, though it is a new phenomenon, cannot be equated to fascism nor does it present the nation with any imminent threat of fascism.

To maintain that McCarthyism in its present phase is the instrumentality of fascism is to impute to it characteristics it does not possess. It would imply, above all, that it is a well-organized and integrated movement. It is not. McCarthyism has no recognized press of its own, no rounded ideology, no party of its own, no tight internal discipline, no acknowledged and consciously organized leadership. It continues to function within the framework of both parties, whereas every powerful fascist movement we know of has been conceived outside the framework of traditional bourgeois democratic parties.

Of greater import is the absence of those social conditions which have been proved essential to the rise of a powerful fascist movement. Fascism, as we know it, comes to power in periods of irreconcilable class conflicts and economic disintegration. The bourgeoisie does not turn to the mailed fist because of intellectual conviction or boredom with bourgeois parliamentarianism. It resorts to fascism out of necessity—when its life is menaced by its native working class and its economic functioning is paralyzed.

Fascism, by definition, presupposes the ruthless suppression of the working class, not only as a contender for power, but as an independent political force. But fascism, again by definition, imposes restrictions on the rights of individual capitalists, limiting their area of political and economic maneuverability. The bourgeois sacrifices in the interests of the bourgeoisie, placing power in the hands of a totalitarian elite, under which he may writhe, but seeing in it the only means of personal and class salvation.

We need not go beyond this elementary definition of fascism and its origins to rule it out as a possible evolvement from McCarthyism in the coming period. The American bourgeoisie can find neither reason nor need today to crush the American labor movement as an independent class force. On the other hand the labor movement, 15 million strong, for all its apathy and class collaborationism is anything but an easily crushable force.

While we fail to see wherein McCarthyism can be equated to fascism, we would be guilty of an ostrich-like self-deception not to recognize the seeds of an authoritarian movement in it. More than that, we should not exclude the long-range possibility of this authoritarian movement coming to power, either through a successful struggle for control of the Republican Party or, failing that, through a consolidation of the forces of total McCarthyism in some new alignment of political parties and groups, the precise nature of which is impossible to foresee. This authoritarian government would not necessarily destroy every vestige of opposition political functioning, as is the case with fascism. It would not necessarily be compelled to conduct a struggle for survival with the labor movement; it might instead attempt to neutralize it, partly through threats and in part by persuading the labor movement to accommodate itself. Such an authoritarian regime might liquidate the Communist Party without the total terror of fascism; it might eliminate any bipartisanship in national or foreign affairs without eliminating all other parties; it might attempt to assert its authority over all cultural and social institutions without attempting to incorporate them fully into the state. It would be a repressive government, but not one of total terror.

Senator McCarthy, who represents the most conscious, outspoken and extremist type of McCarthyism, must be given credit for understanding that the limitations of McCarthyism today can be countered or turned to his advantage tomorrow. These boundaries are set by the following: one, as we have already mentioned, is the lack of a social program; and, second, is the current economic recession with no big upswing in sight.

Until recently McCarthy's political pulse has been kept throbbing almost exclusively by the existence of Stalinism. The World Conspiracy of Communism Operating in the United States provided McCarthy with his enormous successes. The fact that his inquisitions proved nothing, exposed nobody, revealed no hitherto-unknown espionage rings, is beside the point. His supporters were cleverly kept under the impression that McCarthy was single-handedly slaying the red dragon which threatened their way of life.

The recession is putting an end to the illusion that McCarthy is saving the republic from chaos. The senator is no less active than last year in his witch hunting; the "Truman-Acheson gang" has been replaced by Eisenhower-Dulles, leaders of McCarthy's own party; thus the "Red Menace" from within is obviously diminished, and, yet, despite all these "achievements" the average American feels immeasurably less secure this year than last.

Nothing is as sobering to the marginal man as having his margin narrowed down. The sound and fury of McCarthy begin to signify to numbers of his supporters exactly what Shakespeare said: nothing. If the electoral success of the Republican Party and McCarthy's free-swinging mace could not somehow keep the high living standard intact then suspicions are naturally aroused: first, about the Republicans; second, about McCarthy's activities. A man waiting on line for an unemployment insurance check is likely to get a little annoyed at another man who makes his fame and fortune by running around with the scalp of an army dentist.

McCarthy may well be no less aware of this limit to McCarthy and McCarthyism in its present form than we are. But he also understands that this economic factor which tends to stall McCarthyism—it can only be stalled, not repudiated, under either party given present conditions—can become the source of added strength for himself. What he requires is the broad social program as yet absent: McCarthy needs to develop views, not only on the menace of Communism, but on the very real and immediate problems which are hitting at the American budget . . .

While McCarthy may develop a social program it would not necessarily presage a break with the Republican Party. On the contrary, there is no reason to believe that he is at all interested in organizationally splitting his party. Despite McCarthy's power as an individual he would be a man without a future if he were now to foster a formal break. It is no accident that McCarthy has conspicuously avoided any obvious identification with reactionary and fascist organizations of the lunatic fringe. He has no direct public contact with men like Gerald Smith or organizations such as the KKK. McCarthy is too clever a politician to acknowledge support from these discredited types . . .

McCarthy's need for the Republican Party is a reciprocal relationship. The Republican Party needs McCarthy. Its leaders are "practical politicians" first and men of principle last. They are well aware of the effectiveness of McCarthy's techniques for winning votes from the Democrats without soiling their own hands. McCarthy's personal intervention in the last senatorial elections in Maryland produced one of the filthiest campaigns in political history. But the result was that Millard Tydings, an extremely conservative Democrat who could not be purged by Roosevelt and Truman, was defeated by McCarthy's candidate. Such services are appreciated by the Republican leadership . . .

McCarthy overreached himself in his attack on the army. It was bad timing from a man who is, after all, ahead of his times. His public stock has dropped considerably—though not as much as the press makes out—and he frightened even his warmest supporters. It will take considerable time for McCarthy to recoup his losses. If only for this mistake, a split with the party in which he takes the initiative is out of the question. If McCarthy is to split with the party he will choose the propitious moment when, following some particularly dramatic event, he feels capable of riding a tremendous wave of mass discontent . . .

The role of the labor movement vis-à-vis McCarthyism has been nothing short of disgraceful. With the exception of occasional speeches and articles, the leaders of organized labor are remarkable only for their do-nothingism. They have made virtually no attempt to actually mobilize the working class against McCarthyism or McCarthy. For a local union to pass an anti-McCarthyist resolution is an occasion for headlines. It is almost as if a truce existed between McCarthy and the labor leadership. McCarthy has shrewdly refrained from attacking the non-Stalinist[5] labor movement as such; the labor leadership in return has placed narrow limits on their anti-McCarthy activities. Yet the labor leadership must be given credit for understanding that the end-all of McCarthy's activities can only be an attack on the free labor movement. The existence of democratic institutions is a necessary element for a free

---

5   Trotskyists frequently used the word "Stalinist" to describe communists and communist parties that remained affiliated with the Soviet Union, particularly through the Third International (also called the Communist International or Comintern) and later the Cominform. The reference here is to labor organizers and leaders who continued to work closely with or through the Communist Party USA.

labor movement, and a free trade union organization is ultimately intolerable to authoritarian movements . . .

Fundamentally, the union leadership is restricted in any fight against McCarthy by its lack of a dynamic, social program. It remains tied to bourgeois politics. It is deeply committed to the Democratic Party, above all to the Fair Deal wing which, when in power, created the acts, the precedents and the mood which fertilized the soil in which McCarthyism and McCarthy could grow like a rank and stultifying bed of weeds. But for all the political infirmity of the American labor movement, it is the only force today which is potentially capable of leading a major struggle against McCarthyism. The truce between McCarthy and the labor movement is tenuous and cannot be maintained permanently if the latter is to preserve its freedom of organization and movement.

McCarthyism has given an urgent note to the need of an independent labor party. Before the war socialists proposed the political organization of the working class in its own party as an offensive class struggle activity. Today, the need for a labor party is made more pressing by its additional importance as a defensive move against the inevitable encroachments of McCarthyism on the free trade union movement. Should the labor leadership fail to educate its rank and file, fail to respond to the need for building a party of labor, but, instead, cower before McCarthy, compromise with McCarthyism and sink deeper into the Democratic Party, then democracy will have been dealt a foul blow. This is not our ultimatum but one presented by the reality of the political character of the permanent war economy.

Alson J. Smith, "The McCarthy Falange," *Christian Century*, December 29, 1954

This investigative report surveys the hard-right scene of the 1950s as it came together for a gathering in New York City. The author outlines its continuities, in terms of personnel and ideology, with the hard right of previous decades. His report tends to support the analysis of Julius Jacobson (see "McCarthy and McCarthyism," in this volume). In particular, it shows the disorganization of the far right in the 1950s and the failure of McCarthyism to cohere into a bona fide movement. The word "falange" in the title is a reference to the Falangists, Spanish fascists active in the Spanish Civil War and beyond. Smith's piece appeared in late 1954, when McCarthy's influence was largely spent; he had been shamed on public television in June of that year by Joseph Welch, head counsel for the US Army, during the senator's probe of the army.

Alson J. Smith (b. 1908) was a freelance journalist, Protestant minister, and independent scholar who perennially covered the far right, dating back to the 1930s. The following report appeared in Christian Century, *a major magazine of mainline Protestants in the United States. Founded in 1884 as the* Christian Oracle, *it has tended toward a liberal bent.*

On February 22, 1939, this writer, then a young and idealistic minister, attended what was called a "George Washington's Birthday Exercise" at Madison Square Garden in New York. A report of that meeting appeared in the March 8, 1939, issue of the *Christian Century* under the title "I

Went to a Nazi Rally." On November 29, 1954, the same writer, with both youth and idealism somewhat dimmed by the years, went back to Madison Square Garden for another rally.

The 1939 rally was sponsored by the German American Bund. It jammed the garden with a marching, shouting, singing mob of anti-Semitic fanatics. This 1954 rally was put on by something called "Ten Million Americans for Justice." It was a meeting to protest the impending censure by the United States Senate of Senator Joseph R. McCarthy. The tub-thumpers for Ten Million Americans had promised to jam the garden with McCarthy aficionados and pack nearby streets with the overflow—a crowd guaranteed to fill the Senate with such trepidation that Unser Joe[1] would be let off with no more than a patty-cake reprimand for using strong language. The rally was proclaimed as the culmination of a campaign to get 10 million signatures to petitions opposing censure. The sponsors promised that announcement of the exact number of petitioners would be a high point of the evening.

Looking over the advance notices, one gathered that this meeting would in some respects parallel the Bund rally of fifteen years before. The New York papers were comparing the two, and the police stated that their preparations to handle the affair would be the same as for the Bund rally and for subsequent Communist shindigs in the same arena. Elaborate plans were made to handle hordes of pickets and counterpickets, crackpots, sightseers, and potential troublemakers—plans involving paddy wagons, troops of mounted police, and scores of plainclothes men both inside and outside the Garden. The police were ready for anything, and the pre-rally fulminations of the McCarthy high command made such precautions appear justified . . .

Empty Seats

Inside, the Garden was almost empty. An attempt had been made to make the vast auditorium look like the scene of a political convention, with state signs spaced at intervals along the mezzanine, and on the main floor little placards bearing the names of cities sending delegations. The "cities" were not impressive, being limited to such centers of

1   "Unser" is German for "our."

culture as Secaucus, Passaic, West New York, Lodi, Fort Lee—all communities within hailing distance. In the farthest reaches of the balcony a large green-and-white sign proclaimed a section of seats as the rallying point for the Irish-American Minute Men of 1949.[2] It remained empty throughout the evening.

A band, nattily accoutered in yellow-and-brown uniforms, entertained the crowd. Ten Million Americans had flown in this musical aggregation from Hortonsville, Wisconsin, for sentimental reasons, Hortonsville being in the neighborhood of Appleton, the mecca of all true believers.[3] It was a high school band, and its repertoire seemed limited to "On Wisconsin." The rendering of this number was greeted with applause and cheers throughout the evening. The apple-cheeked country kids, who had obviously come along just for the ride, seemed curiously out of place.

By eight o'clock, when the meeting was scheduled to start, the Garden was not half full. At 8:25, when Major George Racey Jordan, who was running the show, announced that "a young man will do some entertaining," it was perhaps half filled, and it never got much more than that. The Garden management estimated 12,000 present. Capacity, with standees, is close to 24,000. Nazis, Communists, the Methodists, Jehovah's Witnesses, the Harlem Globetrotters and the New York Rangers have filled this auditorium, to say nothing of Rocky Marciano, Jersey Joe Walcott, and the fanciers of dogs, cats and horses. The first speaker of the evening, Major Al Williams, a World War I ace, said that "a prairie fire is sweeping America and the grass is dry," but the prairie in the vicinity of Eighth Avenue and Forty-Ninth Street seemed to be more than a bit damp.[4]

The young man who entertained turned out to be a goateed bluessinger and bebopper named Hamm. "God bless Joe McCarthy!" he shouted. "Long may he reign over all he surveys!" Evidently Mr. Hamm

---

2   The American Irish Minutemen of 1949 were not the same "Minutemen" named by Robert F. Williams on page 250–51. They were a New York–based organization that campaigned for the unification of Northern Ireland with the Republic of Ireland.

3   Joe McCarthy was born on a farm near Appleton, Wisconsin, and lived in Appleton until entering national politics.

4   Major Alford Joseph Williams was a staunch McCarthy supporter who had been an isolationist before World War II. He was also an aviator, flight trainer, and booster of an independent Air Force.

had Joe confused with some higher authority, a natural error. He announced that he had written a song called "In the Good Old USA" and had sent it to the army so the army band could learn it. Then he said he would "shake, rattle and roll" to the tune of "Tuxedo Junction." The Hortonsville band did not know "Tuxedo Junction," but Mr. Hamm shook, rattled and rolled unaccompanied. He got a scattering of applause.

The Persecution Motif

After the shaking, rattling and rolling had subsided, a Roman Catholic bishop, the Right Reverend Cuthbert O'Hara, was called upon for an invocation. The good bishop had put in two uncomfortable years in a Red Chinese jail, and he now proceeded to tell the Almighty about it, reading from several pages of manuscript. After filing this complaint he demanded redress, which was not immediately forthcoming. Then a Mr. Feeney sang the national anthem, and [the] crowd settled back for the fireworks.

These sputtered fitfully during the evening. Major Al Williams was introduced as a hero who had been "greatly crushed" by some conspiracy. The major hinted darkly of "brainwashing" and cried that "the people who pay for wars and die in wars are determined to speak!" Was there a move to censure Senator Fulbright (Boo!), a typical Rhodes scholar? (Laughter.) No! "They say, 'McCarthy urged soldiers to disregard orders from above.' God knows I've done that for all the years!"

The speeches were all variations on the same theme: McCarthy is being persecuted. The UN is a fraud. "Dissolve those bonds which weaken and destroy devotion to country!" Coexistence is a trap. "Who wants to shake their bloody hands? Flanders!" At the mention of the hated name, a dozen signs appeared reading "Get the Net!" and "Flanders, why don't you censure Paul Revere for disturbing the peace?"[5]

----

5   Senator Ralph Flanders (R-Vermont) was one of the most visible of the anti-McCarthy forces in Congress. In June 1954, he repeatedly insisted in national forums like NBC's *Meet the Press* that the Wisconsin senator represented the face of American fascism. That same month, he called on Congress to strip McCarthy of his chairmanships and introduced a motion for formal censure. Such efforts eventually bore fruit by September of that year.

Roars of laughter, boos. There were howls of derision and catcalls for the *New York Times,* General George Marshall, "Crybaby" General Zwicker, Franklin D. Roosevelt, Harry Truman, Dean Acheson, Professor Albert Einstein, and—second only to the catcalls elicited by the name of Flanders—the president of the United States. "I mean that to go right to the top of this land!" shouted Williams, excoriating those who "reach high places and then forget where they came from." "Down with Eisenhower!" shrieked a prognathous female from the Secaucus delegation.

Cheers for Heroes

The crowd had its heroes, too. There were cheers for "Bill" Knowland, George Sokolsky, Martin Dies, General MacArthur and the late Senator Pat McCarran. And most of all for "Joe." Signs waved madly at every mention of his name—"McCarthy for President in '56," "Young Americans for McCarthy forever and in eternity," "Fight to the death for Joe McCarthy."

There were speeches by a Mrs. Brossard, representing the Daughters of the American Revolution; Major George Racey Jordan and Admiral John G. Crommelin; former New Jersey governor Charles Edison; Professor Godfrey Schmidt of Fordham; a militant young ex-major by the name of Heinle, who had been connected with Radio Free Europe. There were formal platform appearances by Lieutenant General Pedro A. del Valle and by Dr. J. Oliver Buswell, who said he represented the American Council of Christian Churches. There were wire recordings of speeches by the governor of Utah, by General George Stratemeyer, and by Admiral William H. Standley, "one American ambassador who wasn't afraid to stand up to Joe Stalin!" There were introductions of such stalwarts as Westbrook Pegler, ex-representative Hamilton Fish, Archibald Roosevelt, and young Bill Buckley, author of *God and Man at Yale, McCarthy and His Enemies* and other patriotic prose. Not introduced but visible in the audience were the Reverend Gerald L. K. Smith, masquerading as a Texas oilman beneath a ten-gallon hat, Joseph B. Kamp, and other veteran conspiracy-smellers.

"The Hidden Force"

The speeches themselves were weirdly inflammatory, being a mixture of Know-Nothing isolationism and immediate blood-and-thunder interventionism. "If we had guts at the top of this land China would be blockaded!" shouted Williams. "Get in the first blow!" advised Professor Schmidt—an admonition which drew from the back of the mezzanine a stentorian Brooklynese "Foist tings foist!"

There was an ugly moment when a lady *Life* photographer was almost mobbed and had to be escorted from the hall to the accompaniment of cries of "Kill the Communist!" and "God bless America!" There was a dramatic moment when a searching spotlight probed through the crowd and located a minor hero, Roy Cohn, who was invited to the platform for a few impromptu remarks, which he made from notes. "Give 'em hell, Roy," shouted the crowd. "Pour it on!" Signs, not altogether impromptu, announced that Roy Cohn would be "our next senator." There was a touching moment when the "big surprise," announced early in the evening, finally appeared. It was Jean McCarthy, who blushed prettily and tried to ignore the bleats of "Where's Joe?" and "We want Joe!" The crowd had confidently expected the "surprise" to be Joe himself; when it turned out to be his wife, his followers were not as cordial as they might have been.

It was Admiral Crommelin—far and away the most impressive speaker in this strange mélange—who produced the phrase that would seem to be the key to an understanding of what makes this McCarthy falange tick. That phrase, which he used again and again, was "the hidden force." The "hidden force" was the secret, malevolent frustrator of good patriotic Americans, the recognizers of Soviet Russian back in 1933, the insidious power corrupting the State Department and seeding it with homosexuals and security risks. It was the "hidden force" that defeated the Bricker Amendment, dragged the country into World Wars I and II, unified the armed services (Crommelin was forced to retire for opposing unification), denied reinforcements to Dien Bien Phu, and now calls for "coexistence" and the censure of Joe McCarthy. History is simple: the hidden force defeats America on land, on the sea and in the air.

In order to understand the appeal of the hidden-force theory to the crowd in Madison Square Garden and to the McCarthy falangists everywhere, it is necessary to scrutinize closely these people for whom the junior senator from Wisconsin is an object of almost religious veneration.

Who Follows in His Train?

By and large, the people demanding to know "Who promoted Peress?" and "Why don't they censure Flanders?" and crying "God bless Joe McCarthy" are the same people who were peddling *Social Justice*, hollering up Father Coughlin, and scrawling anti-Semitic filth on subway posters back in 1939. They are older now. One of the characteristics of this crowd in Madison Square Garden was its lack of youth. It was predominately a middle-aged and elderly crowd. Such young people as were present ran to pimply-faced youths in leather windbreakers—a genus indigenous to New York's Middle West Side—and fresh-faced girls in convent-school uniform. Like the old "Christian Fronters" the crowd was 90 percent Irish in background, and as it filed into the Garden one might have been pardoned for asking, "What time does the bingo start?" In a city like New York, which is the largest Jewish and the largest Negro metropolis in the world, and the second- or third-largest Italian, it is odd that there were so few Jewish, Negro and Italian faces in evidence.

In a city with almost 2 million people of Protestant background, the only Protestant present and identifiable as such was the Reverend Mr. Buswell, representing a fundamentalist minority. There was a slight Teutonic tinge to the crowd, a throwback to the old Bund and America First days. Next to the Irish majority, the most obvious element in this falange was the "Old American" of the patriotic-societies variety, the type that haunts the genealogical room of the New York Public Library. Ham Fish is a good representative of this ingredient in the blend, and Mrs. Brossard is another. These are the 200 percent patriots who welcome any allies in their continuous and long-standing warfare against the "hidden force."

The one other recognizable component of the crowd at Madison Square Garden was the merest sprinkling of die-hard adherents of the late Senator Robert Taft.[6] They were quiet and well dressed. Some of

---

6   Robert A. Taft (1889–1953) served as a US Senator (R-Ohio) from 1939 until his death in 1953. Before the bombing of Pearl Harbor, he was a leading congressional

them wore huge orange buttons with the word "Taft" in blue, the same buttons that were so prominent at the Republican National Convention at Chicago in 1952. These were the Constitutionalists, the people whose voices are Senators Knowland, Bricker and Dirksen.

Expensive Frustration

The McCarthy falange, then, is made up—at least in its East Coast corps—of a large nucleus of irritable, middle-aged and elderly people of Irish background, surrounded by a scattering of professional patriots, disgruntled ex-army and navy officers, remnants of the old German American Bund, a few Taft isolationists, and a minuscule fringe of priests and recent parochial- and convent-school graduates who have absorbed a certain amount or pro-McCarthy fanaticism from their teachers and spiritual mentors.

What is it that all these people have in common, the thing of which Joe McCarthy is a symbol, the element that lends credibility to the hidden-force theory of recent history?

It is simply this: all these people are frustrated. Fifteen years ago the scapegoat held responsible in their twisted imaginations for defeating them in their hopes and dreams was the Jew. Today it is the "hidden force," and most of them are convinced, in spite of their momentary affection for Roy Cohn, Dave Schine and Rabbi Ben Schultz, that there is a Hebrew hidden somewhere in the hidden-force woodpile. Father Coughlin with his *Social Justice* and his "Christian Front" spoke directly to this frustration. In the Promised Land, these people have not been able to obtain the promised things. They are still, by and large, economically depressed, still living in the crowded tenements and row houses of Brooklyn, Manhattan's West Side, the cheap Jersey bus-commuting communities, the West Roxbury and South End sections of Boston. They have lost hope. Significantly, their own sons and daughters are not with them in the McCarthy falange, because they are young and still have hope. McCarthy, these frustrated, aging Irish people feel, is one of them.

---

isolationist opposed to any form of economic or military aid for nations fighting Germany and Japan, arguing that war would transform the United States into a socialist dictatorship.

He speaks for them. Like them, he is a good Catholic who is being bilked at every turn by the "hidden force." He is the Coughlinite prototype battling for "social justice."

For the few priests and the pimply-faced young men and fresh-faced convent-school girls who follow them, McCarthy is the stalwart Catholic crusader seeking to reclaim the Holy Land from the infidels. When a New York monsignor told a communion breakfast that a $5 million fund had been raised to "get" McCarthy, he was speaking (with no knowledge of the facts) for this minority of the priesthood. It *is* a minority—there is no unanimity within the Roman Catholic Church on McCarthy. He is attacked and defended with equal vigor inside the church.

Blue Bloods at Bay

Most frustrated are all the Old Americans, the genealogical fetishists. Oddly enough, many of them are also economically depressed, and those who aren't are scared to death that they will be if the "hidden force" is able to hang on to the power to tax. For them, the whole significance of life is in the past. They have Abraham for their father, and if God is able of these stones to raise up children unto Abraham, then they are against God. They are the self-constituted keepers of the national heritage, and any revolutionists more recent than 1776 above the Mason-Dixon line, or 1865 below it, are anathema to them. Unable to comprehend the dynamics of the heritage they think of themselves as preserving, they are dragged along protestingly into a future which they do not understand and of which they are afraid. Afflicted with infantilism, they are firmly fixated in the glorious past and have no intention of going forward or letting the nation go forward if they can prevent it. Which they can't. Hence the frustration, compounded by the incomprehensible fact that their blue blood has not automatically brought riches, recognition and social prestige.

The frustration of the Bundists, the ex-officers and the isolationists is too obvious to call for analysis. History has defeated them; they know it but cannot accept it emotionally.

Some observers are talking about the McCarthy falange as the possible beginning of a third party. True, Huey Long was able to build a powerful political machine of a lumpenproletariat not unlike the McCarthyites, with the secret backing of some moneyed people who bear at least a superficial resemblance to the Texas oil tycoons who allegedly supply Senator Joe with funds. But Huey Long was a political organizer of genius. McCarthy has shown no ability as an organizer, a builder. He is a crafty exploiter of fears, a bandwagon rider sensitive to the mood of the horses; but over the long haul he could not appeal to large and politically potent segments of American life—the South, labor, the Negroes, the Jews, the Protestant farmers of the Midwest, the Citizens for Eisenhower crowd, the "eggheads," the youth.

Not a Revolution

Neither is the McCarthy falange a revolutionary cabal. It is more a band of raggle-taggle gypsies. It is a loud, nagging nuisance, but it is not a revolution. Such political significance as it has is given to it not by McCarthy, but by Knowland, Dirksen, Bridges and their ilk.

It was possible to loath and fear the Bundists back in 1939. But when they are seen close up one can neither loath nor fear these frustrated whiners about the "hidden force"; one can only pity. They are our real have-nots, psychologically and economically. Third parties and revolutions have to be made of sterner stuff.

Incidentally, they didn't get their 10 million signatures. *Life* says they got "just over two million."

Asa Carter and Jesse Mabry, "The Southerner," *Southerner*, March 1956

Asa ("Ace") Earl Carter (1925–1979) was a speechwriter for then-governor George Wallace of Alabama, the most visible opponent of the civil rights movement in the 1960s. In this role, Carter helped Wallace pen his infamous "Segregation Now, Segregation Forever" speech of January 1963. In the 1950s, Carter was a right-wing radio personality in Birmingham, Alabama, where he formed the North Alabama Citizens' Council, a more radical offshoot of the White Citizens' Councils.

Carter was a virulent anti-Semite and secret admirer of Adolf Hitler. He was the leader of a particularly vicious Klan militia, responsible for the public beating of Nat King Cole in Birmingham in 1956 and for the castration of black civil rights activist Edward Aaron. Carter personally shot two Klansmen who questioned his leadership.

Carter also wrote the screenplay for The Outlaw Josey Wales *(1976), and, paradoxically, wrote the bestselling memoir* The Education of Little Tree *(1976), about an oppressed Cherokee boy.*

This piece appeared in the first issue of the Southerner, *a white supremacist periodical he founded to further the aims of the North Alabama Citizens' Council. Jesse Mabry was his coeditor.*

The Southerner is known. His place of origin is instinctively thought of as being the South of the United States of America. No other section in any land has earned for its inhabitants the meaning that is embodied in the term "Southerner."

Through his veins flow the fire, the initiative, the stalwartness of the Anglo-Saxon. Proof of his enviable reputation is the attack upon him. From such, has been coined the words "redneck," and "woolhatter," "cracker," and "hillbilly." He has accepted them for what they are: For "redneck," takes mind of the toil beneath God's sun and with His good earth, of that he feels no shame; the "wool hat" has been his way, with little money, of wearing something "special" to God's house on Sunday morning; the "cracker" he adopts as his calling card of delicate cocksureness; and if "hillbilly" he be, then he exults in the high whine of the fiddle's bow that calls up the sound of the fierce Scot blood that sounded the bagpipe of battle and lamented in the ballads of yore.

The Southerner is proud. Proud of his race. Proud that he bends his knee but to God; proud of his independence. He is the powerful core of these United States that spell doom to those of dictatorial mind. And his pride is sunk deeply in the traditions built for him by his fathers and mothers of the Southland. The Southern woman that protected that race in a prostrate and vulture-ridden Reconstruction when lesser women of a lesser breed would have yielded into the easiest path of degradation.

The Southerner's tradition is marked high on the walls in the hall of battle. From his past, Jeb Stuart led the most fierce cavalry charges known to man. John Mosby's daring has never before or since been approached. The hell-for-leather fighting of the men of Lee, of Jackson, of Forrest, of Early and Hood, of Johnson and Wheeler were those same "rednecks" that inspired Rudyard Kipling to write that there in the Southland lived the greatest fighting breed of man in the world. The Southerner proved worthy of those words. Odds meant little or nothing . . . and in the end, he snatched victory from defeat by starvation, through the sheer will of his devotion to cause and strength of sinew and heart.

The odds today mount steadily against the Southerner's philosophy of race and passion for freedom against his moral standard and devotion to Christianity. The enemy has been allowed to mount his odds, we believe, because the Southerner has not been allowed to read the facts and gain the truth . . . and so determine his aim. His spirit had grown rusty in the corner; his attitude grown more irresponsible through guidance of a "free press," that no longer is free . . . afraid to print of the truth . . . with mercenary abandon using vicious propaganda to change the character and principles of the Southerner.

This we cannot bear. That so proud a race sink into the toils of atheistic mongrelization, carrying with it the hope of Christianity, for lack of the facts, for want of the truth.

We, in choosing the *Southerner* for the title of this publication, do so with sincere prayer in our hearts that we shall have the strength to match the standards and character of its namesake.

We are pledged to print the truth, regardless of the powerful men or organizations that truth touches.

In full faith that the Southerner will, when informed, again take his rightful position, not in defensive evasiveness, but in full thundering charge, we begin this publication.

And as the working man of the South once more turns his hard hand to the saving of a race and freedom, we will count it a blessing and an honor to be numbered among him. To be a member of his ranks, a brother of his blood, there can be no honor greater, no reward richer.

Robert F. Williams, from *Negroes with Guns,* 1962

Activists in the antifascist tradition have often engaged in conventional political forms like coalition building, picketing, and lobbying. But another strand of that tradition has also emphasized the need to physically confront fascists in public, and those wanting to find antecedents to that strand before the 1980s should not overlook Robert Williams (1925–1996) and his controversial book Negroes with Guns. Williams explicitly called out his white supremacist enemies in the Klan and in the Minutemen as "fascists."

Published at a high point of the civil rights movement, Negroes with Guns furthered, by leaps and bounds, a growing public critique of nonviolent civil disobedience as the only valid strategy of the black freedom struggle. Malcolm X and his criticisms of Martin Luther King Jr. were already well known by the time of its publication, and Williams's book would inspire the formation of the Black Panther Party a few years later, in 1966.

Martin Luther King Jr. denounced Williams, yet even King distinguished between "pure nonviolence," "violence exercised in self-defense" and "violence organized as a tool of advancement, as in warfare." King saw violence in self-defense as justifiable in certain contexts.

Williams, in giving his book the provocative title "Negroes with Guns," knew he was striking a nerve lodged deep in the American psyche. The slave codes that followed the defeat of Bacon's Rebellion in 1676 established gun ownership as the privilege of whites, thus forging a psychological link *between guns and white, male identity that remains alive and well in the contemporary United States.*

Robert F. Williams (1925–1996) served in the US Army during World War II and voluntarily enlisted in the Marine Corps in 1954 (he was soon discharged for his criticisms of its racism). In 1956, he took leadership of the National Association for the Advancement of Colored People (NAACP) chapter in his hometown of Monroe, North Carolina, and proved a very capable organizer, boosting its membership from six to two hundred. Williams expanded this work by starting a local branch of the National Rifle Association called the Black Guards; its members received weapons training so that they could defend black citizens, whose calls to the police were generally ignored. Facing near-constant death threats, Williams fled the United States in 1961 with his wife and two children to avoid kidnapping charges, which were later dropped. The Williams family went into exile in Cuba, and then in China, before returning to the United States in 1969.

Prologue

Why do I speak to you from exile?

Because a Negro community in the South took up guns in self-defense against racist violence—and used them. I am held responsible for this action, that for the first time in history American Negroes have armed themselves as a group to defend their homes, their wives, their children, in a situation where law and order had broken down, where the authorities could not, or rather would not, enforce their duty to protect Americans from a lawless mob. I accept this responsibility and am proud of it. I have asserted the right of Negroes to meet the violence of the Ku Klux Klan by armed self-defense—and have acted on it. It has always been an accepted right of Americans, as the history of our Western states proves, that where the law is unable, or unwilling, to enforce order, the citizens can, and must, act in self-defense against lawless violence. I believe this right holds for black Americans as well as whites.

Many people will remember that in the summer of 1957 the Ku Klux Klan made an armed raid on an Indian community in the South and were met with determined rifle fire from the Indians acting in self-defense. The nation approved of the action, and there were widespread expressions of pleasure at the defeat of the Kluxers who showed their courage by running away, despite their armed superiority. What the nation doesn't know, because it has never been told, is that the Negro community in Monroe, North Carolina, had set the example two weeks before when we shot up an armed motorcade of the Ku Klux Klan, including two police cars, which had come to attack the home of Dr. Albert E. Perry, vice president of the Monroe chapter of the National Association for the Advancement of Colored People. The stand taken by our chapter resulted in the official reaffirmation by the NAACP of the right of self-defense. The Preamble to the resolution of the Fiftieth Convention of the NAACP, New York City, July 1959, states: "We do not deny, but reaffirm, the right of an individual and collective self-defense against unlawful assaults."

Because there has been much distortion of my position, I wish to make it clear that I do not advocate violence for its own sake or for the sake of reprisals against whites. Nor am I against the passive resistance advocated by the Reverend Martin Luther King and others. My only difference with Dr. King is that I believe in flexibility in the freedom struggle. This means that I believe in nonviolent tactics where feasible; the mere fact that I have a sit-in case pending before the US Supreme Court bears this out. Massive civil disobedience is a powerful weapon under civilized conditions where the law safeguards the citizens' right of peaceful demonstrations. In civilized society the law serves as a deterrent against lawless forces that would destroy the democratic process. But where there is a breakdown of the law, the individual citizen has a right to protect his person, his family, his home and his property. To me this is so simple and proper that it is self-evident.

When an oppressed people show a willingness to defend themselves, the enemy, who is a moral weakling and coward, is more willing to grant concessions and work for a respectable compromise. Psychologically, moreover, racists consider themselves superior beings and are not willing to exchange their superior lives for our inferior ones. They are most vicious and violent when they can practice violence with impunity. This we have shown in Monroe. Moreover, when because of our self-defense there is a danger that the blood of whites may be spilled, the local authorities in the South suddenly enforce law and order when previously they had been complacent toward lawless, racist violence. This too we have proven in Monroe. It is remarkable how easily and quickly state and local police control and disperse lawless mobs when the Negro is ready to defend himself with arms. Furthermore, because of the international situation, the federal government does not want racial incidents which draw the attention of the world to the situation in the South. Negro self-defense draws such attention, and the federal government will be more willing to enforce law and order if the local authorities don't. When our people become fighters, our leaders will be able to sit at the conference table as equals, not dependent on the whim and the generosity of the oppressors. It will be to the best interests of both sides to negotiate just, honorable and lasting settlements.

The majority of white people in the United States have literally no idea of the violence with which Negroes in the South are treated daily— nay, hourly. This violence is deliberate, conscious, condoned by the authorities. It has gone on for centuries and is going on today, every day, unceasing and unremitting. It is our way of life. Negro existence in the South has been one long travail, steeped in terror and blood—our blood. The incidents which took place in Monroe, which I witnessed and which I suffered, will give some idea of the conditions in the South, conditions that can no longer be borne. That is why, one hundred years after the Civil War began, we Negroes in Monroe armed ourselves in self-defense and used our weapons. We showed that our policy worked. The lawful authorities of Monroe and North Carolina acted to enforce order only after, and as a direct result of, our being armed. Previously they had connived with the Ku Klux Klan in the racist violence against our people. Self-defense prevented bloodshed and forced the law to establish order. This is the meaning of Monroe and I believe it marks a historic change in the life of my people. This is the story of that change.

Chapter 6, "The Monroe Case: Conspiracy against the Negro"

I have a picture taken from a recent issue of the *Toronto Star* of members of the so-called US Minutemen, the fascistic organization that is in fellowship with the John Birch Society.[1] The photograph shows the

---

1   The Minutemen were an anticommunist militia formed by Robert DePugh in Norborne, Missouri, in the early 1960s. Their membership peaked at 25,000 before they were finally shut down by federal prosecutors in 1968. They trained for guerilla warfare in the event of a Communist invasion or a black uprising and distributed anticommunist, racist, and anti-Semitic literature. DePugh maintained friendly contacts with George

Minutemen in training in the state of Illinois. Not the state of Mississippi, not the state of Alabama or South Carolina, but the state of Illinois. These people are equipped with machine guns and automatic rifles, including the Johnson automatic rifle, and they are firing US Army 6.5-millimeter mortars. They are firing these mortars on prepared ranges and firing live ammunition. Where did they get these mortars? Where did they get this ammunition? No surplus stores in the United States sell mortars or live shells. Where did they get their machine guns and automatic rifles, many models of which still are in use by the United States Armed Forces? Unlike our weapons, automatic rifles and machine guns may not be owned by civilians. This is specified by Federal law.

These men are wearing standard steel helmets and are dressed in surplus uniforms of the US Army. The only difference is that they have their own Minutemen insignia. These men have raised and mobilized their own private army. Some of the 5,000 men recruited in Monroe to attack the Freedom Riders were components of this fascistic Minutemen organization.

Nobody was upset about this. None of these pious-sounding newspapers, so interested in the welfare and the security of the American people, breathed a word about Minutemen being brought into Monroe. These Minutemen have been arming and training with heavy weapons in the field. What is the reason for this? Why has this been tolerated in the United States? The Minutemen say that they are mobilizing to fight Communism or possible invasion of the United States by the Communists. Wouldn't an American be naive indeed to believe that if the United States Marine Corps, the infantry, the navy, and the air force couldn't stop some sort of invasion, how in the hell could a few old women in tennis shoes from the John Birch Society and their corps of Minutemen stop them?

Anyone who can think logically can see that the racist Minutemen are being armed and prepared for pogroms. They are becoming a fascist vanguard that will someday be turned loose on all Afro-Americans and white Americans who get out of line. And to get out of line means to petition militantly for constitutional rights. These Minutemen types will

---

Lincoln Rockwell's American Nazi Party and the leaders of the nascent Christian Identity movement. He was sent to prison in 1968 on weapons and conspiracy charges after sending death threats to twenty US legislators who voted to abolish the House Un-American Activities Committee.

be the people who do the dirty work. Just as there were special units to man the gas furnaces for the Jewish people in Nazi Germany, so "special units" will develop to handle "troublemakers" in a fascist America. This must be done outside of the jurisdiction of the armed forces because the US Armed Services are integrated. But the Minutemen organizations are not integrated. It will be like the French Army and the OAS in Algeria.[2] They will look the other way, like the Wehrmacht and the SS corps in Hitler's time. The armed services of the United States, the police officials, the Justice Department will look the other way and say, "We're sorry, but we can't catch these people. We're sorry, but we've done everything we can do to prevent violence." The Minutemen have pure, 100 percent, all-American weapons, and the newspapers have barely found cause to denounce their activities.

But when the Negroes of Monroe, outnumbered and outarmed, gallantly rose to defend their homes, their families, and their persons, their efforts at self-defense were scorned by the press and they were smeared with the insinuation that their weapons were furnished by some insidious Communist conspiracy.

All the American people, not just Afro-Americans, must realize that if we had not been armed in this city of Monroe, Union County, North Carolina, last August 27, there would have been mass bloodshed. There is only one reason why the racist mob lost its nerve in their projected attack on the Negro community. Knowing as they did that we were well armed, they found it impossible to stomach the thought of violence.

---

2   The Organisation Armée Secrète (OAS) was a French right-wing paramilitary formed as a last-ditch effort to prevent Algeria's independence from colonial rule. In 1961 and 1962, and mostly after the ceasefire, they killed several thousand people in France and in Algeria through executions and terror attacks.

PART IV

The Politics of Backlash and a New United Front, 1968–1971

Asian American Political Alliance, "Concentration Camps, USA," June 28, 1968

Like many members of the Black Panther Party, which inspired its forma-tion, the Asian American Political Alliance (AAPA) perceived US history as an ongoing precondition for fascism. This 1968 statement by the alli-ance was occasioned by a move in Congress that year to draft an Internal Security Act reminiscent of the McCarran Act of 1950. The original was intended to suppress, arrest, intern and deport political dissidents, espe-cially communists. Its provision for "emergency detention" in Title II was sufficient for young Asian American radicals to foresee a parallel between the new legislation and an American history of anti-Asian racism in the form of World War II–era Japanese internment camps—or concentration camps, as they are referred to throughout this essay.

The alliance itself had been formed just one month earlier and was based in Berkeley, California. Members included veterans of the Black Panther Party and the anti-war movement, and of the Chinese Students Association at San Francisco State University. Opposition to the war in Vietnam and support for the national self-determination of oppressed nations were foundational political positions of the alliance. In the same year, the alliance joined the Third World Liberation Front, known for lead-ing the San Francisco State strike that effectively created the first ethnic studies programs in the United States.

The AAPA's argument that the new Internal Security Act could result in arrest and detention of Asian and Asian American activists was rooted in analysis of the state as a repressive, racist and frequently violent apparatus for the discipline and punishment of people of color. The arrest and deportations under the McCarran Act of the Trinidadian Marxists C. L. R. James and Claudia Jones were living memories for student revolutionaries. Ultimately, Japanese American activists were critical in the campaign to repeal Title II, which they achieved through an act of Congress in 1971.

On May 6, 1968, Edwin E. Willis, D-LA, chairman of HUAC [House Un-American Activities Committee], issued a sixty-five-page report entitled *Guerrilla Warfare Advocates in the United States* which caused a good deal of controversy. The *Washington Post* of the same day carried an article about it under the caption "HUAC Would Intern Negro 'Guerilla.'" Locally the *San Francisco Chronicle*, also on the same day, carried a similar article under the caption "Probers Suggest Detention Camps." The press release of the report itself stated "that mixed Communist and black nationalist elements are today planning and organizing paramilitary operations and that it is their intent to instigate additional riots which will pave the way for a general revolutionary uprising fought along guerilla warfare lines." The avowed aim of this sixty-five-page report was to alert and inform Congress and the American people of this imminent danger to internal security.

The most crucial feature of this report lies in its recommendation for the usage of "detention centers." In case of a national emergency, presumably when guerilla violence has reached uncontrollable proportions, the report states: "The McCarran Act provides for various detention centers to be operated throughout the country and these might well be utilized for the temporary imprisonment of warring guerillas." The McCarran Act (also known as the Internal Security Act) of 1950, as amended, actually does have provisions to detain people under Title II, which is called "Emergency Detention." Under this Title (Sec. 102 (a)) a state of "Internal Security Emergency" can be declared by the president in the event of any one of the following: (1) invasion of the territory of the United States or its possession; (2) declaration of war by Congress; or (3) insurrection within the United States in aid of a foreign enemy. The report of the HUAC, in asserting that this act provides for detention centers, of course has the third and last emergency in mind.

Title II (Sec. 103 (a)) goes on:

> Whenever there shall be in existence such an emergency the President, acting through the Attorney General, is hereby authorized to apprehend and by order detain, pursuant to the provisions of this title, each person as to whom there is reasonable ground to believe that such person probably will engage in, or probably will conspire with others to engage in, acts of espionage or of sabotage . . .

After the press release of this sixty-five-page report was issued, fears of detention centers were heightened, and understandably the report received considerable public attention. Prior to May 6, 1968, Attorney General Ramsey Clark, on NBC's *Meet the Press*, on April 7, 1968, is reported to have denied the existence of concentration camps, for rumors of one kind or another about them were widespread even before this report was issued. "Rumors, and fear that arises from rumors," he stated, "are a great threat to us. Fear itself is a great threat and people who spread false rumors about concentration camps are either ignorant of the facts or have a motive of dividing the country." Later, on May 12, 1968, after the issuance of the report, on ABC's *Issues and Answers*, he repeated his view:

> There are no concentration camps in this country. There are no plans to prepare any concentration camps in this country. No concentration camps are needed in this country. We have not had a situation in all of the difficulties that we have faced from the standpoint of riots and disturbances throughout our history, which has indicated a need for any mass detention facilities for American citizens, and I see no such need now.

J. Walter Yeagley, assistant attorney general, who heads the Internal Security Division of the Department of Justice and who hence would be directly responsible for administering Title II, has echoed Attorney General Ramsey Clark's statements. He has categorically denied the existence of any concentration camps as well as any government intent to detain anyone under the provisions of Title II. He had admitted, however, that six detention facilities were maintained up until around 1957 in accordance with its provisions. These six facilities were as follows: Tule Lake, California; Wickenburg and Florence, Arizona; El Reno, Oklahoma; Allenwood, Pennsylvania; and Avon

Park, Florida.[1] Though these facilities were maintained up to about 1957, according to Yeagley, they were never used to detain anyone under Title II, and have been abandoned since or are used for other purposes. He cites two basic reasons why the McCarran Act cannot be invoked. First, "the act requires that each 'detained' person be arrested on a warrant specifying his name and stating the Government's belief that he may engage or conspire to engage in sabotage or espionage." Second, "even if the rioting were formally declared an 'insurrection,' there is no evidence to date that it is or may be fomented 'in aid of a foreign enemy' as required before Title II could be applied." Concluding, Yeagley stated: "I know of no contingency plan for mass Federal detention of Negroes under Title II or any other statute."

So much for Willis's HUAC report and the government response to it. It is true that the government under the provisions of Title II is required to name each person to be arrested and ultimately detained. But this requirement by no means would hinder the government from taking action, for we would be naive not to believe that it does not have a list of militants, black and white, as well as of others who have dissented strongly against the Vietnam War and racism. In addition, even though the government has to state its belief that the arrested person is about to engage in, or conspires with others to commit, acts of sabotage or espionage, as we have already seen, it is under no final obligation to produce the source of its evidence for its belief. For the provisions of Title II in fact place the burden of innocence upon the suspected person, judging him as guilty unless he himself can prove otherwise, with the government itself under the obligation of stating only its probable belief and no more.

That there are not detention camps at present, as the attorney general's office states, is beside the point. The important point is that the McCarran Act provides for detention centers and that, if arrests are made under its Title II provisions, then they could be built with relative ease. Japanese Americans were first assembled in horse stables, and then "relocated" to detention centers which were built within a month. The definition as to when there is a state of emergency, particularly the third

---

1   The camps at Tule Lake and Forence had also been used to incarcerate Japanese Americans during the war.

and last one, which states in the event of "insurrection within the United States in aid of a foreign enemy," thus becomes of paramount importance. How is "in aid of a foreign enemy" to be interpreted? The HUAC report mentions groups such as the Revolutionary Action Movement (RAM) and the Progressive Labor Party and such individuals as Stokely Carmichael and Thomas Hayden. Now, depending upon the interpretation, any number of other groups and individuals besides these specifically mentioned could be included. Does it include the Black Panther Party here in Oakland which has become affiliated with SNCC [Student Nonviolent Coordinating Committee], and hence with Stokely Carmichael? In this connection it should be remembered that even Reverend [Ralph] Abernathy has been accused of being a Communist and that Japanese Americans were alleged to be aiding a foreign enemy, which allegation became one of the ostensible reasons for their "evacuation."

Thus the key issue is not whether or not Title II of the McCarran Act can be invoked or not. It is rather the very existence of the act itself which provides for detention centers and which therefore permits someone like Willis to suggest their usage. Some say that the McCarran Act is a product of the McCarthy era, dismissing it at that. We of the Asian American Political Alliance believe, as long as it is in effect, that it can be, and for that matter will be, invoked against black militants as well as white radicals. Moreover, given the current assumptions of American foreign policy, we see the clear possibility of a major war with Communist China; and if such should come to pass, then we do not preclude the possibility of Chinese Americans being placed into detention camps in the same way Japanese Americans were during World War II. And so we of the Asian American Political Alliance demand that all politicians take an unequivocal stand on this issue. Are they in favor of the repeal of the McCarran Act or not? Rumors about detention camps will not disappear by simply stating arguments that it will not or cannot be invoked. Instead they will increase, especially when one considers that a new Internal Security Act of 1968 is now being produced which will in effect make acts of dissent equivalent to treason (see Sec. 2988, introduced by Senator Eastland of Mississippi on February 19, 1968). Only with its actual repeal will the legal justification for political prisoners disappear, and the Asian American Political Alliance demands that it be.

Kathleen Cleaver, "Racism, Fascism, and Political Murder," *Black Panther*, September 14, 1968

White backlash. Men picketing an event commemorating the centennial of W. E. B. Du Bois's birth at Carnegie Hall, with Martin Luther King Jr. as keynote speaker, February 23, 1968. The *Daily Worker* and *Daily World* Photographs Collection, box 90, folder 17, Tamiment Library, New York University.

After the black freedom struggle became more militant and class focused following key civil rights legislative victories in 1964 and 1965, many whites outside the South turned against the movement. They increasingly consented to new state policies regarding working-class people of color—from lifting their burdens through civil rights and social democratic legislation, to a new strategy of ghetto "containment" using the iron fist of mass incarceration.

Kathleen Cleaver's editorial registers this political shift. As importantly, it signals a recurrent theme in African American antifascism when she writes, "Black people have always been subjected to [a] police state and have moved to organize against it, but the structure is now moving to encompass the entire country." If liberalism reproduces a dual system of political subjects—one group with "rights" and another consigned to zones of precarity and exclusion—fascism represents a violent intensification of this system. In fascism, according to this analysis, the pressure exerted against the traditionally ghettoized by the former liberal state is dramatically extended (possibly to genocidal levels), while at the same time, the fascist state widens its circle of terror, however unevenly, to enclose formerly privileged sectors as well. The process starts, according to Cleaver, with the elimination of revolutionary leadership.

Kathleen Neal Cleaver (1945–) was a leader in the Black Panther Party, serving as its communications secretary beginning in 1967. After a shootout with police, her husband Eldridge Cleaver—also a Black Panther leader—went into exile in Algeria, and she joined him there in 1969. They returned to the United States in 1975. In the late 1980s, Cleaver earned a law degree from Yale University and entered the legal profession, serving in the US Court of Appeals, among other positions. At the time of this publication, she is a senior lecturer in law at Emory University.

The Black Revolution is a struggle for survival, first and foremost. It is not white racism but white racists who are killing black people in the most blatant to the most subtle ways, from shooting us in the streets like dogs to immobilizing us in the political hierarchies of the mother country's government. The black leader who moves for political power is dealt with on whatever level the establishment racists feel he is posing the most threat: Thurgood Marshall was placed on the Supreme Court, Adam Clayton Powell was kicked out of Congress. [H.] Rap Brown is jailed on the flimsiest pretext, Malcolm X was assassinated. Whereas Roy Wilkins and Whitney Young are given the full range of the mother country's resources to gun their game on their brothers, Huey Newton must be shot in the streets and lynched in the courts. It is the guns of the racists, their bullets tearing through the flesh of our leaders, that have to be dealt with. The leadership of the racists, the federal, state, and city governments with their armed forces dispatched to the black community with orders of "shoot to kill," is destroying the leadership of the black struggle in order to be able to deal directly with the unorganized, defenseless, divided black masses.

The present black population in this country, approaching some 50 million, is more united and more aggressive and larger than it has been at any other time in the history of this country, while the present white population is decreasing and its government is under siege all over the world, the most hated power on the face of the earth. The key to attaining the political power that our history and culture and strategic location guarantee us is practical, competent, revolutionary national leadership that can direct the masses to satisfy their basic political desires and needs in an organized fashion. What guarantees success to such leadership is revolutionary ideology, or an understanding of how to move systematically for power, a basic program, or an understanding of what to move for and when, and an organizational structure that can put this understanding in motion.

The calculated and systematic destruction of the leadership of the Black Panther Party and harassment of its members in the Bay Area follows a national pattern of political repression taking place at this time. In every black community across this country where there is identifiable organizational leadership exerted by the black militants, it is being jailed, framed, shot, murdered, eliminated. These moves are being coordinated centrally in Washington, DC, and are all directed toward the same end: setting the stage for genocide . . .

The assassination of King followed by systematic mass arrests and shooting of radical organizers throughout the country in April indicates a timetable schedule directed toward removing militant leadership from the streets by the beginning of the summer. This will leave the black masses in an unorganized, defenseless, divided state during the summer, at which point the police plan to move directly against the black community.

Masses Not Asses

As long as only a small fraction of the black population expected to have decent housing, food, clothing, education, employment, protection from harm, and some measure of dignity, the system could afford to function comfortably allowing a small elite group of house Negroes these benefits as the price of controlling their oppressed brothers and sisters, forcing them to be satisfied with their poverty, starvation, misery, and persecution. But, when the masses of blacks start demanding basic needs be fulfilled, the power structure is in trouble because it requires a basic redistribution of the wealth, the land, and the power in order to make this a reality.

The color line is the basis upon which wealth and power are distributed in this country; racism on the part of white institutions and white citizens forces black people to remain poor and powerless. All blacks have a ceiling on the amount of power and wealth they can amass that is unchangeable, that is maintained by the organized force and violence of the governments. Racism is maintained with armed force on the local level by the police departments.

Political power, the control of the institutions in the society, determines to what extent racism is allowed to affect black people, determines how much freedom of action the racists have against black people. Political power is now in the hands of a racist leadership which is determined to prevent black people from satisfying their basic political desires and needs, because this leadership wants to remain in control of the land and wealth and political power that rightfully belongs to black people . . .

Destroy Leadership

Just as the Vietnamese people refuse to be controlled by the capitalist, racist American government, and are fighting to retain control of their own country, black people in America are fighting to have control of the communities in their hands. With a potential mass of 50 million blacks moving together to control their communities across this nation, the first assault by the political leadership of the racists is to destroy the leadership of the black struggle in order to be able to move against the masses without organized resistance. Nationwide repression against militant black organizers and spokesmen has been escalated in the black communities in the past few months in order to stop the organization of the black community. Leadership becomes secondary once the community is organized in a manner to take power; but leadership is primary during the initial 'period of organizing the masses. It is at this period now when leadership is most crucial to the black masses in order to initiate their political organization that the federal, state, and city governments are moving most rapidly against black leaders. An organized black community united around basic political desires and needs as outlined in the program of the Black Panther Party is the only power that the state cannot destroy when the community is prepared to defend itself against the attacks of the police. This is the creation of black power, the first step toward obtaining control over the entire black community.

The advent of fascism in the United States is most clearly visible in the suppression of the black liberation struggle in the nationwide political imprisonment and assassination of black leaders, coupled with the concentration of massive police power in the ghettos of the black community across the country. The police departments nationwide are preparing for armed struggle with the black community and are being directed and coordinated nationally with the US Army and the underground vigilante racist groups for a massive onslaught against black people. But, the billy clubs and mass arrests and guns are no longer just for black people; the white peace movement and the student power struggle are also beginning to get a taste of police violence. State power is being imposed upon the black community and the white peace movement through the organized force and violence of the police departments. Jails are becoming increasingly familiar with political prisoners, and the court system is being warped to serve the needs of the repression. With the economic and political system of the United States under violent attack the world over, the national response has been a tightening of state control over all aspects of life and a vicious and powerful assault on all forms of political dissent. Just as the US Army is attempting to settle a political question of self-determination through force and violence in Vietnam, the city, state, and federal governments across the country are meeting political dissent with police violence . . .

There will be no protest, for to dissent will be to die. This has already started on a sporadic scale in the spontaneous but condoned murdering of young black men in the streets daily all over the country. But the overt military dictatorship has yet to come. The very same solution that Nazi Germany proposed to the German people—kill the Jews to solve the economic and political problems of Germany—will be employed in the United States with even less difficulty: kill the niggers. Once the country pulls itself out of its disastrous defeat in Vietnam, it will be able to direct the full weight of its military power against the black struggle and settle the issue of racism and white supremacy once and for all.

New Phase

The assassination of Dr. Martin Luther King at this point marked the initiation of a new phase in the advance of police power at the decision-making level, a further step toward the complete police state. Dr. King was tolerated and even encouraged by the political leadership of the racists as long as he advocated nonviolent means of gaining civil rights. He was not moving for political power, he wanted the power structure to make the decisions and take the action, and he was not disturbing the economic arrangements that the power structure was based on. But when he joined the peace movement he became a political threat to the establishment because he held the allegiance of millions of black people. He had also begun to move toward the alliance of the black with the brown peoples in the United States. And when he deepened his crusade for justice to be based on poor people, the final project that caused his assassination, the establishment was forced to eliminate his threat. For the crux of the political arrangements in this country are based on the distinction between the rich and the poor. The poor whites and poor blacks are exploited by the same white capitalists who maintain a racist antagonism between the two groups, so that the poor blacks are always victims of the poor white racists, and the poor whites are so busy carrying out racist acts they cannot see that they are victims of the wealthy white capitalists. Both poor whites and poor blacks are powerless; racism prevents them from combining their strengths to gain a redistribution of wealth and power. Dr. King had begun to initiate organization projects among poor whites as well as poor blacks shortly before his assassination. The proposed Poor People's March on Washington that he was planning was a major threat facing the federal government that they had been unable to head off or buy out. The assassination of Dr. King only four weeks before this march was no accident . . .

Freedom or Death

The day when the state and its police power ceases to protect the community but in turn attacks the people of the community has arrived in this country. This is the first stage of building a total police state. Black people have always been subjected to [a] police state and have moved to organized against it, but the structure is now moving to encompass the entire country. The elimination of black leadership—from Dr. King to Eldridge Cleaver, Adam Clayton Powell to Huey P. Newton—is designed to throw the black community into chaos. Intensified and concentrated police power in the black community is designed to impose total control. The next step is GENOCIDE. The black community faces two alternatives: total liberation or total extinction.

Black Panther Party, "Call for a United Front against Fascism," *Old Mole*, July 1969

Cover of *Basta Ya!*, August 16, 1969. Part of the short-lived, cross-racial United Front against Fascism.

In July 1969, the Black Panther Party (BPP) hosted its "United Front against Fascism" conference in Oakland, California. The purpose of the conference was to pull together radical allies in a unity front against an intense racial backlash that the Panthers saw as a reincarnation of fascism. Indeed, urban riots and the radicalization of the black freedom struggle had stoked white racial anxieties in the late 1960s. The year 1968 had also seen the election of Richard Nixon, the assassinations of Martin Luther King and Robert Kennedy, and the rise of white supremacist George Wallace to the national stage. All of these developments translated into increased repression of the Black Panther Party by the FBI and by local and state police, including the murder of Panther leader Fred Hampton in his sleep by the Chicago Police.

The conference did not result in the broad unity front that the Panthers desired. But in the wake of the conference, the BPP organized under the banner of antifascism for at least a year. They established National Committees to Combat Fascism (NCCFs) all over the United States, which effectively became local branches of the BPP. The membership of the NCCFs were open to all groups, but remained almost exclusively African American.

This call was published in the Old Mole, *a paper of the Students for a Democratic Society that was widely read in white radical circles in the Boston area. Notable here is the Panthers' resurrection of antifascist theory and strategy from the 1930s left, including the explicit use of Georgi Dimitrov's 1935 definition of fascism. One notable divergence, however, is their notion that racial genocide forms the ultimate horizon of fascist politics.*

The call for "law and order" is just a disguise to hide the intended genocide of Black people and repression of all progressive revolutionary forces that seek to change this decadent society. Historically, if we examine the existence of Black people, we will find a blatant history of murder and violence inflicted upon us by the oppressor class in this society—the brutality of slavery, the lynchings of the twenties and thirties, and the constant day-to-day brutality inflicted upon our people by the racist police force. Because of the rise in political awareness of Black people, the high degree of student activism and the overall expansion of progressive forces, this government is finding it necessary to drop its disguise of democracy and go openly into FASCISM. The assassination of Martin Luther King, the assassination of Malcolm X, the imprisonment of Huey

P. Newton for his political beliefs, the occupation of Wilmington, Delaware, by the National Guard for one year after King's death, the 14,000 troops at the Chicago Democratic Convention, the necessity for the exile of Eldridge Cleaver, the national repression of the Black Panther Party, the attack on the Republic of New Africa's convention, and the brutal attack on the people of Berkeley by 7,000 national guardsmen.

Fascism is the open terroristic dictatorship of the most reactionary, most chauvinistic (racist) and the most imperialist elements of finance capital. It does not stand above both classes, the proletariat and the bourgeoisie, nor is it super-class government, nor government of the petty bourgeoisie or lumpenproletariat over finance capitalism. Fascism is the power of finance capital itself. FINANCE CAPITAL manifests itself not only as banks, trusts and monopolies, but also as the human property of FINANCE CAPITAL—the avaricious businessman, the demagogic politician, and the racist-pig cop. FASCISM is the organization of terrorist vengeance against the working class and the revolutionary section and intelligentsia.

The Black Panther Party is calling for the creation of a UNITED FRONT AGAINST FASCISM. We are asking all progressive elements of this society to forget our ideological differences and pose a UNITED FRONT against the racist police in this country.

A national conference for a United Front Against Fascism will be held in Oakland, California, July 18, 19, 20, and 21. Advance registration fee is four dollars (six dollars at the conference). Check-in for the conference is the Panther National Headquarters, 3106 Shattuck Avenue, Berkeley, CA 94705.

ALL POWER TO THE PEOPLE
The Black Panther Party

Penny Nakatsu, speech at the United Front against Fascism Conference, July 1969

Penny Nakatsu delivered this speech at the Panthers' United Front against Fascism conference in Oakland, California, during the summer of 1969. At the time, Nakatsu was a student at San Francisco State College, where in 1968, along with two other Japanese American women, she had started a branch of the Asian American Political Alliance. She took part in the famous San Francisco State strike as well.

The piece is notable for illustrating that for people of color at various historical moments, the experience of racialization within a liberal democracy could have the valence of fascism. That is to say, while a fascist state and a white supremacist democracy have very different mechanisms of power, the experience of racialized rightlessness within a liberal democracy can make the distinction between it and fascism murky at the level of lived experience. For those racially cast outside of liberal democracy's system of rights, the word "fascism" does not always conjure up a distant and alien social order.

On the question of male supremacy and male chauvinism, as an Asian woman, I can speak well and long. I can speak well and long of the heroic women who have died combating racism and imperialism. I could speak of women like Iva Toguri D'Aquino, who spent sixteen years in an American racist prison for a crime for which she had no part in. I could speak of a sister who died in the 1950s struggles, [died in] Tokyo, died [in] the struggle against the re-ratification of the United States–Japan

Security Pact. And I could speak well and long of the heroic struggles of our courageous Vietnamese sisters, whose example I hope all women can well follow and learn from. But I will not.

What I came here to speak of today is a story that many of you may not know of, may have forgotten, may not remember. The story begins in 1942—many of the elements of the story are duplicated here, here and now in the year 1969. The dates 1942, 1950, 1969, taken together as a sum total, equate American fascism today. In case many of you have not caught on to what I'm referring to, I'm speaking of the incarceration of more than 110,000 people, human beings, for the crime of having yellow faces, of having Asian names, in World War II . . . There was no 1950 McCarran Internal Security Act at that time to put my people, our people, into what were euphemistically termed "relocation camps."[1] There are ten of these camps. I will not call them relocation camps. I will not call them detention camps. I will call them the concentration camps they were and are and [that] still exist today.

I come from a generation of children born in concentration camps. Many of these places you will find no longer exist on the map. We were born in places with names like Manzanar, Tule Lake, Topaz, Rowher, and on and on. In 1942, the presidential mandate issued by President Roosevelt empowered the racist military under the leadership of General [John L.] DeWitt to incarcerate 110,000 people—more than two-thirds of whom were American citizens. Many of these people remained in these concentration camps for the duration of the war. All of them received between twenty-four and forty-eight hours' notice to report to the nearest military authorities, to report their belongings, to dispose of their beloved possessions within the span of twenty-four and forty-eight hours. How generous, how magnanimous our government was. How magnanimous our government will be when it calls on us to report. When it calls on us, we will not be sitting in our homes, talking. We will

---

1   As the AAPA-authorized piece ("Concentration Camps, USA") in this volume illustrates, the Internal Security Act of 1950 was a source of anxiety for Asian American activists who feared it as the legal basis of a new internment. This threat was revived when the chairman of HUAC advocated its use against domestic radicals in May 1968. Title II of the 1950 act allowed for the use of emergency detention to incarcerate people deemed a national security threat. To comply with the act, the federal government created seven detention centers in the 1950s, using the internment camps of World War II as template (and in some cases literally using the same facilities), though these camps were never used under the terms of the 1950 Act.

be prepared to move. The lesson that I hope we can learn from 1942 is not to wait, not to wait until we have positive, irrevocable proof of the racism, and the all-encompassing determination of our monopolistic capitalist system to suppress all movements, all people who will work for social change, who will work for liberation, who will work for the defeat of fascism and imperialism.

"UFAF Conference,"
Old Mole, August 1969

The following account of the Black Panthers' United Front against Fascism (UFAF) conference appeared in the Old Mole, *a paper of the Students for a Democratic Society that was widely read in radical circles in the Boston area.*

As has been noted elsewhere in this volume, in forming their own United Front in 1969, the Panthers resurrected analyses of the Communist Party USA, reaching out to personnel who were active during the Popular Front period. Interestingly visible in this piece is how their fellow radicals subjected the Panthers to some of the same critiques leveled at the earlier Popular Front: namely, that they watered down their previously revolutionary language and demands in the interests of overly broad coalition building. Following the conference, many whites in the New Left, while continuing to rhetorically support the Panthers as a vanguard, increasingly disdained the shift as "reformist."

Indeed, the Panthers had a modest legislative goal in mind when they assembled the UFAF: decentralized policing, wherein black communities would control police in their communities and whites would control police in their own communities (a legally drawn petition for a referendum on community policing in the city of Oakland was already in place at the time of the conference). The nonrevolutionary nature of this goal illustrates the larger organizational context out of which their antifascist turn emerged. At the beginning of 1969, under the leadership of Bobby Seale and David Hilliard, the party began to shift its emphasis from paramilitary tactics to a community service orientation. As the group swelled with new recruits following the "Free Huey" campaign of 1968, Seale and Hilliard devised an organizational structure more suited to a disciplined, national party rather than a loose, Oakland-based group.

The Old Mole's account of the conference should also serve as a reminder to contemporary readers that movement building has never been easy.

Wherever they have organized, the Panthers have been hit hard by the Man: beaten, framed, jailed, held under huge ransoms, murdered. Systematic repression has threatened their very survival. The Panthers have always believed in the necessity of joint struggle with whites against American racism and imperialism. They felt that the best defense against their own destruction would be a "United Front against Fascism" and, accordingly, called a conference in Oakland to organize such a front.

The conference began on July 19. Eighty percent of the delegates were white. The program stressed the need for unity; chairman Bobby Seale stated in his opening speech that this was no place for "ideological quibbling." There were few workshops or discussions planned for participants. The conference consisted of a solid schedule of speeches on topics such as: "Students and Education vs. Fascism," "Workers vs. Fascism," "Doctors vs. Fascism," and "Religion vs. Fascism."

No Disruptions

Before the conference participants agreed that absolutely no disruption would be tolerated, since the attack on fascism was so crucial. On the first evening Progressive Labor / Worker Student Alliance (PL-WSA) members were identified by SDS [Students for a Democratic Society] and subsequently ejected from the conference by the Panthers.

Seale surprised the audience by referring to "policemen" and "cops" rather than "pigs," and by hailing "progressive forces" without mentioning socialism or revolution or armed struggle. He stressed that fascism exists in this country and must be combated *now*, before the arrival of concentration camps. The radical movement, he urged, must move to defeat fascism by organizing for community control over decentralized police forces.

Seale was followed by Herbert Aptheker, who spoke on "Historical Aspects of the Rising Tide of Fascism Today."[1] Aptheker droned on for an hour, irritating many who were worried that Communist Party influence might swing the political line of the United Front to the right. Furthermore, the women's panel, inserted into the program at the last minute and postponed until last on the evening's schedule, was being threatened with extinction by Aptheker's verbosity. As angry women began to stand up in protest, they were forcibly seated by Panther monitors, trying to prevent disruptions.

Masai, a Los Angeles Panther who was moderating the meeting, called the protesting women "pigs and provocateurs." The main speaker of the women's panel, Roberta Alexander, stressed the tensions inside the party over the question of male supremacy and called on men and women to struggle against the problem.

None of the women had wanted to disrupt the conference or to withdraw their support for the Panthers, but various groups disagreed about the appropriate response to the problems of male chauvinism internal to the movement. Women's caucuses met continually during the conference, sharing their experiences, setting up national committees and discussing the politics of the UFAF.

The UFAF Program

Speeches continued according to schedule on Saturday. During an afternoon session in Bobby Hutton Memorial Park, PL-WSA members were physically attacked when they refused to stop leafletting against the conference and the Panthers. More violence erupted on Sunday morning when PL returned to leaflet.

By Sunday night, many of the delegates had left the conference before hearing the United Front program, as presented by Bobby Seale at the closing session. The UFAF program calls for decentralization of police

---

1   Herbert Aptheker (1915–2003) was a Jewish American writer, organizer, and independent scholar. He joined the Communist Party USA in 1939 and remained active in the Party for most of his life. He saw combat in Europe with the US Army during World War II. He wrote more than fifty books, many of them on African American history, including the pioneering *Negro Slave Revolts in the United States 1526–1860* (1939).

forces and community control, with the right to hire police officers from the community. This is to be accomplished by referendum campaigns organized by Committees to Combat Fascism in black, brown and white communities. These committees are to initiate petition campaigns to educate and involve people around the police-control demand.

Panthers stressed that white as well as black workers come under attack from fascist police and thus need to fight and control them. They explained the need for legal tactics as an educational necessity at this time.

Seale reminded his audience that conferences would have to be held every three or four months in order to implement the program. "At the next conference," he predicted, "we'll be back here 15,000 strong, and we're not going to miss a single worker in the country."[2]

Many of the delegates left the conference confused and disappointed. The radical movement feared that the Panthers' UF tactic was attempting to enlist liberal support at the expense of revolutionary militancy.

SDS supports self-determination and community control in colonized black and brown communities, but not in white communities where racism and white supremacy must be fought. In a statement after the UFAF conference, the National Interim Committee of SDS says:

> We support completely the demand for community control of decentralized police in the black and brown communities, and will help by building support for that demand in white neighborhoods. At the same time we cannot support the demand for "white community" control and we therefore urge local and regional SDS organizations to work within the National Committees to Combat Fascism to change the wording of the petition. This will also be done on a national level. We also urge that SDS chapters undertake campaigns around pig repression.

---

2   There was never a follow-up conference. Be that as it may, the Panthers set up National Committees to Combat Fascism across the country, which were essentially branches of the Black Panther Party.

Les Evans, "Alliances and the Revolutionary Party: The Tactic of the United Front and How It Differs from the Popular Front," *Education for Socialists*, October 1971

Coalition building has always been central to the antifascist tradition. But how do you build them, and how do you enter into coalitions with other organizations that do not share all of your values? The Marxist left has debated these questions for over a century, yet very little of this debate is accessible to twenty-first-century activists on the left.

The tactic of the "United Front" was first elaborated by Leon Trotsky and expanded most fully within the Trotskyist tradition. Trotskyists generally contrasted it with the "Popular Front" or People's Front policy of Soviet-backed Communist parties in the second half of the 1930s. In left parlance, a "United Front" is typically a smaller coalition limited to left and radical organizations that unites around a discernably left-wing platform. A "Popular Front" is a broader coalition among radical and nonradical organizations, in which the left compromises much more in terms of both the platform and the unifying principles.

This piece is based on two talks that Evans delivered earlier in the year before it appeared in an educational bulletin of the Socialist Workers Party (SWP). The SWP is a small but intellectually vibrant Trotskyist organization founded in 1938; it enjoyed a rise in membership in the early 1970s, a time of growing labor militancy.

In the European movement history that he recounts, Evans uses "reformist" to refer to Social Democratic parties of the Second International (democratic socialists) and "revolutionary" to refer to Communist parties of one stripe or another. Readers should keep in mind that in many

European countries following World War I, Communist and Socialist parties were quite large and deeply embedded in working-class culture; thus, when building coalitions, they were able to bring far more to the table than were their counterparts in the postwar United States.

The labels "revolutionary" and "reformist" might ring strange to twenty-first-century American ears. Nonetheless, the piece offers food for thought and a forgotten history to anyone interested in building antifascist coalitions, especially coalitions that unite left-wing organizations with less radical ones.

In discussing the question of the united front, we should bear in mind at the outset that this is a discussion about tactics, one of the most important tactics in the political arsenal of the revolutionary party . . .

What Is the United Front?

The revolutionary party sets itself the task of organizing the whole of the oppressed, first and foremost the industrial working class, for the socialist overturn of the capitalist system. But except in a prerevolutionary situation the party can expect to count in its own ranks and among its followers only a minority of the working class and sometimes a numerically insignificant minority in relation to the population.

For sectarians the thing to do in such a situation is very simple: you unfurl your revolutionary banner and wait for the masses to come to you. Passive sectarians such as the SLP [Socialist Labor Party] announce their presence by putting out their newspaper and an occasional leaflet. The more active variety, such as the Progressive Labor Party or the Workers League, attempt to initiate actions in the name of their own group or of organizations created and controlled directly by their group.

Of course the revolutionary party sees as one of its central activities the circulation of its press and occasionally helps to set up committees that for one reason or another do not extend far beyond the party's immediate members or sympathizers. But it does not have any illusions that by these means alone great masses can be won to fight for socialism.

Revolutionists participate directly in existing mass organizations of all kinds where, in counterposition to the reformist leaderships, they propose campaigns of action around concrete immediate or transitional

demands that can involve the members in struggle. This also is a necessary though by itself insufficient course.

The question remains how the revolutionary party, disposing of
limited forces, can draw into action genuine masses in defense of their
interests against the capitalist rulers. The majority of workers and their
potential allies, the students, oppressed national minorities, women as
an oppressed sex, the so-called middle classes, the peasantry in those
countries where it remains a significant section of the population, do
not yet agree with the party's full program and are not prepared to follow
its call to action. They are influenced to a greater or lesser extent by
reformist or even directly bourgeois leaderships that have no intention
of organizing mass struggles.

But the failure to reply massively to the threat or reality of imperialist
war, to attacks on basic democratic rights, or on the standard of living of
the working class, weakens the revolutionary party as well as the position of the proletariat vis-à-vis the bourgeoisie. Thus the need to unite
the whole of the working class or whatever sector can presently be won
to struggle around anti-capitalist demands is an objective necessity that
faces the party as a prerequisite of its future growth.

The tactic of the united front was developed by the leadership of the
Communist International under Lenin and Trotsky in 1921–22 to meet
the challenge of this vital task facing the Communist parties of Europe.
The revolutionary wave of the post–World War I period had passed and
a measure of capitalist stability had been restored. The bourgeoisie was
on the offensive against the workers' organizations. The left, both politically and in the narrower sphere of the trade union movement, was
dominated by mass radical parties, generally the social democrats.

There were no mass ad hoc formations of struggle such as the anti-
war movement or the women's liberation which we have seen in the
present radicalization. These have taken form outside of any political
party in part because the great mass of youth and others who have been
radicalized entered the political arena in the absence of mass socialist or
communist parties that would appear as the natural champions of their
demands.

On the one hand this meant that in the twenties the focus of the
united front tactic was to find a basis of common action between mass
working-class parties; hence, from the organizational point of view, it

had a more obviously proletarian character than the united fronts we enter into today, when the trade unions are locked in a bureaucratic stranglehold and remain outside of politics. But it also meant that the Communist Party, which in almost every country represented a minority of the politicized workers, had to forge an alliance with the powerful bureaucracy of case-hardened reformists which controlled the much larger Social Democratic parties, which were imbued with a thoroughly class-collaborationist and anti-revolutionary outlook.

The united front tactic was first proposed in December 1921 and the details of its implementation worked out at the Fourth World Congress of the Communist International in November 1922. It was denounced at the time by ultraleftists in the world communist movement, who saw in it a capitulation to reformism. Lenin and Trotsky demonstratively described themselves as representatives of the *right* wing of the Comintern in this debate to indicate their impatience with this sterile sectarianism. The most succinct statement of the tactic is to be found in Trotsky's article, "On the United Front," based on his report for the leadership to the enlarged Plenum of the Executive Committee of the Comintern which convened in February 1922.

> "Does the united front extend only to the working masses or does it also include the opportunistic leaders?" Trotsky asked. "The very posing of this question is a product of misunderstanding," he replied. "If we were able simply to unite the working masses around our own banner or around our practical immediate slogans, and skip over reformist organizations, whether party or trade union, that would of course be the best thing in the world. But then the very question of the united front would not exist in its present form."

There are two sides to the united front. On the one hand it allows the most massive mobilization of the working class in defense of its immediate interests by bringing together on a single issue or limited set of issues organizations that have fundamental programmatic differences on other questions. From this standpoint the whole purpose of the united front is precisely for the revolutionists to take the initiative in forcing the reformist leaderships into a common coalition, even against their will. For the very reason that workers still follow the reformists, it is impossible to go over the heads of the reformist leaders by appealing directly to the ranks of these organizations. This latter policy was tried by the Communist Party in Germany in the early 1930s under the ultra-left slogan of the "United front from below," with the disastrous result that there was no common struggle against Hitler by the Communist and Socialist parties. Inherently the united front means negotiations with and agreements with the reformist tendencies.

The other side of the united front tactic is that in the course of united struggles the revolutionists have the best opportunity to work with the rank-and-file members of the reformist organizations or with unaffiliated radicals—the independents—and to demonstrate in action that the revolutionists are the best builders of the struggle. In the course of this experience the authority of the reformist leaders can be undermined and recruits made to revolutionary socialism.

Doesn't this policy involve concessions to the reformists in order to secure agreements with non- and even anti-revolutionary forces? Yes. Inevitably concessions must be made to preserve the alliance, and Marxists must carefully weigh at each step how much can be given while still preserving the anticapitalist thrust of the agreed-on actions.

There is a very useful discussion of this question by Lenin in an article written in April 1922 entitled "We Have Paid Too Much." The Comintern was seeking to establish a united front with the Second International. The Social Democrats, without promising any specific common actions, demanded a series of conditions for continuing the negotiations. The Bolshevik representatives to the negotiations reluctantly agreed. Lenin objected, not that the concessions as such were unprincipled, but that nothing had been received in return.

The key to the united front is that its axis be action against the ruling class and that the concessions made to hold it together not undercut its central purpose. By choosing single-issue demands such as "immediate withdrawal from Vietnam" or "abolish the abortion laws" that directly oppose one or another aspect of bourgeois policy, the revolutionary party through the united front is able to lead far-larger masses in action on particular demand within the *party's* program than it could in any other way. The reformist organizations, subject to pressure from their own ranks, are forced to join in, but would not themselves initiate such actions on these kinds of demands.

Furthermore, in the process of successful and significant struggles a political climate is created that encourages the working class to further tests of strength with the bourgeoisie and is propitious for the further direct growth of the revolutionary party.

Is the United Front Limited to Single-Issue Coalitions?

The single-issue united front is, of course, the easiest to maintain and has the greatest programmatic clarity. The ultimate aim of the united front, however, is to unite the whole of the working class against all sectors of the capitalist class. As long as its central anti-capitalist direction is unequivocal, there are circumstances where the united front tactic can be applied to electoral blocs or even to coalition governments of the left. The slogan "All power to the Soviets," for example, was first raised by the Bolsheviks when they still constituted a minority in the Russian soviets (workers councils), which were dominated by the representatives of the reformist socialist parties. Even after the October Revolution the Bolsheviks for a time participated in a united front government with the left wing of the Social[ist] Revolutionary Party.

But a united front government is the last step before the overthrow of capitalism. A revolutionary party cannot join a government which merely administers the capitalist state.

What Is the Popular Front?

The so-called People's Front preached and practiced by the pro-Moscow and pro-Peking Communist parties has nothing in common with the Leninist policy of the united front. The essence of the People's Front is a coalition between the left parties and the liberal bourgeoisie. It is based on the *program* of the liberal capitalists and is aimed only at extracting certain reforms from the "right wing" of the capitalist class. In this country the Communist Party loyally applies the People's Front policy through its work in the Democratic Party, where it gives its support to the candidates of this capitalist party on the basis of *their* program. It seeks to mobilize the working class not to break with capitalist politics but to support one capitalist politician against another in the hope of being paid off in minimal concessions after the "good" capitalist is elected.

A genuine workers' government would be clearly distinguished from all varieties of People's Front both by its program and its deeds. It would move rapidly to disfranchise the capitalist rulers, to nationalize industry, to dismantle the repressive apparatus of the capitalist state, and to create or to strengthen armed bodies of workers to administer the new workers' state.

It is our conviction, confirmed by the whole history of the revolutionary movement, that such a transition cannot be accomplished by electoral means alone but requires the revolutionary mobilization of the working class in its own self-governing organizations or councils and with its own armed power. A hallmark of the People's Front, even of the left-sounding variety, is its hostility to such independent organizations of the oppressed and its refusal to challenge the bulwarks of capitalist rule, the old police and the army.

That both a workers' government and a pro-capitalist people's front might contain many of the same parties is a fact that mystifies sectarians who want neat formulas and schemas to cover all contingencies. This was no puzzle at all to Lenin and Trotsky, who urged the Communist parties of Europe to force the reformists into a united front coalition as the best way to prevent them from joining a coalition with the liberal capitalist parties. At that time the policy later to be put forward by Stalin under the name of the People's Front was defended by the reformists under the name of the "Left Bloc."

Trotsky in his report on the United Front cited above characterized this "Left Bloc" as a "bloc between the workers and a certain section of the bourgeoisie against another section of the bourgeoisie," that is, a coalition based on the defense of bourgeois property and the bourgeois state. Revolutionists, he said, must counterpose to this "a bloc between all the sections of the working class against the whole bourgeoisie."

. . .

It is here that the question of single-issue and multi-issue takes on another dimension. A governmental bloc or common agreement to support certain candidates in an election implies support to a multi-issue program, to the whole program on which the candidates stand. If one or another capitalist politician chooses for whatever reason to declare support for a single-issue united front action, such as an anti-war demonstration, they objectively serve to build the united front because no concession is made to them whatever on their pro-capitalist program. Membership in the anti-war movement is not conditional on anything except opposition to the imperialist war in Vietnam, a demand that is contrary to the interests of the capitalist class as a whole.

Trotsky was quite clear on this question in his discussion of the People's Front policy of the Stalinists in France, in his article "'Committees of Action'—Not a 'People's Front'" written in 1935. "The proletariat," Trotsky wrote, "does not deny anyone the right to struggle side by side with it against fascism, the Bonapartist government of Laval, the war plot of the imperialists, and all other forms of oppression and violence. The sole demand that class-conscious workers put to their actual or potential allies is that they struggle *in action*."

At the same time he made it plain that he did not expect much from those few bourgeois forces that might agree to support concrete workers' actions: "When struggle is in question," he declared, "every worker is worth ten bourgeois, even those adhering to the united front."

In relation to the petty bourgeoisie, however, Trotsky took a different attitude, posing the necessity of winning them in larger numbers to the Committees of Action.

"To be sure," Trotsky wrote, "in the election of Committees not only workers will be able to participate but also civil service employees, functionaries, war veterans, artisans, small merchants, and small peasants. Thus the Committees of Action are in closest harmony with the tasks of the struggle of the proletariat for influence over the petty bourgeoisie."

Such committees or coalitions organized around concrete demands of struggle can thus unite broad forces. Just as plainly, there must be a far-greater agreement to begin to consider a more far-ranging coalition. A political party or an electoral bloc stands on a social program for administering the state power. The first question that must be posed here is whether this program is for or against the continuation of the capitalist system and the state apparatus. Thus the very same people who can agree with us that the United States should get out of Vietnam may be prepared to vote in an election for liberal Democratic Party politicians or to participate in a coalition, such as the Peace and Freedom Party, that in no way programmatically or in deeds opposes capitalism as such, but only seeks this or that peripheral reform.

What Is the Popular Front?

In the second talk of this series I would like to give some concrete examples of the Popular Front in practice. Here I am going to discuss it as a theory and how it was propounded by the Stalinists.

As you know, between 1929 and 1934 the Comintern under Stalin's leadership went on an ultraleft binge, closely resembling the politics of Progressive Labor today, with the exception that these were mass parties united in a worldwide organization. During this so-called Third Period of the Comintern the united front was rejected on the spurious grounds that the seizure of power was on the order of the day. Instead of proposing unity with the Social Democrats in Germany against the threat of Nazism, the Communist Party at Stalin's instigation denounced the reformists as "social fascists" and even declared them, not Hitler, to be the main enemy.[1] The Stalinists claimed that it was more revolutionary to appeal directly to the workers and to the rank-and-file members of the Social Democratic Party than to conclude a common agreement with the reformist leaderships. This policy of the "united front from below" was not a united front at all but an appeal to the mass of followers of the Social Democrats to abandon their party and accept the program and leadership of the Communist Party, which they were not willing to do.

If the Communist Party had proposed a genuine united front to the Social Democrats, there is no doubt that the masses of Social Democratic workers would have welcomed this proposal with open arms and exerted great pressure on their leadership to accept. If a united front had come into being, it could have taken serious and successful measures to prevent the Nazis from coming to power. And even if the Social Democratic leaders had refused the proposals for common action, the Communist Party would have been in the strongest-possible position to appeal over their heads to the masses of Social Democratic workers.

But the ultraleftism of the Communist Party guaranteed that the working class would be left divided in the face of the common fascist

---

1   In February 1932, a year before Hitler's seizure of power, German Communist leader Ernst Thälmann argued that since fascism is capitalism in disguise, the Party must attack it at the root by directing its energies against the Social Democrats, who, as "the moderate wing of fascism," were ultimately the greatest obstacle to revolution.

enemy. That experience showed how ultraleftism, as well as reformism, can open the door to the victory of fascism.

. . .

After Hitler had consolidated his rule in a bloodless takeover in 1933, the Kremlin bureaucracy reacted by a sharp swing to the right, searching for bourgeois allies to protect it from the menace of German fascism. The turn was made at the Seventh World Congress of the Communist International in 1935. The doctrine of "collective security" was adopted there, calling for military alliances between the Soviet Union and the Western bourgeois democracies against Hitler.

. . .

Stalin bluntly told the Communist parties in the countries where he was seeking governmental allies to avoid embarrassing the liberal regimes and to refrain from socialist propaganda in the armed forces . . . This so-called anti-fascist People's Front was nothing but a coalition of the Stalinists, the reformists, and the liberal bourgeois parties programmatically committed to the preservation of capitalism and absolutely opposed to socialist revolution under any circumstances.

The American CP [Communist Party] applied this policy by agitating in the CIO [Congress of Industrial Organizations] against the creation of an independent labor party and for political support to the Roosevelt government. With the exception of the brief interlude of the Stalin-Hitler pact, from 1939 to 1941, during which time Roosevelt suddenly became a fascist in the CP press, the CP has followed this same class-collaborationist course down to the present day. Its only departure from the Democratic Party fold had been in a few abortive experiments in creating a third, more liberal capitalist party, notably in the Progressive Party effort in 1948. After mobilizing its supporters to vote for the "progressive" Henry Wallace, who had been Roosevelt's vice president, the whole thing ended in a debacle when Wallace came out in support of Truman's counterrevolutionary invasion of Korea in 1950.[2]

---

2   After the announcement of the Popular Front line in 1935, the CPUSA, at the urging of Dimitrov, initially worked with other organizations to form an independent farmer-labor party. However, they found the Soviet-led call for a third party to be impractical in the US context. The CP only switched to clear support of Roosevelt after 1937 when it was clear that he wanted to take action to curb fascist expansion abroad. Also, Wallace's Progressive Party campaign ended in profound electoral defeat in 1948—it was only *after* the debacle that Wallace took a right turn.

PART V

Anti/Fascism in the Age of Neoliberalism

Ken Lawrence, "The Ku Klux Klan and Fascism," *Urgent Tasks*, no. 14, fall/winter 1982

The National Anti-Klan Network was formed in late 1979 in the aftermath of the November 3, 1979, massacre of four Communist Workers Party members by Klansmen and neo-Nazis in Greensboro, North Carolina. The infamous "Greensboro massacre" occurred when the CWP called a "Death to the Klan" march in response to a rash of Klan violence across the South. Longtime Southern civil rights activist and journalist Anne Braden was a founder of the network.[1]

Ken Lawrence (1942–) was a civil rights activist in the 1960s and later a freelance journalist, researcher, organizer, and lecturer devoted to anti-Klan and anti-racist work. His speech below was one of three presented at the 1982 national meeting of the network in Atlanta on June 19, 1982. In it, Lawrence offers a materialist history of the Klan as a subset of twentieth-century American fascist movements. He argues that the Klan that carried out the Greensboro attacks was unlike its predecessors of the 1920s, which primarily undertook bourgeois electoral strategy—successfully—as a means of building social power. The modern Klan, he argued, is effectively a street movement with fascist aspirations.

As evidence, Lawrence cites the popularity of anti-Semitic and white supremacist pamphlets in the Klan movement, singling out William Luther Pierce's notorious white supremacist novel The Turner Diaries *(1978), a narrative account of a fascist takeover of the United States. The Turner*

---

1   Ultimately, none of the killers served any jail time.

Diaries *became widely infamous in 1995 when white supremacist Timothy McVeigh claimed it as inspiration for blowing up the Alfred P. Murrah Federal Building in Oklahoma City, Oklahoma. In Turner's novel, the fascist revolution includes a suicide bombing of the Pentagon.*

Urgent Tasks, *the journal that published Lawrence's speech, was operated by the Sojourner Truth Organization. The STO was formed in 1969 as a new communist organization out of the remnants of SDS. Centered in Chicago, where* Urgent Tasks *was published, its small membership concentrated on interracial industrial shop floor organizing, centering the role of white supremacy in dividing workers under capitalism. The journal included as editor Noel Ignatin (aka Ignatiev) a former leader of Students for a Democratic Society and later author of* How the Irish Became White *(1995).*

The National Anti-Klan Network survived until 1985, when it became the Center for Democratic Renewal. The Sojourner Truth Organization dissolved in 1986. Lawrence, a longtime civil rights activist and founder of the Deep South People's History Project, later directed the American Friends Service Committee's anti-surveillance project in Mississippi.

Our movement has done a good job of surveying the history of 115 years of Ku Klux Klan racist terror—seeing how it developed and how it was stopped in the past. We have fairly well internalized most of those lessons and put them into practice in many ways, but if we are going to achieve a truly successful strategy to counter the Klan we have to understand not only how the Klan is the same organization of racist terror that it has been for 115 years, but also what is distinctive about it today that it wasn't 115 years ago.

Today the Ku Klux Klan is probably (I say probably because there are some qualifiers to this, but I think we can generally agree it is) the main face of militant fascism in the United States. That is such a commonplace for us to say that we almost don't think about it when we say it. So I ask you to think about it for a minute . . . because the Klan was not always a fascist organization. Yes, it was always a racist terrorist organization, but it was not always a fascist organization. The Ku Klux Klan was born in 1866. Fascism was not born until the ruins of World War I darkened Europe. The Klan was around for a half century before fascism existed in the world, and the Klan actually taught the fascists a great deal in their early years.

So when we think about it that way, let's compare what were the Klan's politics in its different resurgent periods of the past with what are its politics and its aims and strategies today.

In the 1860s the Klan ... was led by the notorious General Nathan Bedford Forrest of the Confederacy. Forrest's military strategy, as every Southerner knows, was to be "fustest with the mostest"—he wasn't known as a military genius. It seems sometimes like a third of the counties in the South are named for him. Streets are named for him, housing projects are named for him, parks are named for him. He is known everywhere. Well, who was General Forrest? Before the Civil War he was the largest slave trader in Memphis, and during the war he was its greatest war criminal when he ordered the massacre of the garrison that was guarding Fort Pillow, the black troops who surrendered to his much-larger force. Rather than accept their surrender he ordered them slain to the last man, then gloated to his diary how the blood of the dead soldiers dyed the Mississippi River red. That's who General Forrest was. When he took over leadership of the Klan in 1867, it represented the guerrilla continuation of the war he had tried to fight as a Confederate general. In essence, he exchanged his Confederate grey for a white sheet. The earliest Klan, then, was a restorationist movement of the Confederacy.

The Invisible Empire was something quite different when it arose in the 1920s. It was essentially a bourgeois, nativist movement. As the Southern Poverty Law Center film documents so well, in fact, the KKK had the potential to go further than it actually did, because the truth is not only that in many places you had to be a Klansman to be elected to office, and you certainly at least had to have the active endorsement of the Klan, but the Klan came very close to capturing, on separate occasions, the national Democratic and Republican Parties. That's what kind of a movement it was. It was a right-wing, white supremacist, but essentially mainstream bourgeois movement. That is, it intended to control, through the traditional political legal apparatus, the politics of the United States government and as many state and local governments as possible.

When the Klan was resurgent in the 1960s, it was essentially a backward-looking movement, attempting to preserve what was most reactionary and most peculiar of the institutions of the segregated white South. It was under that banner, represented everywhere by the battle flag of the Confederacy, that it went out and did its beatings, bombings, lynchings, mutilations, and castrations.

It is something quite different today.

Today, it is as likely to fight under the banner of the twisted cross, the Nazi swastika, as under the banner of the Confederacy. In fact, it is the genius of the Klan leaders today that they have managed to merge these two movements into a single whole, and to create a coherent ideology out of those two divergent strains.

The fascist movement has a somewhat-different history in this country. There is no way I can cover it in a brief talk, but some highlights are essential if we are to understand this, particularly since I think two extremes of this organization have somewhat misread the history—the history of the 1930s especially.

The fascist movement got its real insurgent birth in the United States from Henry Ford through his newspaper the *Dearborn Independent* . . .

Built on the movement that Henry Ford founded, the fascists, but not the Klan, flourished in the 1930s. It is well to remember that one of the largest mass movements in the United States, and one of the few outside of the mainstream political parties that was capable of packing Madison Square Garden in those years, was Father Coughlin's Christian Front. Huey Long built a similar movement in the state of Louisiana, which was led by the notorious anti-Semite Gerald L. K. Smith, who became one of the most important figures in the reconstitution of the fascist movement in the 1950s and gradually bringing it into concert with the Ku Klux Klan over a period of time.

So we need to understand not only the Klan history, but also the quite-independent fascist history, which have merged to become a single movement with an ideology that is quite different from the ideology of the Confederacy of Nathan Bedford Forrest, or the nativism of David C. Stephenson, the Klan leader of the 1920s who was the main political figure in that rebirth, or even of Sam Bowers and Robert Shelton of the 1960s. Today many of those key figures of the sixties have accommodated themselves quite well to this new ideology of fascism, which they did not previously profess in their earlier guise. Thus we see the rise in North Carolina of the United Racist Front, which carried out the Greensboro massacre[2]

---

2   As noted above, on November 3, 1979, the Communist Workers Party of the US organized a "Death to the Klan" march through a low-income neighborhood in Greensboro, North Carolina. The CWP had formed out of an organization called "Workers' Viewpoint Organization," which had organized earlier demonstrations against Klan violence in Alabama and Mississippi. Klansman and Nazis met the marchers with rifles, shooting and killing four of them. Fourteen were charged with crimes in connection with

and which represents, I think, the peak of their ability to fuse these two movements.

The Ku Klux Klan did not become fascist overnight, and the development was uneven.

Naturally, racists, even when divided by important points of ideology, have considerable political agreement of which they are conscious. So it is no accident that one of the leading fascist organizers of the thirties, Gerald L. K. Smith, also was a close kin to the Klans of the fifties and sixties, and that most of the Klans borrowed heavily from his journal, *The Cross and the Flag*.

The earliest attempt at merging the two movements was in 1940 at Camp Nordland, New Jersey, when the German American Bund and the Ku Klux Klan met, 3,500 strong, on a Bund platform beneath a fiery cross. Anti-Semite Edward James Smythe presided, having spent three years working to consummate such a coming together. Arthur H. Bell, the KKK's grand giant, shook hands with August Klapprott, the Bund's vice president, and Klapprott declared, "The principles of the Bund and the Klan are the same."

But that merger was not to be. A storm of unfavorable publicity forced the Klan's imperial wizard, James Colescott, who had originally authorized participation in the meeting, to recant, and to repudiate the Nazis. Eventually Colescott's literature listed fascism among the foreign "isms" the Klan officially opposed, and Smythe's dream was stillborn.

But from that time on, some of the most committed Nazis viewed the KKK as their most likely road to power. Among these was J. B. Stoner, who was a Klan *kleagle* (organizer) in Tennessee during World War II, but was also organizing a "national anti-Jewish political party" and distributing the *Protocols*.[3] In 1958 the National States' Rights Party was founded by Edward Fields, who had worked with Stoner in the forties, and Matthias Koehl. (Koehl later succeeded George Lincoln Rockwell as head of the American Nazi Party.)

Stoner's Nazi sympathies were never veiled—he told the *Atlanta*

---

the shootings. They were found not guilty on all counts after a jury trial.

3   First published in czarist Russia in 1905, *The Protocols of the Elders of Zion* remains the urtext of modern anti-Semitism. It purported to be the transcript of a secret meeting of Jewish "elders" who plotted world domination through economic manipulation, media control, and a general sowing of dissent. To this day, it feeds the conspiratorial imagination central to anti-Semitism.

Constitution in 1946 that Hitler had been too moderate and that his party wanted "to make being a Jew a crime, punishable by death." But he also practiced law jointly with KKK leader James Venable of Atlanta. During the early years of the NSRP, Stoner's role was low profile (the 1958 Birmingham church bombing for which he's been found guilty was committed during this period), but he eventually emerged as its national chairman and main spokesman.

The United Racist Front, a Klan/Nazi umbrella organization formed in September 1979 in North Carolina, carried out the Greensboro massacre in November of that year, and NSRP leaders Stoner and Fields saw the opportunity to hasten the fascist development of the whole movement. Fields organized the New Order Knights of the Ku Klux Klan, combining the two movements in the name. Though considered by Klan watchers such as the Anti-Defamation League as a relatively insignificant splinter, this was actually a shrewd tactic.

The New Order Klan simultaneously projected its politics (by organizing a union, then calling a strike to protest the hiring of Mexican workers at the Zartic Frozen Foods plant in Cedartown, Georgia) and promoted "Klan unity" (by inviting leaders of the various Klan factions to a meeting to "honor" two of the Greensboro killers). These moves paid off handsomely as one local Klan leader after another has aligned himself with Stoner and Fields.

What is the difference, then, between this new guise of the Klan and the past that I have talked about? One difference—and this is one thing I've learned from the writings of David Edgar[4]—is that the role of racism, and the role of anti-Semitism and the role of scapegoating in general, is quite different ideologically for a fascist movement from that of a right-wing conservative movement or a traditional Klan-type movement. That is, it is not to put people in their place. It is not to make a sub-class out of them and to exploit, or superexploit, their labor. It is genocidal. It is exterminationist.

I urge everyone, despite its horror, to acquire the manual of the current Klan/Nazi strategy, and to understand what that strategy is. That

---

4   David Edgar (1948–) is a British playwright, activist, and organizer. In 1982, he gave a speech, "The International Face of Fascism," to the same National Anti-Klan Network Conference in Atlanta at which Lawrence delivered this address. He is also author of the book *Racism, Fascism, and the Politics of the National Front*.

book is the novel *The Turner Diaries*, written by William Pierce of the National Alliance under the pseudonym Andrew MacDonald.[5] It is a stirring call to power. To cast it in literary terms, it is the flip side of *The Iron Heel*. Where Jack London projected a look back at the revolution of the future to see its horrors, William Pierce uses that device to show how the revolution that creates the New Order comes into being.

Upon reading this book you will find that the strategy described is very similar to the strategy of the Nazis in Europe, which ideologically is summed up by the person responsible for creating it, a French fascist, Michel Faci, who uses the nom de guerre LeLoup. He calls it the "strategy of tension." The Bologna and other bombings are attempts at social destabilization, which have as their assumption that the fascist movement has reached its peak "respectable" strength and that now is the time to polarize society and build on the fears, the tensions, and the disarray that can be created by disrupting the fabric of politics as usual. That's the politics of *The Turner Diaries*.

The book begins, for example, after a period of difficulty and repression of the right, with bombing the FBI building in Washington. It goes from there onward to a situation of nuclear war, which is launched not by the government but by the fascists who seize control of the nuclear weapons. Let me read you just a couple of passages.

Pierce has many dialogues where he differentiates between the politics of his movement and the conservatives. He always personifies those political views, as any good novelist does:

> He didn't understand that one of the major purposes of political terror, always and everywhere, is to force the authorities to take reprisals and to become more repressive, thus alienating a portion of the population and generating sympathy for the terrorists. And the other purpose is, to create unrest by destroying the population's sense of security and their belief in the invincibility of the government.

---

5   William Luther Pierce (1933–2002) was the founder in 1974 of the anti-Semitic, neo-Nazi National Alliance, itself derived from the National Youth Alliance, part of the remains of George Wallace's 1968 presidential campaign. *The Turner Diaries* first appeared in serial form that same year in *Attack!*, the newspaper of the National Alliance. It was published as a book in 1978, and over the next twenty years sold over 500,000 copies. Historian Kathleen Belew wrote that Pierce's novel "worked as a foundational how-to manual for the [White Power] movement, outlining a detailed plan for race war."

Other passages in here indicate a similar desire to destabilize society and view that period of destabilization very much as the secret National Front document quoted by David Edgar described the situation they anticipate arising in England. The culmination of this he describes as follows:

August 1, 1993. Today has been the Day of the Rope—a grim and bloody day, but an unavoidable one. Tonight, for the first time in weeks, it is quiet and totally peaceful throughout all of southern California. But the night is filled with silent horrors; from tens of thousands of lampposts, power poles, and trees throughout this vast metropolitan area the grisly forms hang.

In the lighted areas one sees them everywhere. Even the street signs at intersections have been pressed into service, and at practically every street corner I passed this evening on my way to HQ there was a dangling corpse, four at every intersection. Hanging from a single overpass only about a mile from here is a group of about 30, each with an identical placard around its neck bearing the printed legend, "I betrayed my race." Two or three of that group had been decked out in academic robes before they were strung up, and the whole batch are apparently faculty members from the nearby UCLA campus.

He describes how they did this:

Squads of our troops with synchronized watches suddenly appeared in a thousand blocks at once, in fifty different residential neighborhoods, and every squad leader had a long list of names and addresses. The blaring music suddenly stopped and was replaced by the sound of thousands of doors splintering, as booted feet kicked them open . . .

One of two things happened to those the troops dragged out onto the streets. If they were non-Whites—and that included all the Jews and everyone who even looked like he had a bit of non-White ancestry—they were shoved into hastily formed columns and started on their no-return march to the canyon in the foothills north of the city. The slightest resistance, any attempt at back talk, or any lagging brought a swift bullet.

The Whites, on the other hand, were, in nearly all cases, hanged on the spot. One of the two types of pre-printed placards was hung on the victim's chest, his hands were quickly taped behind his back, a rope was thrown over a convenient limb or signpost with the other end knotted around his neck, and he was then hauled clear of the ground with no further ado and left dancing on air while the soldiers went to the next name on their list.

The hangings and the formation of the death columns went on for about 10 hours without interruption. When the troops finished their grim work early this afternoon and began returning to their barracks, the Los Angeles area was utterly and completely pacified. The residents of neighborhoods in which we could venture safely only in a tank yesterday were trembling behind closed doors today, afraid even to be seen peering through the crack in drawn drapes. Throughout the morning there was no organized or large-scale opposition to our troops, and by this afternoon even the desire for opposition had evaporated.

That's a little more than you probably wanted to hear; it more than I want even to consider, but I think it's important to understand what that strategy is. It's very different from bombing a church here, lynching a civil rights worker there, in order to keep people in their place. It is actually a vision of seizing control of the entire society, exterminating minorities and Jews and creating something quite different.

To accomplish that strategy, which they are deadly serious about, something quite different from their previous approaches to organization and mass political action are necessary—and are in effect now.[6] One area of that work that I've followed carefully has been the gun shows throughout the South and how they recruit through them.

I want to show you two documents, both popular pamphlets I've bought recently at gun shows. One is a manual that shows how to convert semiautomatic weapons to fully automatic machine guns with parts that are commonly available for sale without any records being kept at these gun shows. The other is a book entitled *Elementary Field Interrogation*, which is a torture manual, literally. It is written,

6   Using *The Turner Diaries* as their blueprint, a goup of white supremists founded a terror group called The Order at the Aryan Nations compound in Idaho in 1983. Over the next two years, this terror cell perpetrated a string of crimes including robbery, counterfeiting, bombing, and murder.

according to a publicity blurb put out by the publisher, by a former Phoenix Program interrogator for the CIA during the Vietnam War who has now dedicated his services to the fascist movement. There are plenty of illustrations of these tortures, in case you can't figure it out for yourself from reading the text. They are sufficiently horrifying, more so even than some passages from *The Turner Diaries*, that I won't read them to you. But I urge you to familiarize yourself with this grizzly stuff anyway.

The night riders and lynch mobs of the past had no need for torture manuals or machine guns. But the fascist paramilitaries who train in the Klan, Nazi, and "survivalist" camps in preparation for what they call "the coming race war" do need them. These are significant differences from the KKK's previous incarnations, and we need to understand them.

Then of course, the other thrust, the ideological thrust that David Edgar told us about, is the so-called Historical Revisionist movement. This is the latest copy of their journal, which looks quite scholarly and impressive—the *Journal of Historical Review*. The envelope in which it arrived bears a nonprofit organization postmark from Torrance, California—Liberty Lobby's West Coast headquarters of Willis Carto— which means they have a 501(c)(3) tax exemption. Pierce's National Alliance does not have such a tax exemption right now, but the ACLU has a case in Federal District Court in Washington suing to get him one, so he will probably have one soon.

Now, the traditional Klan did not need this kind of document—a torture manual. It did not need this kind of document—a document about creating fully automatic weapons to build an army with. It did not need to deny the Nazi Holocaust. And it did not have books like *The Turner Diaries*, which all of the resurgent Klans, every one of them from Edward Fields to Don Black to Bill Wilkinson, use as their manual. In fact, they all have bulk discount prices for copies of it which, among other things, proves that they are considerably more unified as to program and strategy than they ostensibly appear to be. They didn't need those in the past, because they had a different program then. Therefore I want to suggest that our program has to learn not only what we know and what we try to practice based on the movements of the past that successfully defeated the Klan in its earlier guises, but also the lessons that have been learned, sometimes under quite-different circum- stances, by antifascists both in this country and around the world.

I'm not going to spin that program here.

It's going to take some time to do it, some debate. I hope that we're ready for debate. It's taken us three years to get to that point, but I think we're ready.

I do want to say, though, that it's going to take a more unified movement than the one we have thus far built. This is much too small a meeting. I don't want to take anything away from the accomplishments, particularly of the work that Lyn Wells[7] and others have done to bring people here, but we all know this is too small a meeting. It needs to be much bigger. And one of the reasons is that this movement, our anti-Klan, anti-fascist movement, is fragmented right now—I believe needlessly so. There is a considerable amount we can do to try to heal that fracture and make it a stronger movement. For my part, I gave a talk somewhat similar, but on a different theme, at the national conference of People United—the other national anti-Klan coalition—in Baltimore a few months ago, and stressed basically the same thing. The two national coalitions should get together. There is plenty of evidence we can. A lot of people from People United are here at this conference, and some of our members were at the other one. Many of us belong to both coalitions. Whatever the reasons may have been in the past that kept our movement fractured, they aren't valid any more. If we're going to defeat a newly resurgent fascist Klan, we need the strongest possible movement we can have.

---

7   Lyn Wells was at the time of the meeting director of the National Anti-Klan Network. In March of 1982, Wells had written to US Attorney General William French Smith on behalf of the Women's Appeal for Justice in Chattanooga, a group formed after the murder of four black women in that city by Klansmen in 1980. Wells helped to head up the NAKN organizing for this meeting, which occurred three months later.

Barbara Ehrenreich, foreword to *Male Fantasies*, by Klaus Theweleit, 1987

Barbara Ehrenreich (1941–) is an American writer, speaker, and activist who has spent most of her life working and writing outside of academe. Of her twenty-one books, her most famous is Nickel and Dimed: On (Not) Getting By in America *(2001), recounting her experiences as an "undercover" minimum wage worker in the United States. She was very active in the Democratic Socialists of America in the 1980s and 1990s.*

The piece below is her foreword to the English translation of Klaus Theweleit's Male Fantasies, Volume 1: Women, Floods, Bodies, History, *first published in German in 1977. Theweleit's two-volume work remains the most famous theorization of fascist masculinity available in the English-language world. Yet Ehrenreich's foreword should be seen as an important intervention in its own right, one that reframes the meaning of* Male Fantasies *from an American socialist-feminist perspective, distilling its lessons for US history.*

Ehrenreich raises a provocative question about fascism that is not emphasized in other pieces in this collection: What if we look at fascism as a form of desire? To address it, one must take seriously the gender of fascism, something that far too few works in the US antifascist tradition have done. Ehrenreich, following Theweleit, sees a link between fascist masculinity and everyday acts of "banal sexism," yet she refuses the move famously made by Betty Friedan in The Feminine Mystique *(1963) of conflating the Holocaust with everyday treatment of women.*

The foreword also speaks to early twenty-first-century conversations about "permanent war" in the United States: namely, how a militarized culture works to create forms of manhood with devastating consequences, both at home and abroad. It dovetails with historian Kathleen Belew's recent observation, in the American context, that the experience of war can sharpen, solidify, and quite literally weaponize fascist sensibilities, at least within a small but influential minority of veterans. One way to curb fascism, then, is to stop war.

The fantasies with which this book is concerned belong to a particular group of men: members of the Freikorps, the volunteer armies that fought, and to a large extent, triumphed over, the revolutionary German working class in the years immediately after World War I.[1] The Freikorps were organized by officers returning from the war, in which many of their leaders had commanded "shock troops," trained to penetrate the lines of trench warfare with sudden, daring assaults. Most of the men who organized the Freikorps and were recruited to them belonged to a class that has no precise analogue in American history: a kind of rural "petty bourgeoisie" with semifeudal traditions. Hired by the socialist chancellor Ebert to bring order to revolutionary Germany in 1918 (he did not trust the regular army, with its working-class rank and file), the Freikorps became roaming, largely autonomous armies, each commanded by its own charismatic leader. Between 1918 and 1923, they fought Polish communists and nationalists, the Russian Red Army and Latvian and Estonian nationalists in the Baltic region, and the German working class throughout Germany.

The Freikorpsmen fought, first of all, because they were paid to, and, by the standards of postwar Germany, were paid generously. They fought also for revenge, believing that the German army had been betrayed in

---

1 Immediately after World War I, Germany faced a left-wing and communist revolution on several fronts, driven by workers and returning veterans. Sometimes called "the German Revolution of 1918–1923," it included the January 1919 uprising, the Bavarian Council Republic, and the revolutionary conflict in the Ruhr Valley in 1920. Many of its participants aimed to create a direct democracy of workers' and soldiers' councils like the simultaneous Bolshevik Revolution in its infancy. This insurgency was violently suppressed by the forces of a short-lived coalition between the Social Democrats, the conservative establishment, and the proto-Nazi Freikorps, described in this piece. Karl Liebknecht and Rosa Luxemburg, the most visible symbols of this revolutionary ferment, were murdered by the Freikorps on January 15, 1919.

World War I—"stabbed in the back," as it was so often said—by the communists, with their internationalist ideology, as well as by the vacillating socialists and other, insufficiently resolute, civilian forces. But they fought, most of all, because that was what they did. Robert Waite, in his classical history of the Freikorps, quotes a member of the famous Ehrhardt Brigade, a man who had started his military career in World War I at the age of sixteen:

> People told us that the War was over. That made us laugh. We ourselves are the War. Its flame burns strongly in us. It envelops our whole being and fascinates us with the enticing urge to destroy. We obeyed . . . and marched onto the battlefields of the postwar world just as we had gone into battle on the Western Front: singing, reckless and filled with the joy of adventure as we marched to the attack; silent, deadly, remorseless in battle.

For the American reader, the most important thing about the Freikorpsmen is that they managed to survive the relatively warless years between 1923 and 1933, becoming the core of Hitler's SA and, in several cases, going on to become key functionaries in the Third Reich. The author of the above quote, for example, became the supreme SA leader for Western Germany; another Freikorps leader, Rudolf Höss, later commanded the death camp at Auschwitz. There is still some debate over how critical the Freikorps were to the rise of Nazism, but a recent and impressively exhaustive study by Richard Hamilton suggests we ought to focus less on the mass social-psychological appeal of fascism, and give more credit to the organizational strength and armed might of the Freikorps. Certainly the Nazis themselves were proud to claim the ruthless Freikorpsmen as their comrades and progenitors.

So these are the men we are dealing with—men who were first soldiers in the regular army, then irregulars serving the cause of domestic repression, and finally Nazis. They are men for whom the period between 1914 and 1945 was continuous, almost-uninterrupted war, in no small part because they made it so. I should add that there may have been as many as 400,000 of them, or according to another estimate, no more than 50,000.

Hold on to this information—it may provide you with an illusion of security in what follows. We set out to read about fascism in a hardheaded, instrumental frame of mind. After all, we know the last chapter, which is the Holocaust, which is "unthinkable," so we command ourselves to think as hard as possible, to ask the right questions, to run through a checklist of morbid possibilities. Confronted with a group of fascist, or in this case, soon-to-be-fascist personnel, like the Freikorpsmen, we want to know, above all: what kind of men they were. And we want to know for the sound, pragmatic reason that we would like to be able to detect any similar men in our contemporary political world, and do our best to expose and isolate them. That is, we approach the subject of fascist men with the mindset of a public health official: we want to get near (to the toxin or the protofascists) in order to get as far away as possible. And that, unfortunately for the composure of the reader, is exactly what Klaus Theweleit will not let us do. He looks too close and consequently draws us in too far. So you will want to look up from these pages from time to time and try to reassure yourself that you are reading about a certain group of men, of a certain class and nationality, who lived at a certain time now two generations behind us.

There are other, far less disconcerting, ways to approach the study of fascism. There are liberal sociological theories of totalitarianism; there are Marxist theories of fascism as the inevitable outcome, given certain "conjunctures," of the course of capital accumulation. The problem is that these theories have very little to tell us about what we ultimately need most to understand, and that is murder. In the sociological or Marxist worldview, fascist murder appears either as an instrumentality— the terrorist spectacle required to maintain absolute authority—or as an intrusion of the "irrational," which, for most social scientists, is also the unknowable. Then there are the psychoanalytic theories of fascism, which at least have the merit of addressing the "irrational" as a subject of inquiry. The problem here is that, too often, fascism tends to become representational, symbolic. In the commonplace attenuated version of psychoanalytic theory that most of us have unthinkingly accepted, fascism is "really" about something else—for example, repressed homosexuality. Fascist murder becomes a misdirected way of getting at that "something else"—a symbolic act, if not a variety of performance art. Such an account goes almost as far as the stock Marxist theories in obliterating the human agency in fascism: we "know" what the fascist really wants (but is too deluded or psychotic to go after), just as we "know" what the masses really need (but are, once again, too confused or foolish to fight for). We know, and are therefore human; they, fumbling in darkness after what-they-do-not-know, can only be objects of our knowing, hence not fully human. Reassuringly, the "unthinkable" becomes also the "inhuman."

As a theory of fascism, *Male Fantasies* sets forth the jarring—and ultimately horrifying—proposition that the fascist is not doing "something else," but doing what he wants to do. When he throws a grenade at a working-class couple who are making love on the grass, he is not taking a symbolic stand against the institution of heterosexuality. When he penetrates a female adversary with a bullet or bayonet, he is not dreaming of rape. What he wants is what he gets, and that is what the Freikorpsmen describe over and over as a "bloody mass": heads with their faces blown off, bodies soaked red in their own blood, rivers clogged with bodies. The reader's impulse is to engage in a kind of mental flight—that is, to "read" the murders as a story about something else, for example, sex . . . or the Oedipal triangle . . . or anything to help the mind drift off. But Theweleit insists that we see, and not "read," the violence. The "bloody mass" that recurs in these men's lives and fantasies is not a referent to an unattainable "something else," and the murders that comprise their professional activity are not mere gestures. What is far worse, Theweleit forces us to acknowledge, these acts of fascist terror spring from irreducible human desire. Then the question we have to ask about fascism becomes: How does human desire—or the ceaseless motion of "desiring production," as the radical psychoanalytic theorists Deleuze and Guattari call it—lend itself to the production of death?

You will see at once that this question applies to much more than twentieth-century German fascism—as if that were not enough. The Freikorpsmen were not the first men in history to make war—or death production—into a way of life. For my generation of historians (in which I claim membership only as an amateur), the history of war and warriors has taken second place to social history—the attempt to reconstruct how ordinary people have gone about their business, producing what they need and reproducing themselves. Reinforced by Marxism and later feminism, we have rejected the conventional history of "kings and battles" for the "hidden history" of everyday life, almost to the point of forgetting how much of everyday life has, century after century, been shaped by battles and dominated by kings or warrior elites. It has not been stylish to pay attention to those warrior castes who neither planted nor herded, but devoted their lives to pillage and forgotten causes: the illiterate Greek chieftains on their decade-long excursion to the plains of Asia Minor; the tribal bands of Northern Europeans who raided Rome and then its Christian outposts; the Asiatic "hordes" who swept through medieval Europe; the Crusaders who looted the Arab world; the elite officership of European imperialism; and so on. These were men—not counting their conscripts and captives—who lived only parasitically in relation to the production of useful things, who lived for perpetual war, the production of death.

Then in our own time—and I write in a time of "peace," meaning that the wars are so far "local" and endured only by peripheral, or Third World, people—what do we make of the warrior caste that rules the United States and, in combination with its counterpart in the Soviet Union, rules the world? These men wear civilian clothes or well-pressed uniforms; they go home at night to wives and children. Yet are they not also men who refuse, at all costs, to disarm? Men who have opted for perpetual war—the "cold war" of nuclear terror? In fact, their relationship to production is not only parasitical: they have succeeded in enlisting the human and mechanical energy of production for the cause of death. The mounted warriors of remote history looted farms in order to continue their conquests (and further looting); our executive warriors pave over the farm and build a munitions factory. In my country, as more and more human and material resources are appropriated by the warrior caste, it becomes harder and harder to draw the line between production, as an innately purposeful human activity, and the production of death.

Perhaps because we have not spent enough time studying the warriors of the past, we do not have a psychology with which to comprehend our own warrior caste. We are watching them now in a time of little murders—Vietnam, El Salvador, Lebanon—just as Theweleit watches the Freikorpsmen engaged in what are comparatively minor skirmishes. In both cases, we know the last chapter: the Holocaust, Armageddon. So do our warrior leaders. Are they "evil"—which is a way of saying that their motives lie outside "normal" human drives and desires, that they themselves are inhuman? Or are they only absentminded, lacking the imagination or powers of concentration to broach the "unthinkable"? Or is it just possible, Theweleit forces us to ask, that they are human beings (i.e., not totally unlike ourselves) doing, more or less consciously, exactly what they want to do?

So the question posed by the Freikorpsmen's lives—the question of
how "desiring production" becomes death production—is of more than
historic interest, more than a matter for specialists. You will have some
premonition of the answer from the subject Theweleit takes up at the
beginning: not how the Freikorpsmen thought about fighting, or about
the fatherland, or how they felt about Jews or workers, but how they felt
about women. Here I cannot give you a shortcut to Theweleit's conclusions (in fact, there are no "conclusions," only more and more paths to
follow). But I will say that, for the feminist reader, some of these paths
will begin to look familiar, and you will find yourself following them
with a sense of foreboding: the Freikorpsmen hate women, specifically
women's bodies and sexuality. It would not be going too far to say that
their perpetual war was undertaken to escape women; even the moth-
erly battlefront nurse is a threatening intrusion in the unisexual world of
war. This hatred—or dread—of women cannot be explained with Freud's
all-purpose Oedipal triangulation (fear that heterosexual desire will
lead to punishment by the father, homosexual yearnings for the father,
or some such permutation of the dramatic possibilities). The dread
arises in the pre-Oedipal struggle of the fledgling self, before there is
even an ego to sort out the objects of desire and the odds of getting
them: it is a dread, ultimately, of dissolution—of being swallowed,
engulfed, annihilated. Women's bodies are the holes, swamps, pits of
muck that can engulf.

In the Freikorpsman's life, there are three kinds of women: those who
are absent, such as the wives and fiancées left behind, and generally
unnamed and unnoted in the Freikorpsmen's most intimate diaries; the
women who appear in the imagination and on the literal battlefront as
"white nurses," chaste, upper-class German women; and, finally, those
who are his class enemies—the "Red women" whom he faces in angry
mobs and sometimes even in single combat. The best category is, of
course, absent women. But then, women of the white-nurse variety are
never entirely present; they are indistinct, nameless, disembodied. In
fantasy, the good woman, the white nurse, has no body at all; there is
only a smooth, white plain. In fantasy, she is already dead.

The Red woman is a more obstinate case. She is vividly, aggressively
sexual; in fantasy, always a whore. Her mouth is enormous, spewing out
insults at our Freikorpsmen as they attempt to ride, straight-backed,
through the city streets. The Red woman is, in addition, armed, or is so

at least in fantasy: she might have a gun under her skirt, or she might lead the Freikorpsmen through a dark passageway to an ambush. In other words, there is no distinguishing her sexuality from the mortal danger she presents. So when the Freikorpsman kills her (as he will do over and over in these pages), he kills her in what appears to him to be self-defense. In the brief moment of penetration—with bullet or knife—he comes close, thrillingly close, to her and the horror of dissolution. But once it is over, he will still be intact, erect (and we must imagine, quite clean and dry), and she will be—a "bloody mass." With her absent, the world becomes "safe" and male again.

Feminist readers will recognize, in Theweleit's men, the witch-hunter, for whom female sexuality and power is evil incarnate . . . or the rapist who mimics (and often accompanies) murder with sexual inter-course . . . or the garden-variety sadist, who finds relief in images of women battered and humiliated . . . or . . . But let us come back to the issue of what kind of man we are talking about. We are, remember, deal-ing with the Freikorps, the vanguard of Nazism, and we know that what they are about is not a witch hunt. In the 1920s, the time of these "fanta-sies," they are at war with the communists, and beyond them, the entire politicized German working class. And what they will finally undertake is not "sexocide," as some feminists have termed the witch hunts of sixteenth-century Europe, but genocide. What is the connection?

Here Theweleit takes us beyond any ground so far explored by femi-nist theory: from the dread of women to the hatred of communism and the rebellious working class. I will not retrace his path, because my job is not to convince you, but only to prepare you. Always bear in mind that primal fear of dissolution. Communism—and this is not the communism of Lenin or Stalin, but the communism of Rosa Luxemburg, the most potent and horrifying of the "Red women," and even, briefly, of Wilhelm Reich—represents a promiscuous mingling, a breaking down of old barriers, something wild and disorderly. ("Represents" is too weak a word. This is what communism promises the oppressed and, we must imagine, usually hungry, working class of postwar Germany.) The Freikorpsmen recount with icy horror a working-class seizure of a castle, where the occupiers proceed to glut themselves, fornicate indis-criminately (this is the Freikorpsmen's account, anyway), and find a hundred ways to desecrate this tower of feudal, nationalist pride. To the Freikorpsmen, the Reds, like individual women, are a nameless force that seeks to engulf—described over and over as a "flood," a "tide," a threat that comes in "waves." A man must hold himself firm and upright, or be "sucked in" by this impure sea . . . All that is rich and various must be smoothed over (to become like the blank facades of fascist architecture); all that is wet and luscious must be dammed up and contained; all that is "exotic" (dark, Jewish) must be eliminated.

Now, having come so close to the "last chapter," we can no longer postpone the question of which men we are talking about and whose fantasies these are. For if the fascist fantasy—which was of course no fantasy for the millions of victims—springs from a dread that (perhaps) lies in the hearts of all men, a dread of engulfment by the "other," which is the mother, the sea or even the moist embrace of love . . . if so, then we are in deep trouble. But even as I say that, I am reminded that we who are women are already in deep trouble. As Theweleit says, the point of understanding fascism is not only "because it might 'return again,'" but because it is already implicit in the daily relationships of men and women. Theweleit refuses to draw a line between the fantasies of the Freikorpsmen and the psychic ramblings of the "normal" man: and I think here of the man who feels a "normal" level of violence toward women (as in, "I'd like to fuck her to death") . . . the man who has a "normal" distaste for sticky, unseen "feminine functions" . . . the man who loves women, as "normal" men do, but sees a castrating horror in every expression of female anger . . . or that entirely normal, middle-class citizen who simply prefers that women be absent from the public life of work, decisions, war. Here Theweleit does not push, but he certainly leaves open the path from the "inhuman impulse" of fascism to the most banal sexism.

I think it should be said though—especially since Theweleit himself does not say it—that the equation does not work both ways. It would be a perverse reading of *Male Fantasies*, and a most slovenly syllogism, which leaps to conclude that "all men are fascists" or that fascism and misogyny are somehow the "same thing." The fascist enterprise was not, after all, a modern witch hunt, and the Jewish (and communist) men who fell victim to it were not substitute women, symbolic whores, or anything of the kind, but real men whose crime was their Jewishness, or their politics. Neither feminism nor antifascism will be well served by confounding fascist genocide with the daily injuries inflicted by men on women—and I urge the feminist reader to resist the temptation to do so.[2] The problem is not that any comparison "trivializes" the Holocaust (we need comparisons if we are to inch our way up to some comprehension of the "unthinkable"), but that we need to preserve the singularity of the horrors we seek to understand. One example: the Freikorpsmen do not rape the "Red women" they capture; they beat them or kill them. We may say that rape is like murder, but it is not the same as murder. And the Freikorpsman's predilection for murder, over rape, turns out to be a clue.

There is a further bit of historical specificity to keep in mind: these Freikorpsmen do not emerge on the plain of history fresh from the pre-Oedipal nursery of primal emotions, but from the First World War. That war was a devastating experience not only for the men who lost, like these, but for those who "won." It was the first modern technological war, the first war to produce its own specific psychosis—"shell shock." Obviously very few of the survivors—and only an elite minority of the Germans—went on to create fascist movements. But in considering the so far unending history made by men of the warrior caste, it may be helpful to recall that it is not only that men make wars, but that wars make men. For the warrior caste, war is not only death production, but a means of reproduction; each war deforms the human spirit and guarantees that the survivors—or some among them—will remain warriors. I do not offer this as an "excuse" (there are none) but as a thought that may have practical value: if we cannot, certainly not in one generation, uproot the murderous fantasies, we can at least try to stop the war.

The fantasies are another problem. If I may extrapolate from the work of the American feminist theorists Dorothy Dinnerstein and Nancy Chodorow, it seems to me that as long as women care what we are in this world—at best, "social inferiors," and at worst, a form of filth—then the male ego will be formed by, and bounded by, hideous dread. For that which they loved first—woman and mother—is that which they must learn to despise in others and suppress within themselves. Under these

---

2   Betty Friedan's famous book *The Feminine Mystique* (1963) contained a chapter entitled "Progressive Dehumanization: The Comfortable Concentration Camp," comparing the plight of suburban housewives with that of concentration camp prisoners. Both housewives and internees, Friedan wrote, "were forced to adopt childlike behavior, forced to give up their individuality and merge themselves into an amorphous mass." As Kirsten Fermaglich has observed, the comparison drew surprisingly few critiques in its day, even from mainstream reviewers.

conditions, which are all we know, so far, as the human condition, men will continue to see the world divided into "them" and "us," male and female, hard and soft, solid and liquid—and they will, in every way possible, fight and flee the threat of submersion. They will build dykes against the "streaming" of their own desire. They will level the forests and pave the earth. They will turn viciously against every revolution from below—and every revolution starts with a disorderly bubbling over of passion and need. They will make their bodies into hard instruments. They will confuse, in some mad reverie, love and death, sex and murder. They may finally produce the perfect uniformity, the smooth, hard certainty that transcends anything that fascism aspired to: a dead planet.

. . .

It is Theweleit's brilliance that he lets us, now and then, glimpse [an] other fantasy, which is the inversion of the fascists' dread: here, the dams break. Curiosity swims upstream and turns around, surprising itself. Desire streams forth through the channels of imagination. Barriers—between women and men, the "high" and the "low"—crumble in the face of this new energy. This is what the fascist held himself in horror of, and what he saw in communism, in female sexuality—a joyous commingling, as disorderly as life. In this fantasy, the body expands, in its senses, its imaginative reach—to fill the earth. And we are at last able to rejoice in the softness and the permeability of the world around us, rather than holding ourselves back in lonely dread. This is the fantasy that makes us, both men and women, human—and makes us, sometimes, revolutionaries in the cause of life.

Stuart Marshall, "The Contemporary
Political Use of Gay History:
The Third Reich,"
from *How Do I Look? Queer
Film and Video*, 1991

The Silence = Death graphic adopted by ACT UP as its logo.
Created by the Silence = Death Project, New York, NY, 1986.

By the late 1980s, the LGBT movement had become the most visible bearer of antifascist politics in the United States. When the AIDS activist organization ACT UP adopted the pink triangle as a logo in 1987, it became the only major US postwar movement to evoke fascism in one of its major symbols. The pink triangle graphic, created by the Silence = Death collective in New York, recalled the historical incarceration of gay men in Nazi concentration camps, where homosexuals were forced to wear pink triangle badges as markers of their crime against the state. The symbol had first been adapted by the gay and lesbian movement by West German activists in the mid 1970s. With increasing frequency in the mid and late 1980s, American gays and lesbians drew upon new archives of "the gay Holocaust," opened up by post-Stonewall historiography, and evoked the memory of the Nazi persecution of homosexuals as they confronted the AIDS crisis and the Christian right. In the process, they also injected into liberal America a notion of the Christian right as the new face of fascism—a notion that is far from groundless.

Stuart Marshall's piece is a particularly lucid example of the movement's effort to uncover a forgotten history of Nazi persecution, a history that had largely been overlooked, even by gay liberation in the late 1960s. Marshall asks quite directly: What can we learn from this history in the late twentieth century? Although he is critical of the use of the pink triangle by the movement, he nonetheless sees the history of Nazism as absolutely vital for understanding homophobia in the present. The essay is also crucial for anyone wishing to understand the eugenicist history behind the neo-Nazis' infamous fourteen words ("We must secure the existence of our people and a future for white children").

Stuart Marshall (1949–1993) was a British independent writer and filmmaker and a person with AIDS. His documentary work Bright Eyes, *produced by BBC's Channel Four, pushed back against dominant, pathologizing representations of people with AIDS—the disease that later claimed his life. The piece below was first published in a collection of essays by the now-defunct Bay Press in Seattle.*

In 1983 I made a proposal to Channel Four Television in England for a program about media representation of AIDS. At that time, only two television documentaries about AIDS had been broadcast on British television. Although these demonstrated an emerging televisual agenda, I decided to confine myself to the horrific printed journalism about AIDS that had begun to dominate British tabloids. The upshot of this proposal and the subsequent research was the videotape *Bright Eyes* (1984), in which I sought to deconstruct the journalistic representations to reveal their historical determinations. Stated concisely, the point I wanted to make was that the historical construction of homosexual identity as an inherently pathological subjectivity formed the powerful subtext of contemporary journalistic representations of AIDS as "the gay plague." According to this subtext, if homosexuality was a diseased form of subjectivity, then it was inevitable that this condition would eventually reveal itself in a medically identifiable form of morbidity . . .

What, then, are the possible relationships between a presentation of the worst kind of tabloid AIDS journalism and a partial history of the demise of the German homosexual rights movement? There is a strong clue to this when the Hirschfeld character [in *Bright Eyes*] describes an anti-homosexual media smear campaign that was conducted by the French and Italian press in the 1910s in the attempt to discredit Kaiser Wilhelm II . . . The sequence registered my fears that the international lesbian and gay rights movement might suffer a fate in the 1980s similar to the eventual demise of the German movement in the 1930s, when it was totally destroyed by the Nazis.

There were other relationships as well. At that time in Britain, the right was demanding that people with AIDS (PWAs) be quarantined, a demand that evoked the specter of condemning social undesirables to the concentration camps. My intention at that time, however, was not to draw a parallel between the AIDS epidemic and the Holocaust—a point to which I will return in greater detail.

Several years after completing *Bright Eyes*, I submitted a proposal to Channel Four Television for *Desire* (1988), a film about the experiences of lesbians and gay men under National Socialism. My reasons for proposing this project were complex. On a personal level, I felt I was not done with this subject, or rather it was not done with me. On a political and intellectual level, I thought it was necessary to examine the particular period of history that has provided the gay rights movement with potent symbols—the pink and, more recently, the black triangles—symbols with which, in Europe and North America at least, we have often represented our common movement for liberation. The symbols of the Nazi persecution of homosexuals have been given a privileged status in contemporary gay politics since the late 1970s. I wanted to discover some of the historical facts—if you will excuse me such a positivist endeavor—that lay behind the use of these symbols in contemporary political discourse. It seemed necessary to confront the fact that although these pink and black triangles had become such a common form of self-identification within the gay and lesbian communities, they had extracted from a specific historical and political conjuncture that lay outside the life span and therefore beyond the memory of the contemporary generation of gay activists. Furthermore, this history, precisely because it was gay history, had not been documented in a form accessible to the kind of analysis that could usefully inform contemporary political practice. My goal, therefore, was to lay out this history in such a way that it could resonate with our contemporary experience.

I was curious as to why the pink triangle had been taken up by the gay movement at a time of its greatest optimism for the future of lesbian and gay civil rights. Other symbols, such as the butterfly and the lambda, had been considered as well, but had never found widespread popularity. I had never felt comfortable about the use of the pink triangle in contemporary gay politics. After all, this symbol represented the limit point, the inconceivable and unspeakable possibility of annihilation. I wanted to know why such a horrific symbol had gained currency for representing our commonality, our hopes, our struggles, our belief in a better future. I wanted to tease out the political meanings and effects of using for affirmative group identification an image that was once so cruelly used to stigmatize gay men in the Nazi death mills.

During the filming of *Desire*, I began to acknowledge a repressed agenda, which became painfully clear to me in the course of conducting one particular interview. While making the film, I met some extraordinary elderly lesbians and gay men who thrilled me with their dignity and courage. One man, Gert Weymann, who survived this period as an active gay man, ended his harrowing account of persecution by saying, "It was very hard then, but it was easier to survive Nazism than it is to survive AIDS." Suddenly part of my investment in this project was made clear to me. It was the pressing need to discover for myself, in the context of the AIDS crisis, what it was like to survive that limit point, that inconceivable experience of terrifying persecution. What price was paid? What were the strategies of survival? How deep were the scars? Who lived and who died, and why? . . .

A simple example of the problem [of historical memory] relates to the AIDS activist group ACT UP's use of the pink triangle (albeit ironically inverted) in conjunction with the legend "SILENCE = DEATH." Herr Weymann told a very different story. According to him, the only way to avoid the concentration camps and death was precisely to remain silent. Those lesbians and gay men who lived to tell their tales survived by subterfuge, self-concealment, and secrecy. Both his testimony and the testimony of another gay man, who was tortured by the Gestapo in its attempt to gain a confession of homosexual activities and the names of homosexual partners, demonstrated that at that time the equation would have been "SILENCE = SURVIVAL."

It might be argued that my objection is nothing more than an academic one to the powerful rhetorical deployment of a potent symbol to galvanize a community and express its fears of annihilation. Such an argument is encapsulated in the slogan "Never again." It is my contention, however, that we must examine this period of gay history to determine whether the analogy holds, and if so, what possible lessons and survival strategies can be learned. The analogy proceeds from a commonly held belief that the Nazi treatment of homosexuals was a form of *genocide*—the annihilation of a *race*—and thus comparable to the Nazi treatment of Jews and Gypsies. Furthermore, the analogy equates the Nazi state's extermination of homosexuals and the contemporary liberal democratic state's treatment of PWAs. It can, of course, be argued that the juxtaposition of the legend "SILENCE = DEATH" and the pink triangle can produce meaning on a number of different levels, and it is clear that the inversion of the pink triangle is intended to skew its meaning. But even though the meaning of the pink triangle has been changed by its use in the context of the gay liberation movement, it is apparent that among AIDS activists a contemporary perception of its earlier historical meaning is being called upon to produce a specific ideological effect. This intended effect is the evocation of a "memory" of mass extermination.

I hope that the following remarks will not be construed as an attack upon the dynamism, the energy, the political importance, and the successes of the AIDS activist movement in general, or of ACT UP in particular. I offer them simply as a series of reflections.

Returning briefly to my earlier comments on *Bright Eyes*, I would like to restate a commonplace observation of social constructionist theory. The contemporary homosexual identity was first formulated in the late 1860s by European medics intent on extending their purview, their domain of professionalism, and their arena of social power by increasingly medicalizing aspects of human behavior that had previously been supervised by the church. This medicalization of homosexuality—a transition from notions of sin within ecclesiastical law to notions of sickness and deviancy within criminal law—is part of a general process of the medicalization of deviancy that was to result in a proliferation of new social identities, a whole new species of human beings. The new characters to be added to the social drama were, among others, the prostitute, the criminal, the mentally enfeebled, and the drunkard. Within the realm of sexual deviancy, the process of categorization was to become so refined that by the end of the nineteenth century, sexologists such as Havelock Ellis and Krafft-Ebing were to describe literally dozens of sexual types, all of which were absolutely characterized by sexual proclivities. It is important to note that this process constructs and categorizes not only the deviant but the norm itself . . .

Nineteenth-century criminal anthropologists, sexologists, and medics attempted to categorize and classify social deviancy by using models that vacillate between notions of personal identity, physiological specificity, racial characteristics, psychological complexes, subclasses of the population, genetic predispositions, and patterns of criminal behavior . . .

Running through discourses of physiognomy and social categorization is the notion of racial similarity. In the case of [English eugenicist Francis] Galton, there are a number of photographic studies of "the Jewish type," for example. It is important to note the broader social backdrop to this scientific behavior was the expansion of European imperialism. There is a complex and self-validating interrelationship between attempts to categorize, control, and regulate the colonized subjects of imperialism "abroad" and the potentially rebellious, politically seditious subjects of the social underclass "at home." . . . Attempts to describe social differences by the use of racial analogies do not absolutely characterize all work of this kind, but they do form a dominant discourse that was eventually to be rationalized as the discourse of eugenics. Hence the physiology of social deviancy was profoundly inflected by a racial understanding of social groupings, behaviors, and demographic patterns.

Foucault has noted that attempts to control and categorize deviant social behavior through the construction of a deviant identity also open up the possibility of a reverse discourse, a political struggle, based upon and made possible by the construction of the deviant identity. Thus the nineteenth-century German homosexual rights movement proceeded from the new notion of a homogenous homosexual identity, but contested the social persecution of individuals characterized by this identity. Magnus Hirschfeld, the leader of the liberal-left wing of the German homosexual rights movement, was very much a man of his time. As a physician and sexologist his struggle for equal rights for homosexuals was based on an absolute acceptance of the medical science of his day. But Hirschfeld made use of a contradiction internal to the discourse of deviancy in order to construct a reverse discourse of resistance to the process of social stigmatization . . .

Hirschfeld employed the notion of the "naturalness" of nature in order to argue that if the homosexual was constitutionally homosexual then he was only doing what came "naturally," and therefore he should not be discriminated against for being true to "his nature." . . .

By Hirschfeld's time, it is evident that a separate homosexual identity had been constructed and that this was an essential aspect of homosexual subculture and self-acknowledgment. This is clearly obvious in the right-wing German homosexual rights movement, which saw itself as a movement of a particular and special people and which adopted the name Gemeinschaft der Eigenen (community of the special).

Though this reverse discourse of struggle has provided gay men and lesbians with a variety of political possibilities, ranging from Hirschfeld's liberal movement of the beginning of the century to the 1970s gay liberation movement (whose name also reflects the influence of Third World Marxist liberation struggles of the same period), we are still employing a problematic agenda of sexual identity and community, an inherited agenda that determines the very terms of our self-recognition and our discourse of contestation. Perhaps the most problematic aspect of this agenda is the nature of our own community, how we define ourselves *as* a community. Precisely because the nineteenth-century discourse slid between conceptions of race, community, subculture, underclass, and criminal conspiracy, we have inherited imprecise and sometimes mutually contradictory options to conceptualize our society.

It is precisely this problem that Nazism set out to address in its attempts to eradicate homosexuality. In order to produce a range of regulatory strategies toward homosexuality, Nazism made use of a variety of *understandings* of our society and our individual appearances, understandings that reflect the numerous conceptualizations of homosexual identity and homosexual society available within scientific discourse at the time. To understand the complexity and sophistication of the Nazi position, it is essential to comprehend the particular form of racial eugenics developed by Nazi scientists and the Nazi state.

It is clear that eugenics had many different faces, including, for example, the arguments put forward by the British birth control movement's struggle for women's reproductive rights. In this case, the eugenic argument for the need to control and develop racial purity and strength was deployed in a form that gave individual women the right to choose motherhood. The fascist development of eugenics, however, denied women control of reproduction and lodged all power in the state, supported by legal and penal power structures. In this case the purification of the race not only depended upon the absolute extermination of those other "races" to be found "like a disease within the social body"— the Jews and the Gypsies—but also required the imposition upon all "true Aryans" of a duty to reproduce prolifically.

It is often stated that abortion and contraception were outlawed by the Nazi state, but this is only partly true. In 1943, after three years of preparation, a law was indeed introduced for the "Protection of Marriage, Family, and Motherhood," calling for the death penalty, "in extreme cases," for carrying out or aiding abortions. However, this legislation covered only the abortion of an "Aryan" fetus. In fact, in June 1935, aborting "defective pregnancies" on grounds of race hygiene, which was already in practice, had been legalized. For Jewish women, or Aryan women who were pregnant by a Polish worker, for example, abortion was then required by law. In July 1933, the cabinet, led by Hitler, had passed the "Law for the Prevention of Hereditarily Diseased Offspring," which was used to limit the propagation of "lives unworthy of life." Paragraph 12 of this law allowed the use of force against those who did not consent to being sterilized. This law was used to deny reproductive rights to "Aryans" who were criminal, disabled, or mentally disturbed (and eventually the long-term unemployed and the work-shy). Also in 1935, a law against "habitual delinquents" legalized castration of men in specific cases. This was extended to women in the form of ovariectomy and sterilization by X-ray in 1936. Only after having experienced three cesarean births was a woman entitled to an abortion, and then only on condition that she accepted sterilization. Between 1934 and 1937, about eighty men and four hundred women died in course of sterilization. Furthermore, hundreds of thousands of Jewish women who entered the extermination camps but were not sent immediately to the gas chamber were forcibly sterilized by X-ray. Many of them were unaware of the meaning of the "treatment" they were being given.

The eugenic control of the population was therefore twofold. On the one hand, it required genocide—the mass extermination of the Jews and the Gypsies, and forced sterilization for those who would be used as labor but not allowed to reproduce. On the other hand, for Aryan women there was an enormous social pressure to have as many children as possible, and this demand frequently contradicted the official Nazi position on the sanctity of the family. Pregnancy outside marriage was to some extent sanctioned, and the notorious Lebensborn institutions were set up to provide illegitimate mothers with social support when they were rejected by their families. It is well known that Lebensborn were to come into their own when privileged young SS officers fulfilled the demands of the chief of the SS, Heinrich Himmler, that every good SS officer should father at least three children. "If both parents are pure Aryans," Himmler stated, "illegitimate children should be accepted with as much joy as legitimate offspring."

It is true that Himmler, when speaking about homosexuals, frequently employed racial eugenic analogies: for example, "We must exterminate these people root and branch." He also described homosexuals as "symptoms of dying races" and conjured up an image of an early, pure Teutonic race that drowned homosexuals in bogs. But this is nothing more than political rhetoric appealing to the discourse of racial purity already in place. No real parallel can be drawn between the extermination of Jews in the Final Solution and the extermination of homosexuals. The extermination of Jews was conceived by the Nazis precisely as the extermination of a "race," which unless sterilized and gassed would continue to propagate its putative racial characteristics. The problem with homosexuals, as far as the Third Reich was concerned, was the fact that they supposedly did *not* reproduce. In this sense, they did not propagate themselves or their "race." Hence this remark, from the speech of Himmler's just quoted: "Just think how many children will never be born because of this." According to Rudolf Diels, the founder of the Gestapo, Hitler "lectured me on the role of homosexuality in history and politics. It eliminated from the reproductive process those very men on whose offspring a nation depended." First and most important, then, homosexual men were not available for the propagation of the Aryan race. From this perspective, we can see that the regulation of homosexuality was understood as part of eugenic politics only by way of reproductive politics. On October 26, 1936, Himmler established the Central Agency for Jointly Combating Abortion and Homosexuality. It was headed by SS Captain Josef Meisinger, whose previous job had been administering the redistribution of property confiscated from Jews.

But this is not the full story. Whereas it is clear that the Nazis saw homosexuals as constitutionally deviant, they also simultaneously made use of a much more modern theory of homosexuality, a theory not of racial or even sexual identity, but rather a theory of sexual desire. Homosexuality as a non-identity-specific desire was frequently represented by disease analogies. For example, again from the same speech by Himmler: "Just think how a people can be broken in nerve and spirit when such a plague gets hold of it." Or Hitler: "Once rife, it extended its contagious effects like an ineluctable law of nature to the best and most manly of characters." As I said, there is a long Western European sociological tradition that describes the effects of homosexuality as a moral contagion. This is not specific to Germany, but its manifestation there was more complex. For Hitler, paradoxically it would seem, it is the best and most manly of characters who are vulnerable to the disease of homosexual desire. Homosexuality is therefore made to bear a historical anxiety in German culture about masculinity, femininity, and the nature of friendship. The anxiety may be couched in the language of disease and contagion, but this language simply covers over a contradiction fundamental to Nazi attitudes toward masculinity.

The Nazis appropriated a history of male friendship popularized in eighteenth-century literary society that included the open display of affection as well as the writing of what can best be described as love letters. From the Napoleonic Wars to the First World War, romantic friendship was politicized into comradeship—the mutual bonding of men in the service of the state. This is the origin of the *Männerbund*, or "male bonding," which was to form such a powerful ideology in German culture. The Nazis aestheticized and eroticized the Männerbund as part and parcel of their overvaluation of the masculine fighting man. They produced endless representations of male beauty for the populace to identify with or to idealize, most notably through their official art, which made frequent references to Hellenic Greek art and culture (a fascination of right-wing German cultural commentators).

The overvaluation of masculinity carried within it, however, the possibility not just of identification but also of object choice. It is absolutely clear that the German language of male comradeship was shot through with homoeroticism. In German philosophy and culture, eroticism connoted a desexualized relationship; it was about a cosmological love relation and not about sexual desire. But homoeroticism can easily become transmuted into homosexual desire, and this was the root of the Nazis' problem. Homosexual desire radically challenged the fixed relationships between the sexes fantasized by the Nazi state as an absolute difference between the maternal, reproductive desire of the woman and the domineering, active desire of the man. As Himmler stated, "It would be a catastrophe if we foolish males wanted to make women into logically thinking instruments . . . If we try to masculinize them, well, there we conjure up the danger of homosexuality." "If a man just looks at a girl in America, he can be forced to marry her or pay damages . . . therefore men protect themselves in the USA by turning to homosexuals . . . Women in the USA are like battle axes—they hack away at the males."

The recognition that the finest fighting men of the German nation might be open to the influences of homosexual desire produced a violent paranoia about homosexuality in the Third Reich. The Nazis promoted all-male organizations, which were constantly open to accusations of homosexual perversion. From very early on, the Hitler Youth was commonly referred to as the "Homo Youth." . . .

This fear had existed among the Nazis for some time. In 1928, Adolf Brand of the Gemeinschaft der Eigenen canvassed all German political parties for their views on the reform of Paragraph 175, the law that made homosexuality a criminal offense. The Nazi Party replied as follows:

It is not necessary that you and I live, but it is necessary that the German people live. And it can only live if it can fight, for life means fighting. And it can only fight if it retains its masculinity. And it can only retain its masculinity if it exercises discipline, especially in matters of love. Free love and deviance are undisciplined. Therefore we reject you, as we reject anything which hurts our people. Anyone who even thinks of homosexual love is our enemy.

It is this focus of paranoia about the possible promotion of homosexuality among the members of the leading male Nazi organizations that explains the lack of uniformity in the Nazi persecution of homosexual men. In the SS—the most prestigious Nazi organization—homosexual offenses were punishable by death. There was no trial; the individuals involved were immediately executed. In the army, homosexuality was dealt with slightly more leniently. In civil society, the due processes of law were meticulously used, followed by imprisonment. In the early days of the regime, only habitual offenders were sent to the concentration camps. Second offenders were sometimes punished by castration. As Himmler gained power, however, he used the so-called *Schutzhaft*, or "protective custody," to enable the police to rearrest homosexuals after their release from prison and specified that they should be sent to Level Three camps—the death mills: "After serving the sentence imposed by the court, they will, upon my instructions, be taken to a concentration camp and there shot while trying to escape." . . .

Professor Rüdiger Lautmann of Bremen University has established from official records that between 5,000 and 15,000 homosexual men were sent to concentration camps. In the period of the Third Reich, 50,000 men were sentenced for homosexual offenses by the courts. It is therefore clear that only a minority of convicted homosexuals, all of whom must have been known to the Gestapo, were sent to concentration camps. This information has been available since the late 1970s. In 1985 the German gay historian Manfred Herzer stated that a description of the life of homosexual men in the Nazi state was not exhausted with their unspeakable suffering in concentration camps. In fact, some homosexual men who survived the period reminisced about the brown dictatorship as the "happiest time of their lives." This is incompatible with the usual clichés "according to which the unimaginably demonic Nazis launched an entirely unique and unparalleled holocaust against gays in which the pink triangle was to have even more horrible connotations than the yellow star."

Herzer's observation takes me back to my original question about the use of the pink triangle in contemporary gay politics. Why did this symbol [that] represented only the extreme point of the Nazi regulation of homosexuality gain currency to represent gay people's commonality, our hopes, our struggles, and our belief in a better future? The answer to this question may be revealed in the very terms I have just used to ask this question. I think there is, and always has been, a fundamental problem about the status of the word *our* in this formulation. In what way are we a "we"? What is the common denominator of our putative community? . . .

From the very beginning of the homosexual rights movement, there has been a very real problem, not only from a theoretical but also from an organizational point of view, about the roots of our commonality. Nothing anchors our bonding other than our sexual desires. We come from different classes, different ethnic backgrounds, different genders, and different positions of social privilege. The sexual liberationists and libertines of the 1970s saw sexual desire as a great leveler of these differences. Many gay male theorists argued that at the level of organs connecting with organs, social, racial, and class differences were erased. The bathhouse was seen as the privileged site of this collapse of difference, the place where democracy of desire reigned supreme. In the world outside, however, these differences returned. These problems are not, of course, specific to the lesbian and gay movements. After the heady heyday of "sisterhood," second-wave feminism was riven with questions of class and racial difference.

For gay people in the 1970s, then, the mistaken belief that homosexuals had been massively exterminated as a group by the Third Reich filled an enormous gap. This mythical genocide of homosexuals provided us with a group identity similar to that of the Jews. The pink triangle expressed our commonality as victims; we could recognize our community through the eyes of our Nazi persecutors. How potent, then, the use of the pink triangle in the midst of a health crisis that represents, in our worst fears, the annihilation of our community. Hasn't history repeated itself? Have we not found ourselves again faced by the genocidal actions of a fascist state?

Every political movement requires its points of imaginary identification. Using the term in the sense given it by Jacques Lacan, the *imaginary* is a necessary fiction that is required not only for the construction of the subject as distinct from an external world of objects, but also in order for any political rallying and action to take place. It would be naive to suggest that an effective political movement could be based entirely upon the recognition of difference. A passionate identification of similarity is an absolute necessity. This political identification does not and cannot exhaust our subjectivities . . . The very use of the word *gay* has been an effective means of insisting upon the complexity of subjectivities over and above the reductive notion of identity implicit in the term *homosexual*. AIDS education campaigns that target gay men have had to address these issues on a day-to-day basis. They recognize that there is no singular gay community and that many of the men who most urgently need to be reached are those who do not identify as gay and who do not participate in gay subcultures.

I believe that problems arise when we [reactivate] the horrifically stigmatizing pink triangle in order to reunite our political struggles against AIDS around the central figure of the victim of the fascist state. Clearly the fact that this symbol is being used in the context of an angry and powerful political movement shows that certain paradoxes are consciously being used. But this grounding symbol, which has already been used historically to unite gay people around the idea of a group experience of persecution, is now being reinvested with an intensified experience of victimization horribly linked to questions of survival, of life and death. It seems entirely inappropriate to me to compare the complex and sometimes murderous actions of a fascist state toward homosexuals to the contemporary response of a supposedly liberal democracy to a health crisis in a number of populations it actively discriminates against. But more important, lost in the analogy are all those aspects of difference and subjectivity that identity politics subordinates and suppresses precisely to ensure political solidarity and action. This has, on a subtle level, far-reaching and possibly reactionary consequences.

What PWAs have in common with homosexuals at the time of the Third Reich is not the status of concentration camp victim. Rather it is being a recruit within the complex and contradictory regime concerning the state's regulation of desire by means of moral, legal, and ideological manipulation of a society's anxieties about sex and deviancy. The parallel is to be found in the positive and negative pressures to conform to a politically defined imaginary moral norm, and the construction of the hierarchy of susceptibilities, vulnerabilities, predilections, and fears of reprisal used by Nazism to construct different levels of disposability within a population. It should not be forgotten that the system of colored triangles was used by the Nazis to construct a hierarchy of differences within the enclosed society of the concentration camp. This system not only allowed the Nazis instantly to determine the disposability of a prisoner, but also produced a consciousness of divisions among the prisoners themselves, which, by working on preexisting social, religious, and racial differences, set the inmates against each other in a world of dog-eat-dog.

AIDS has resulted in the regulation of desire throughout the entire population. We cannot understand this if we focus on genocide metaphors. People with AIDS are not of a piece. The simplest division of this population into guilty and innocent victims within dominant regimes of representation shows how contemporary society itself constructs and capitalizes upon differences. It is for this reason that I have difficulties with the notion of a singular AIDS community. Although this notion may be an important imaginary point of identification for political struggle, it cannot account for the different experiences of AIDS even within New York City . . .

I am utterly convinced of the appropriateness of the legend "SILENCE = DEATH," but I am unconvinced about anchoring this equation to the pink triangle. The powerful message contained in the slogan is the necessity of representation, but the use of the pink triangle immobilizes representation by locking it into an agenda of victimization and annihilation . . .

There is a pressing need for a range of representations of AIDS. We need to find languages and images that begin to approach the complex and contradictory reality of AIDS. I don't believe this language can be homogenous and consistent. By necessity it must be polysemic, multiple, and perhaps, when it speaks about difference, contradictory. I would like to suggest that the most useful, confirming and productive forms of representation for us to develop will be those that help us understand and respect our differences while at the same time suggesting a multiplicity of mutually supportive political and cultural strategies. Although the political issues of AIDS are of enormous immediate concern to the gay communities, they can also fruitfully be linked to far-wider political struggles around the politics of health care as they affect many other sectors of the population.

Anti-Racist Action,
Anti-Racist Action Primer,
1999

The logo of Anti-Racist Action.

Founded in 1987, Anti-Racist Action (ARA) was in many ways the first "antifa" organization in the United States. That is to say, it was a radical movement rooted in anarchist and punk subcultures that emphasized direct, public confrontation with the extreme right (though it never limited itself to physical confrontation). The ARA began in a Minneapolis pizza parlor when the Baldies—a multiracial crew of anti-racist skinheads— decided to confront a local group of neo-Nazis who were terrorizing African Americans and leftists. They were aware of the newly revived Anti-Fascist Action in Europe but, according to historian Mark Bray, decided to call themselves "Anti-Racist Action" because they thought the word fascism *sounded dogmatic and leftist in an American context. The early group was most immediately concerned with rooting white suprema- cists out of the punk rock scene, but they also organized in coalition with other groups against police brutality.*

The ARA's decentralized structure was affirmed at the first Midwest Anti-Fascist Network conference in Columbus, Ohio, in 1994. In the second half of that decade, it had expanded well beyond Minneapolis and the punk scene to become a national organization with over 120 chapters and several thousand activists in the United States and Canada. Politically, it was predominately anarchist, though its members were not exclusively so.

The ARA confronted the Klan at their rallies throughout the 1990s, mostly in the Midwest. In 2002, they were part of the so-called "York riot" of York, Pennsylvania, joining local black and Latino residents of a neighborhood where the white supremacist World Church of the Creator decided to hold an event. In the melee that ensued, twenty-five people were arrested.

The ARA had largely fizzled out by 2013, but it laid the groundwork for similar antifa organizations in the United States. The still-active Hoosier Anti-Racist Movement (HARM) in Indiana, for example, was formed along ARA lines, including its "Four Points of Unity."

What Is ARA?

Anti-Racist Action is a network of organizations that fight against Nazi, fascist, KKK, racist skinhead, white supremacist, "Christian Identity," patriot militia, religious right, anti-immigrant, and institutional racism.

ARA is the North American counterpart to the European Anti-Fascist Action (Antifa) movement. ARA chapters are organizing across the United States and in Canada.

ARA organizes against racism, sexism, homophobia, anti-immigrant and anti-Semitic bigotry.

ARA confronts white supremacists, fascists, the religious right and other bigots when they try to organize in our communities. EVERY TIME they come out, we want to be there.

ARA fights institutional racism by cops who want to criminalize young people because of their skin color and the way they dress, the military who target colored and low-income neighborhoods with deceptive promises in order to recruit them into being mercenaries for the New World Order, and the government, which wants to demonize people of color and immigrants as being responsible for the nation's problems.

ARA educates people about racism with information tables at schools, community events and music shows. We publish newsletters that expose racism and racist activities in our communities and discuss ways to fight racism. ARA speakers have spoken about fighting racism at colleges, high schools and community groups.

ARA works with other anti-racist groups in the community to educate and organize against racism.

ARA wants to build a society based on social equality, mutual respect and community cooperation, where people are judged by their character and work together to make things better for everybody.

ARA is a grassroots organization made up of ordinary people from our communities. We are multiracial and multicultural.

ARA is anti-authoritarian. We are a federation of democratic, locally autonomous groups that are free to create solutions to the problems of bigotry and discrimination in their community BY WHATEVER MEANS NECESSARY.

. . .

ARA Today

Today, ARA is composed of over 120 chapters in the United States and Canada. Many chapters are very different from each other, but they are all united around four common principles. These points of unity are:

1. Wherever they go, we go to shut them down.
This means that we believe that the best way to stop white supremacists from organizing is to counter their ideas directly in public. Same-
time-same-place mobilizations make it extremely difficult for the
Klan to rally and for Neo-Nazi skinheads to hold concerts. It shows
people who are curious about white supremacy just how unpopular
an idea it is. Most importantly, it thrusts the problem directly into the
public eye so that everyone knows that terrorists are trying to organize in their community. We do not believe that they will go away if
they are ignored. People ignored Hitler, and the results of that policy
are permanently etched upon the soul of humanity.

2. We don't rely on the cops or the courts.
That doesn't mean that we never go to court or work with the police.
What it means is that we recognize that it is the job of ordinary people
to fight fascism in their community. The police and the courts cannot
legislate away fascism. In some areas, police departments are infil-
trated by white supremacists and the courts are biased. We feel that it
is up to us to stop racist terror. Our reliance on ourselves to defend
ourselves is our bottom line.

3. We defend and support all other antifascists.
An attack on any one of us is an attack on us all. We are committed to
helping defend all people who are fighting against oppression despite
whatever political differences we may have. It is important to have
unity between all people and all struggles. We must stand united.

This support can take many forms. It may be a long campaign
around a series of court battles or may be practical direct support in
the streets. We may be struggling to free a political prisoner or working against police repression of other social justice activists, but the
net policy is the same. We will support anyone working to make the
world better that comes under attack, no matter who they come under
attack from.

*4. We are active with the goal of building a movement against racism,
sexism, homophobia and discrimination against the differently abled,
the oldest, the youngest and the most vulnerable of our society. We fight
for reproductive freedom for women. We intend to win!*

ARA believes that all forms of oppression are intertwined and linked. We believe that they all must be fought in order for a just society to exist. We believe that steady, constant struggle on all these fronts is the proper way to conduct a movement for social justice. Additionally, many ARA chapters have added additional points of unity that are specific and meaningful to their local political work. Since our chapters are all autonomous, we encourage them to develop political programs as they see fit, so long as they continue to adhere to the four basic points.

ARA often works closely in conjunction with other direct action–oriented youth organizations, like Refuse and Resist on the campaign to free Mumia Abu-Jamal. We work closely with Food Not Bombs on the fight against hunger and with Earth First! on direct action environmental campaigns. Because all struggles are interconnected and all these groups are youth oriented, there is crossover and cooperation between them and us on a practical level.

ARA continues to make plans for the future. We will soon be releasing a CD featuring many prominent punk, ska and hardcore [illegible] . . . The CD will include a one-hundred-page booklet on ARA and what you can do to fight fascism. There will be eighteen songs from various acts as well as spoken word pieces and cool vintage movie samples.

Our campaigns to rid certain metropolitan areas of white supremacist organizing continues. We are planning to continue our campaign against the Nazi record label Resistance in Detroit, Michigan, and Windsor, Ontario. Our march and rally in Las Vegas is the beginning of our campaign to free that city of the grip of over 300 hardcore neo-Nazis who are active in violent crime and recruiting and support for the racist movement as a whole. This program will include a diligent effort to force the closure of a Nazi-owned and -operated tattoo parlor, and direct action against key fascist organizers.

Wherever fascism shows its face . . . ARA is on the prowl.

Sam Miller, "Lipstick Fascism,"
Jacobin, April 4, 2017

*Attention to the hypermasculinity, misogyny and sexism of fascist move-
ments has tended to sideline analysis of the role of women in them. Sam
Miller, a New York City–based teacher and left columnist, makes no such
mistake in this essay, first published in* Jacobin. *She argues that white
nationalist and YouTube personality Lana Lokteff has parlayed and recycled classical fascist themes—including the German slogan "Kinder,
Küche, Kirche" (children, kitchen, church)—to become the leading
female voice of the US alt-right. Miller here diagnoses Lokteff's toxic
assemblage of reactionary anti-feminism, racism, Islamophobia, anti-
Semitism and nationalism as a blend of eugenicist romance and male
imitation. Lokteff, who desperately wants to be "one of the boys" of the alt-
right, turns the "fashy" fashion statements of storm troopers into an
aesthetic of feminine mystique: real women stay home and shine jackboots.
Significantly, Miller notes, Lokteff has used media—especially radio—to
propagate her messages across the United States. "Lipstick fascism," for
Miller, is both a style of white supremacy and the name for a pageant of
female reaction where women "lean in" and embrace histories of genocide,
extermination and violent chauvinism.*

*Sam Miller is a school teacher and journalist who regularly contributes
to* Jacobin *magazine and works in Manhattan.*

Anytime they [the left] talk about the alt-right, they make it sound
like it's just about a bunch of guys in basements. They don't mention

that these guys have wives—supportive wives, who go to these meet-ups and these conferences—who are there—so I think it's great for right-wing women to show themselves. We are here. You're wrong.

—Lana Lokteff, cohost of *Red Ice TV*

When we imagine the alt-right insurgency, we likely envision an army of Richard Spencers: angry white men with fashy haircuts marching under the banner of Pepe the Frog.[1] But this image leaves out a sizable and increasingly vocal segment of extremist right politics: women.

Like their male counterparts, these white nationalist and neofascist women reject what they call the "domination of cultural Marxism," portraying leftists as the children of Karl Marx and Lena Dunham, trying to turn the United States into an anti-white cesspool run by Jewish interests that promote race mixing, feminism, and hedonism.

These alt-right women put a feminine spin on the movement's patri-archal and xenophobic rhetoric by emphasizing traditional gender roles and old-fashioned ideals of beauty. They promote the mid-century nuclear family, dreaming of emulating Obergruppenführer John Smith's all-white, American Nazi family on the science fiction show *The Man in the High Castle*.

In this, the alt-right seeks to naturalize what is not only oppressive but also conventional, reminding us that, as shocking as its recent explosion onto the political landscape has been, their ideology is largely recycled.

Make Patriarchy Great Again

Lana Lokteff is the most prominent woman on the alt-right. Of Russian American ancestry, she claims that her family fled "Bolshevism" in Eastern Europe and moved to China, where her father was born. Raised in the American Northwest, she adopted libertarian and anarchist posi-tions before converting to white nationalism.

---

1   "Pepe the Frog" is an animated cartoon frog first created by cartoonist Matt Furie in 2005. The frog initially had no distinguishing political features. Around 2015, the US alt-right movement adopted "Pepe" as a symbol. The animated frog began to appear in Nazi uniforms uttering Anti-Semitic slogans like "Kill Jews, Man." It appeared on the neo-Nazi website *Daily Stormer* until the artist Furie brought legal action and had it removed from the site.

Lokteff cohosts a white nationalist talk show with her husband, Henrik Palmgren. Hailed as the "CNN of the alt-right," *Red Ice* happens to be headquartered in Sweden, where a fair number of alt-right leaders come from. The couple devotes their program to exposing the "cultural Marxist" agenda, which they define as a "metapolitical struggle" of academic and cultural elites meant to subvert white civilization in favor of multiculturalism.

The alt-right woman reduces feminism to the "crazy radical left-wing stuff that we see coming out of Hollywood." She believes that feminist women trample over men to feel important. She thinks that feminism has permeated culture from television to academia, turning all the material taught in schools into crypto-Marxist propaganda. This explains why the most vehement right-wing women support homeschooling and oppose public education.

Lokteff finds feminism to be ultimately self-centered because it focuses on a woman's autonomy instead of the family. The suffrage movement started this trend by transferring the "one vote per family" model to "one vote per woman." Husbands and wives were supposed to vote together, and giving each woman the right to vote stripped the nuclear family of its important function in society, she says. It created divisions from the start, paving the way for single-parent households run by "trashy, drug-abusing" women. The days when the man of the house was the breadwinner and the mother the dutiful wife, pumping out football fields of children, disappeared. Women on the alt-right emphasize the need to rebuild tight-knit, heteronormative white families with traditional values and gender roles.

This kind of family structure entails a natural hierarchy: though, as Lokteff admits, women ultimately decide if the race will continue, they are in fact auxiliary and must accept their inferiority to men. Once you believe that men are born as the dominant sex, then patriarchy becomes natural, normalized, even necessary: inferior women should be "taken care of" by men—a euphemism for subordination.

European men are portrayed as naturally intelligent and strong protectors who build civilizations and provide for their families. Lokteff believes that all women are attracted to masculine strength and valor and should accept their role as the bearer and supporter of children. Indeed, having children *is a must*. If they want their right-wing legacy to live on, white women must get married early and have a big family.

Daniel Friberg—CEO of AltRight.com and one of Lokteff and Palmgren's political collaborators—echoes this advice in his handbook for fascist activists, *The Real Right Returns*. Friberg agrees that the myth of equality between the sexes harms both men and women—especially those men forced to compete with women on the job market.

He argues that there are "fundamental differences" between men and women that cannot be eradicated by "cultural Marxist" propaganda, one of which is women's essentially apolitical stance. Feminism represents the only exception, but for Friberg, "that is the exception that proves the rule." It therefore makes sense that women on the right are underrepresented, because they belong in the home. Women should never make the mistake of trying to act like men, or appropriate their masculine characteristics.

But Lokteff adds something to Friberg's strict demarcation between the sexes. She believes that alt-right women, while internalizing their subordination, can use their femininity to subvert the left. On one episode of [conservative podcast] *Virtue of the West*, Lokteff argues that because a female speaker "doesn't want to dominate anyone physically," she can get away with "a lot more verbally."

Immigration as "White Genocide"

Charges of racism no longer hurt Lokteff. Instead, she says, "I've been called so many names that it actually energizes me now, because I can just treat [critics] like my footstool, step on them and laugh." Her segments on *Red Ice* are filled with invectives against multiculturalism, immigrants, and especially Muslims, who she demagogically scape-goats. She falsely claims that refugees are responsible for a rise in crime across Europe, depicting them as "lazy bums, packing the welfare offices, who flock in for the incentives."

She calls Muslim immigrants "incoming invaders" with no respect for white women. Against this alleged threat, Lokteff tells women to prepare for a race war: "These people risk their lives trying to come to the countries that men built for us. We must be ready to go to battle." She asks: "Has mass immigration by non-Europeans made Sweden a better place with safer streets and more opportunities? The answer is so obvi-ous: it's a big fat 'no.' We offer a simple solution: European countries for European people. If you don't like us, get out."

These sentiments, unfortunately recently echoed by the Dutch prime minister, are hallmarks of the insurgent European right. Lokteff frequently brings up another aspect of this rhetoric, which exaggerates incidents of migrant violence against women: "If the women who were raped got together and made their voices heard *that they were raped by migrants*, it could undo years of a massive cover-up in a matter of minutes." (emphasis added) She fails to mention that violence against refugee homes has spiked across Europe, particularly in Germany.

For Lokteff, a cultural Marxist conspiracy against white identity is driving mass immigration. Marxism's secret plan is "white genocide," enacted through open-border policies that encourage the destruction of homogenous white communities. She argues that cultural Marxism's metapolitical warfare has guilt-tripped white people into privileging non-European identities over white ones.

The alt-right, from Kevin MacDonald to Lokteff, holds that Marxism's ostensible egalitarianism masks an anti-white bias that will plunge white people into extinction. The ideal of a suburban home with a "white picket fence has been traded in for a tiny, carbon-neutral apartment in a diverse neighborhood swarmed with immigrants," says Lokteff. Cultural Marxism emasculates white men, turning them into feminized "beta males" in "skinny jeans who hold signs that say 'refugees welcome.'"

Contrary to Lokteff's racist sensationalism, the actual rate of sex crimes has been more or less unchanged since 2005, according to the Swedish Crime Survey. No legitimate link between increased reports of sex crimes and mass immigration has been discovered; rather, the definition of rape has expanded, which is the proximate cause of increased reports.

Further, according to the Swedish National Council for Crime Prevention, the majority of criminal suspects were born in Sweden and come from Swedish-born parents. The vast majority of people with foreign backgrounds have little contact with the criminal justice system. According to these surveys, most crimes have socioeconomic, rather than racial, motivations.

Of course, Lokteff can denounce these findings as part of the cultural Marxist conspiracy. Instead, she isolates incidents of rape and crime as evidence of an overall pattern that simply does not exist.

The Ugly Obsession with Beauty

According to Lokteff, three things are ingrained into a woman's head that will never disappear: beauty, family, and home. These values comprise the core of what makes white nationalism so appealing to right-wing women. In the alt-right, beauty is embraced—even obsessed over—as the primary force propelling a woman to live her best life.

This ideology has a pseudoscientific foundation. The argument goes that women are biologically wired to desire a mate who can provide her with a safe and comfortable material existence until death. The surest way to accomplish this is by appearing as physically attractive to men as possible.

In almost every single interview and speech, Lokteff stresses how "beautiful" and "attractive" the people of the alt-right are:

> They're smart, beautiful women who understand that mass immigration is not working . . . Nationalism has become the guy that everyone wants. All the girls are starting to eye the bad boy who is the nationalist . . . European nationalists and the alt-right are a very attractive, very sexy bunch. It's a eugenic process. Matches are being made left and right of beautiful couples. Now it's time to procreate.

Following Nietzsche, Lokteff and the alt-right want a transvaluation of values that will replace cultural Marxism with traditionalism. They maintain that Marxism is waging a war against truth and beauty. This argument holds that nature makes some people better than others, producing social "winners" and "losers." Now, the losers are teaming up to tear down the noble and aristocratic winners.

The alt-right believes that envy drives the entire left-wing movement. Lokteff derides feminism as "affirmative action for ugly people," arguing that leftists "push ugly, fat-positive feminists as the beauty ideal and they say it's natural for a husband to dress like a woman or have sex with another man occasionally to prove that he's not homophobic."

In his handbook, Friberg reiterates these points to valorize fascist femininity. His advice to the women of the alt-right is as follows: "Nurture your femininity. Realize that your feminine qualities are your greatest assets. Nurture and develop them. They are also your main weapon in the rather brutal competition which constitutes natural selection, and it is your primary strength in your interactions with men."

Lipstick Fascism

Lokteff's argument is a nonargument. Whether it concerns race or gender, it has no empirical backing. She claims that innocent white people are increasingly victim to heinous crimes at the hands of biologically inferior subhumans, repeating the worst Nazi-inspired propaganda. When it comes to race, she relies on gross stereotypes and scapegoating; when it comes to gender, she makes anatomy destiny. She believes that people who disconnect sex from gender are deeply confused, brainwashed by Marxist propaganda. Her views on gender essentially regurgitate the rhetoric of "*Kinder, Küche, Kirche*" (children, kitchen, church) from 1930s Germany.

Lokteff claims that she just wants to be left alone with her fellow white Europeans to live in peace, arguing that if all races had the option to live in segregation, there would be less violence in the world. Unsurprisingly, she never articulates how we might achieve such a society—but we know from history that attempts to create all-white states quickly turn to ethnic cleansing and genocide. Discounting any possibility of internationalism or integration, Lokteff and her ilk condemn humanity to a racialized Hobbesian war of all against all. Her politics resemble nothing more than zoology: the idea of humanity is liquidated, and all that is left is warring subspecies of animals.

But this is nothing new: behind Lana Lokteff's feminized politics is the same old bloated, beer-guzzling storm trooper who harbors violent male fantasies of protecting white women from the forces of "racial decadence." What was once the threat of "Jewish Bolshevism" has become the threat of "cultural Marxism." This should come as no surprise: after all, "alt" in German means "old."

Enzo Traverso, "Trump's Savage Capitalism: The Nightmare Is Real," *World Policy Journal*, vol. 34, no. 1, spring 2017

In November 2016, Donald Trump was elected president of the United States, against a backdrop of rising far-right nationalist parties in Europe and a resurgence of street-level racism and white supremacy in the United States fueled by his campaign. Before and after his election, the combination of fascist dimensions of Trump's rhetoric and persona with their relationship to new white nationalist movements posed a plausible public question: Was Trump a fascist?

While some have argued yes, Enzo Traverso (1957–) here answers no. Trump, he notes, is a businessman, not a mass leader; a television celebrity, not political ideologue. His essay provides a nuanced analysis of pitfalls of arguing for fascism through historical analogy, while positing a new term for thinking through the potential lineaments of a new fascist movement fueled by Trump: "post-fascism."

Traverso's numerous scholarly monographs on Europe's history of anti-Semitism are vital companions to this piece, as is his 2017 book Left-Wing Melancholia: Marxism, History, and Memory.

During the US presidential campaign, most opinion polls and news outlets predicted a Hillary Clinton victory. At the time, it seemed natural—inescapable, even—that Clinton, a candidate supported by Wall Street, political elites, and the media, would defeat Donald Trump, a reality TV star. When the final results came in, the triumph of an indecent, semi-fascist monster over a former secretary of state produced a vast and prolonged trauma. Prepared for a Democratic victory, many now feel thrown into a counterfactual story, like the postwar America dominated by Nazi Germany and imperial Japan in the television series *The Man in the High Castle*. The verdict was written in advance, and, as a result, the presidency of Donald J. Trump seems like a transgression of the "laws" of history. If one thinks that things should have happened differently, it is difficult to accept that this nightmare is real.

Coming from Italy, a country that experienced twenty years of Prime Minister Silvio Berlusconi—a billionaire TV tycoon, our Trump—I tend to be more blasé, though I recognize that the consequences of Trump's victory are incomparably bigger. But what the media failed to foresee was not a Trump landslide—which did not take place—but the decline of the Democratic vote. Trump received fewer votes than Clinton and fewer votes than Mitt Romney in 2012; it is the Democratic candidate's foundering—Clinton lost many millions of votes that Barack Obama won in 2008 as well as several traditionally Democratic states—that explains his victory. We are not facing the transformation of the United States into a fascist community embodied by a charismatic leader; what occurred is the rejection of the political establishment through mass abstention and a protest vote captured by a populist demagogue in a few key states. In other words, Trump signifies an upheaval at the political level, not a sudden, dramatic change in American society (as the Nazi Party did in Germany, shifting from 2.6 percent to 37.27 percent of the popular vote between the elections of 1928 and 1932).

Sketching Trumpism's resemblance to fascism involves speculation about what the latter would look like in the twenty-first century. Historical parallels allow us to draw analogies rather than homologies; we cannot simply impose the profile of Trump upon a fascist paradigm that appeared in the years between the two world wars. Trump is as far from classical fascism as Occupy Wall Street, Los Indignados, and Nuit Debout are from twentieth-century communism. Nevertheless, Trumpism and the Occupy movement represent a social, political, and even class polarity as deep as the conflict between fascism and communism nearly a century ago. This comparison seems legitimate, even if the modern-day subjects of this opposition reject the historical filiation. Unlike Senator Bernie Sanders, who professes a form of democratic socialism, Trump does not inscribe himself into a fascist tradition. His fascist inclinations can only be deduced from his acts and declarations, not from a political culture he would consciously defend.

During the electoral campaign, many observers highlighted Trump's fascist features in the pages of reputable newspapers. Last May, Robert Kagan—a neoconservative political thinker and one of the ideologues of George W. Bush's invasion of Iraq—wrote an article in the *Washington Post* titled "This Is How Fascism Comes to America." In the *New York Times*, Ross Douthat bluntly asked: "Is Donald Trump a Fascist?" and listed traits that bring him close to the fascist leaders of the 1930s: a charismatic conception of politics, authoritarianism, hatred for pluralism, radical nationalism, racism, xenophobia, misogyny, homophobia, Islamophobia, and a populist style that considers citizens only as a crowd to mesmerize, manipulate, and mislead.

In many ways, Trump does behave like a twenty-first-century fascist. Trump presents himself as a "man of action," not a thinker; he despises intellectuals and does not accept criticism; his misogyny is outrageous; he exhibits his virility with vulgarity and aggression; and he uses racism and xenophobia as propaganda weapons. He wants to expel Muslims and Latino immigrants, depicting them as terrorists and criminals; he defends the police when they kill African Americans, and, by expressing doubts about Obama's birth in the United States, he suggests that African Americans cannot be true Americans. He pretends to defend the popular classes that have been deeply affected by the economic crises of 2008 and the deindustrialization of the country—not by denouncing the main culprit, financial capitalism, but by offering them a scapegoat. His campaign reproduced features of old anti-Semitism, which defined a mythical, ethnically homogeneous national community against its enemies: the Jews. Trump took this model and enlarged the spectrum to include African Americans, Latinos, Muslims, and nonwhite immigrants.

The incredible split between urban and rural America reveals the persistence of a connection between economic crisis and xenophobia. It seems to me that, in Trump's rhetoric, his condemnations of "the establishment" reproduce the anti-Semitic cliché of a virtuous agrarian community rooted in land and tradition, opposed to an anonymous, corrupted, intellectual, and cosmopolitan metropolis. It is not that he dislikes Jewish politicians or representatives of the economic elite— today, his Islamophobia is certainly stronger than his prejudice against the Jews—but rather [that] he portrays the cities as realms of an abstract and ungraspable power generated by media, finance, and culture, which anti-Semitism codified during the past century. Of course, this portrayal does not acknowledge Trump's roots in New York, a city that epitomizes the urban landscape he renounces, nor does it hinder him from having excellent relations with Wall Street—his administration is a gathering of billionaires. The fascists and the Nazis acted similarly in the 1930s, despite vilifying the "parasitic" Jewish elite.

Trump plays the strong, captivating leader who alone is able to save the country through his exceptional, almost demiurgic, faculties. In the purest tradition of charismatic, authoritarian politics, he pretends both to represent a national community and to transcend it as its savior and redeemer. His speeches and meetings recall fascist aesthetics: one could not view the images of his aircraft landing at a rally, surrounded by a cheering crowd, without remembering the opening sequence of Leni Riefenstahl's *Triumph of the Will*, with Hitler flying over Nuremberg to join his waiting disciples at the Nazi congress. Temperamentally Trump is a "decisionist"—a leader who decides and acts without any parliamentary constraints and ignores procedural rules—though he has certainly never heard the name of Carl Schmitt, the theoretician of "decisionism." We can also suppose that many people gathering at his campaign rallies probably exhibit the marks of what Erich Fromm and Theodor W. Adorno called the "authoritarian personality"—the proclivity to submit themselves to an arbitrary, tyrannical rule—but fascism is reducible neither to the character of a political leader nor to the psychological predispositions of his followers.

The fact is, there is no fascist organization behind Trump. He does not lead a mass movement; he is a TV star. From this point of view, he is much more reminiscent of Berlusconi than Mussolini. Unlike Mussolini, he does not come from the left, and unlike Hitler, he is not a lumpen, a marginal figure who discovered politics in a society devastated by war. But like Berlusconi, he is a billionaire (or at least claims to be) whose political activities will permanently collide with his private business. Thus, he would never think to lead a march of black and brown shirts on Washington, simply because he couldn't; there are no sizable organized groups behind him. He was able to channel the dissatisfaction and anger of ordinary people against Washington and Wall Street, but his only tools to oppose "the establishment" are his supposedly unparalleled faculties. The Republican Party he now leads is precisely the opposite of a radical, subversive movement.

Nobody knows what Trump's full program will be, though we've all heard his promises to deport Muslims and Latinos and build a wall at the Mexican border. He announced several authoritarian measures— against Muslims, refugees, Mexican immigrants, abortion rights—that put into question both democracy and the state of law. His cabinet choices for the new administration—notably the extreme-right nationalist Steve Bannon as "chief strategist"—clearly confirm this trend. Economically, though, he merges protectionism and neoliberalism: on the one hand, he wishes to annul the free trade agreement with Mexico; on the other, he wants to deregulate finance and privatize social services, which means abolishing the modest achievements of Obama's health care policies. From this point of view, Trump is much more open to neoliberal policies than the European radical right opposed to the euro and supportive of socialized health care, and far away from classical fascist corporatism (which in many cases established forms of national security). In France, Italy, Austria, Belgium, the Netherlands, and even Germany, the far-right movements claim a kind of xenophobic welfare state. Trump defends a form of authoritarian neoliberalism in domestic policy. Like a populist demagogue, he sets up ordinary people against a so-called establishment, but he does not propose any social policy (even a xenophobic or racist one) to defend them.

Classical fascisms worshipped the state, defended imperialism, and promoted military expansionism. Their foreign policies were oriented toward war and the conquest of the so-called "vital space" (*spazio vitale, Lebensraum*). Trump, by contrast, seems more oriented toward isolationism insofar as he criticizes the war in Iraq and supports an alliance with Vladimir Putin's Russia. In the field of foreign policy, his vision does not transcend his own business interests. Instead of fascism, which strongly affirmed the idea of a national or racial community (*stirpe, Volk*), Trump preaches individualism. All in all, he embodies a xenophobic and reactionary vision of Americanism: a social Darwinist self-made man, the avenger bringing arms, the resentment of a white population that cannot accept ever becoming a minority in a country of immigrants. He won the votes of only a quarter of eligible American voters, and his success gives a voice to the fear and frustrations of a minority, like WASP nationalism did a century ago, when its targets were the Catholic, Orthodox, and Jewish immigrants from Southern and Eastern Europe.

Fascism was a product of the Great War and the collapse of the nineteenth-century European order. Its radical nationalism came out of this global continental crisis, and it adopted a form of militarized politics inherited from the trenches and sharpened in a violent confrontation with Bolshevism. In this cataclysmic content, fascism proposed, in spite of an ideological eclecticism, an alternative to the decaying liberal order. In short, it offered a new project of society and civilization, causing many scholars to speak of a "fascist revolution" or a "third way" opposed to both liberalism and communism. Trump belongs to a different time, and proposes no new model of society or civilization. He can only offer slogans: "Make America Great Again" or "America First." He does not wish to change the American social and economic model, if only because he has enormous private interests to defend in it.

Trump emerges in an age of financial capitalism, competitive individualism, and social precariousness. He does not organize and mobilize the masses; he attracts an audience in an atomized society of consumers. He does not wear a uniform, like Hitler and Mussolini, but instead exhibits his luxurious lifestyle like a stereotype of a Hollywood star. More than a new political project, he represents a neoliberal anthropological model: market, competition, and private interests adopted as a "conduct of life." While the United States has never had a president as reactionary and right wing as Trump, fascist ideas are also less widespread in America today than they were seventy or one hundred years ago, during McCarthyism or the Red Scare. The Bolshevik threat no longer exists, and the specter of terrorism isn't sufficiently frightening for Americans to readily give up their freedoms in exchange for the promises of security.

Finally, Trump's victory has to be inscribed within an international context, between the European refugee crisis, "Brexit," and the next French presidential elections. It belongs to a wave of right-wing, anti-globalization movements. Riding a tide that could upend the transatlantic order, Trump is a danger, and we should prepare for a period of social and political conflict.

Nevertheless, I am not convinced that interpreting him through the old category of fascism can help us to understand the novelty of the Trump era. We tend to depict new political phenomena and objects through the lens of preexisting concepts, but Trump's rise is not a sudden return to barbarism, nor is it a meteor crashing down onto a peaceful country. Rather he is the product of the transformations of capitalism in recent decades. With his nationalist, populist, racist, and authoritarian tendencies, he personifies a form of savage capitalism—a capitalism without a human face. It is not a resurgence of fascism, but something new and not yet realized. For now, we might call it "post-fascism." Since Trump does not respect the rule of law, traditional politics risks are becoming obsolete or, at the very least, largely inadequate. Politics, therefore, is returning to the streets.

Mark Bray, "Trump and Everyday Anti-fascism beyond Punching Nazis," *Roar Magazine*, January 23, 2017

In the days after Donald Trump's election as US president in November 2016, there was an increase in attacks on people of color and religious minorities, especially Muslims, and mass street protests against Trump's victory. Mark Bray's reportage, originally published just three days after Trump's inauguration, is an attempt to capture what might be called the antifascist zeitgeist of that moment. His eyewitness account of the huge national protests in Washington, DC, against Trump in conjunction with the massive Women's March signaled for Bray a rejection of what he here calls the "everyday" aspects of reaction associated with Trump's victory: racism, sexism, misogyny, homophobia, xenophobia. Bray's essay was an attempt to interpret the protests as something like a germinal new united front against Trump and Trumpism, on one hand, and against fascism and neofascism, on the other.

    Mark Bray has emerged as a leading philosopher and historian of the "antifa" phenomenon in the United States. In this essay, he outlines an antifa position on free speech and political organizing that in some ways conflicts with dominant American ideas of liberalism. He is best known as the author of Antifa: The Anti-fascist Handbook, *to date the single most comprehensive study of antifa published in the United States. For publication in this volume, the author has revised the essay from the version that originally appeared in* Roar.

> Either change their views
> Or change your friends
> If you have a racist friend
> Now is the time, now is the time
> For your friendship to end
> —"Racist Friend," The Special AKA

Much attention has been directed toward the anonymous avenger who slugged the white supremacist "alt-right" leader Richard Spencer at the Trump inauguration protest in Washington, DC, and with good reason. Yet the punch heard round the internet was far from the only anti-fascist action taken in DC this weekend.

In order to develop a broad anti-fascist agenda that aims to rip this weed out by the stem, we mustn't overlook more seemingly mundane, even trivial, examples of what I argue amount to everyday anti-fascism that rely on developing an anti-fascist outlook that can hopefully stem the tide of bigotry unleashed by "everyday Trumpism."[1]

Everyday Fascism

If we want to promote everyday anti-fascism, we must first be clear on what everyday fascism can look like (admittedly it can take many forms), and who the everyday fascists are. Although the alt-right makes a lot of noise, those who self-identify with that rather-new label are few.

Yet as Trump rose to power, their ideas filtered through the campaign to ignite reactionary passion among many white Americans who felt alienated about the loss of their "place in the sun." A country that they imagined would remain white, Christian, patriarchal and heteronormative with an eternal manufacturing economy is rapidly disappearing.

In this context, Spencer and the alt-right have made Trump their figurehead in the movement to push back waves of (albeit incomplete) progress that American social movements have made in establishing societal taboos against explicit manifestations of racism, sexism and other oppressive behaviors that have been dismissed as "political correctness."

---

1   Bray credits this phrase to Yesenia Barragan, "Everyday Trumpism, Old and New: This Latina Will Fight Back," *Univision*, November 15, 2016, univision.com.

This has taken many forms—from Trump and his supporters dismissing his boasts about sexual assault as mere "locker room talk," to his disdain for the Geneva Conventions and general opposition to torture, to his comfort with labeling Mexican immigrants as rapists, to his outrage at being named the *Time* magazine "person of the year" rather than the "man of the year."

Much of Trump's popularity stemmed from the relief that many Americans felt in hearing someone in an unquestioned position of authority and prestige say the very things that they had been thinking for years, but that were considered too taboo by society to utter or act upon. Especially after Trump's election, the strength of that taboo was damaged, as more than 867 "cases of hateful harassment or intimidation" were reported within the first ten days after the election.

When we think about everyday fascists, we must bear in mind that the fascist regimes of the past could not have survived without a broad layer of societal support. Over the years, historical research has demonstrated that the process of demonizing the marginalized required the privileging of the favored, making many the explicit or implicit allies of Mussolini, Hitler, and other leaders.

If fascism required societal support for the destruction of "artificial," "bourgeois" norms such as the "rights of man" in developing its hypernationalism, then today we must be alert to the ongoing campaign to delegitimize the ethical and political standards that we have at our disposal to fight back. This is evident in many of the arguments of the far right, but I found one useful articulation of it in the opening of an article from a crappy, generic far-right blog:[2]

One of the best things about Donald Trump's glorious, GLORIOUS election win is how it proved that all the main smears that SJWs [Social Justice Warriors] and "journalists" throw at wrongthinkers— Sexist, Racist, Islamophobe etc—have lost most of their power. After all, Trump was hit with these slurs non-stop during his presidential campaign, even by "respectable" media outlets, and still ended up beating Hillary Clinton decisively. It's about time too, because not only are smears like Racist and Sexist overused, they've basically become intellectual poison.

2   The blog is the *Ralph Retort*, November 16, 2016, theralphretort.com.

After Trump's victory, we have a dangerous mix of mainstream conservatives who don't want to appear racist and alt-right "race realists" who all accuse the "left" of so overusing the term that it is rendered meaningless—in other words, no one is racist anymore (or we're all racist now?). There is a major difference between the previous paradigm—where the left accused the right of being racist, and then the right accused the left of being the *real* racists because they focused so much on race—and a developing paradigm where the alt-right and those they have influenced try to drain the power of the accusation.

The everyday fascists are the ardent Trump supporters who "tell it like it is" by actively trying to dismantle the taboos against oppression that the movements for feminism, black liberation, queer liberation and others have given their sweat, tears and all too often blood to establish as admittedly shoddy, and far too easily manipulatable, bulwarks against outright fascism.

These social norms are constantly contested and are unfortunately subject to resignification in oppressive directions, such as when George W. Bush sold the war in Afghanistan as a crusade for women's rights. Yet the fact that politicians have felt the need to engage on the plains that popular resistance have established means that they left themselves open to political attacks on grounds that they at least tacitly acknowledged. A major concern with Trump and the alt-right, however, is that they hope to drain these standards of their meaning.

Liberals tend to examine issues of sexism or racism in terms of the question of belief or what is "in one's heart." What is often overlooked in such conversations is that what one truly believes is sometimes much less important than what social constraints allow that person to articulate or act upon. This issue is at the center of questions of social progress or regression, and its contours are established through the seemingly infinite networks of human interactions that compose our society.

While one should always be wary about painting large groups of people with a broad brush, it is clear that ardent Trump supporters voted for their candidate either *because of* or *despite* his misogyny, racism, ableism, Islamophobia and many more hateful traits. There is certainly a significant difference between "because of" and "despite" in this context, and sensitivity to the difference should attune us to the importance of mass organizing that can divert potential fascist-sympathizers away from the far right. It is always important to distinguish between ideologues and their capricious followers, yet we cannot overlook how these popular bases of support create the foundations for fascism to manifest itself.

Everyday Anti-fascism

When leftists think of anti-fascism they tend to focus on the movements around the many Anti-Fascist Action groups popularly abbreviated as "antifa." They have undoubtedly played tremendously important roles in resisting the far right around the world and protecting the vulnerable. Here, however, I am interested in the more subtle forms of everyday anti-fascism that deprive the far right of their bases of support in popular opinion. In order to understand what I mean by everyday anti-fascism, let's first take a look at what I call an anti-fascist outlook that provides their foundation.

At its core, anti-fascist politics are about denying fascists a platform in society to promote their politics. This can be done by physically confronting them when they mass in public, by pressuring venues to cancel their events, by shutting down their websites, stealing their newspapers, et cetera. At the heart of the anti-fascist outlook is a rejection of the classical liberal notion incorrectly ascribed to Voltaire that "I disapprove of what you say, but I will defend to the death your right to say it." After Auschwitz and Treblinka, anti-fascists committed themselves to fighting to the death the ability of organized Nazis to say anything.

In theory, American liberalism is allergic to the notion of "discriminating" against anyone based on their politics, and sees the role of government as that of referee in a game that all political tendencies are invited to play (despite the empirical inaccuracy of this dream). Unless they break the law, Nazis can be Nazis. That's just their "opinion," which is just as legitimate as any other in an imagined free market of thought. In contrast, anti-fascism is avowedly political in its determination to deny the legitimacy of Nazi opinions and take seriously the ramifications that such views can and do have in the world around us.

An anti-fascist outlook applies this logic to any kind of interaction with fascists. It refuses to accept the dangerous notion that homophobia is just someone's "opinion" to which they are entitled. It refuses to accept opposition to the basic proposal that "Black lives matter" as a simple political disagreement. An anti-fascist outlook has no tolerance for "intolerance." It will not "agree to disagree." To those who argue that this would make us no better than Nazis, we must point out that our critique is not against violence, incivility, discrimination or disrupting speeches in the abstract, but against those who do so in the service of white supremacy, heteropatriarchy, class oppression and genocide. The point here isn't tactics, it's politics.

If the goal of normal anti-fascist politics is to make it so that Nazis cannot appear uncontested in public, then the goal of everyday anti-fascism is to increase the social cost of oppressive behavior to such a point that those who promote it see no option but for their views to recede into hiding. Certainly this goal had not been fully accomplished by a long shot prior to the rise of Trump, but his election and the growth of the alt-right (at least on the web) has made this task all the more pressing.

The anti-fascist outlook was put into action in many ways during the inauguration protest—from the more visible example of socking Richard Spencer to burning the Trump baseball caps of attendees at the alt-right "DeploraBall," to getting in the faces of Trump supporters heckling the Women's March. Two signs I saw at the Women's March epitomized this perspective. They read: "Make Racists Afraid Again" and "Make Rapists Afraid Again." These slogans point to the fact that, while ideally we could convince all racists and rapists to change their ways, the pressing task for the protection of the vulnerable is to make it so that they think twice before acting.

Demonstrators at the Women's March, Washington, DC, January 21, 2017.
Photo by Mark Bray.

To clarify, I certainly agree that changing hearts and minds is ideal and that it can happen. One striking example occurred with the case of Derek Black, the son of the founder of the Nazi Stormfront site, who disavowed white supremacy through conversations with friends at the New College of Florida.

But apart from the rareness of this development, one point should be remembered: that Derek Black's white supremacist ideas and the anti-racist ideas of the New College students did not meet each other on an equal playing field. Derek Black was embarrassed about being a neo-Nazi, and that fact only came out once others publicized it. Why was he embarrassed? Because Nazism has been so thoroughly discredited that he felt like he was in a tiny minority, at odds with everyone around him.

In other words, the anti-racist movements of the past constructed the high social cost that Black's white supremacist views carried, thereby paving the way for him to open himself up to an anti-racist outlook. Hearts and minds are never changed in a vacuum; they are products of the worlds around them and the structures of discourse that give them meaning.

Any time someone takes action against a transphobic, racist bigot— from calling them out to boycotting their business, to shaming them for their oppressive beliefs, to ending a friendship unless someone shapes up—they are putting an anti-fascist outlook into practice to contribute to a broader everyday anti-fascism necessary to push back the tide against the alt-right, Trump and his loyal supporters. Our goal should be that in twenty years, those who voted for Trump are too uncomfortable to share that fact in public.

We may not always be able to change someone's beliefs, but we sure as hell can make it politically, socially, economically, and sometimes physically costly to articulate them.

Further Reading

The Historical Fascist States

Arendt, Hannah, *The Origins of Totalitarianism* (New York: Harcourt, Brace, Jovanovich, 1973).

Bauerkämper, Arnd and Grzegorz Rossoliński-Liebe, eds., *Fascism without Borders: Transnational Connections and Cooperation between Movements and Regimes in Europe from 1918 to 1945* (New York: Berghahn, 2017).

Bois, Marcel, "Hitler Wasn't Inevitable," *Jacobin*, November 25, 2015, jacobinmag.com.

Gentile, Emilio, *The Sacralization of Politics in Fascist Italy* (Cambridge, MA: Harvard University Press, 1996).

Griffin, Roger, *The Nature of Fascism* (London: Routledge, 1993).

Herzog, Dagmar, *Sex after Fascism: Memory and Morality in Twentieth-Century Germany* (Princeton, NJ: Princeton University Press, 2007).

Hofmann, Reto, *The Fascist Effect: Japan and Italy, 1915–1952* (Ithaca, NY: Cornell University Press, 2015).

Kershaw, Ian, "Hitler and the Uniqueness of Nazism," *Journal of Contemporary History* 39:2 (2004), 239–54.

——, *Nazi Germany: Problems and Perspectives of Interpretation* (London: Edward Arnold, 1993).

Paxton, Robert, *The Anatomy of Fascism* (New York: Alfred A. Knopf, 2004).

Payne, Stanley, *A History of Fascism: 1914–1945* (Madison: University of Wisconsin Press, 1995).

Pelz, William, "Economic Collapse and the Rise of Fascism, 1920–1933," in *A People's History of Modern Europe* (London: Pluto Press, 2016).

Plant, Richard, *The Pink Triangle: The Nazi War against Homosexuals* (New York: Henry Holt, 1986).

Tansman, Alan, ed., *The Culture of Japanese Fascism* (Chapel Hill, NC: Duke University Press, 2009).

Historical Fascist Currents in the United States

Allen, Joe, *When Fascism Was American* (CreateSpace Independent Publishing Platform, 2017).

Carter, Dan, *From George Wallace to Newt Gingrich: Race in the Conservative Counterrevolution, 1963–1994* (Baton Rouge, LA: Louisiana State University Press, 1996).

Diggins, John, *Mussolini and Fascism: The View from America* (Princeton, NJ: Princeton University Press, 1972).

Kühl, Stefan, *The Nazi Connection: Eugenics, American Racism, and German National Socialism* (Oxford, UK: Oxford University Press, 1994).

McVeigh, Rory, *The Rise of the Ku Klux Klan: Right-Wing Movements and National Politics* (Minneapolis: University of Minnesota Press, 2009).

Norwood, Stephen, "Marauding Youth and the Christian Front: Antisemitic Violence in Boston and New York during World War II," *American Jewish History* 91:2 (2003), 233–67.

Simpson, Christopher, *Blowback: America's Recruitment of Nazis and Its Effects on the Cold War* (New York: Collier Books, 1989).

Thompson, Mark Christian, *Black Fascisms: African American Literature and Culture between the Wars* (Charlottesville: University of Virginia Press, 2007).

Warren, Donald, *Radio Priest: Charles Coughlin, the Father of Hate Radio* (New York: Free Press, 1996).

Whitman, James, *Hitler's American Model: The United States and the Making of Nazi Race Law* (Princeton, NJ: Princeton University Press, 2017).

Antifascist Struggle (Europe and Asia)

Balhorn, Lauren, "The Lost History of Antifa," *Jacobin*, May 8, 2017, jacobin-mag.com.

Braskén, Kasper, "Making Anti-Fascism Transnational: The Origins of Communist and Socialist Articulations of Resistance in Europe, 1923–1924," *Contemporary European History* 25:4 (2016), 573–96.

Bray, Mark, *Antifa: The Anti-Fascist Handbook* (New York: Melville House, 2017).

Copsey, Nigel, *Anti-Fascism in Britain* (New York: Palgrave Macmillan, 2000).

Copsey, Nigel and Andrzej Olechnowicz, eds., *Varieties of Anti-Fascism: Britain in the Interwar Period* (New York: Palgrave Macmillan, 2010).

García, Hugo et al., eds., *Rethinking Antifascism: History, Memory and Politics, 1922 to the Present* (New York: Berghahn, 2016).

Liszt, Gabriella, "The Trotskyist Struggle against Nazism in World War II," *Left Voice*, May 8, 2017, leftvoice.org.

Pavone, Claudio, *A Civil War: A History of the Italian Resistance* (London: Verso, 2013).

Renton, David, *Fascism: Theory and Practice* (London: Pluto, 1999).

———, *Never Again: Rock Against Racism and the Anti-Nazi League 1976–1982* (London: Routledge, 2019).

———, *The New Authoritarians: Convergence on the Right London* (Pluto Press, 2019).

Ross, Alexander Reid, *Against the Fascist Creep* (Oakland: AK Press, 2017).

Testa, M., *Militant Antifascism: A Hundred Years of Resistance* (Oakland: AK Press, 2015).

Antifascist Struggle (United States)

Bencivenni, Marcella, *Italian Immigrant Radical Culture: The Idealism of the Sovversivi in the United States, 1890–1940* (New York: New York University Press, 2014).

Bray, Mark, *Antifa: The Anti-Fascist Handbook* (New York: Melville House, 2017).

Burley, Shane, *Fascism Today: What It Is and How to End It* (Oakland: AK Press, 2017).

Ceplair, Larry, *Under the Shadow of War: Fascism, Anti-Fascism, and Marxists: 1918–1939* (New York: Columbia University Press, 1987).

Diggins, John, "The Italo-American Anti-Fascist Opposition," *Journal of American History* 54:3 (1967), 579–98.

Hill, Rebecca, *Men, Mobs, and Law: Anti-Lynching and Labor Defense in US Radical History* (Chapel Hill, NC: Duke University Press, 2009).

Ottanelli, Fraser, *The Communist Party of the United States: From the Depression to World War II* (New Brunswick, NJ: Rutgers University Press, 1991).

Vials, Chris, *Haunted by Hitler: Liberals, the Left, and the Fight against Fascism in the United States* (Amherst: University of Massachusetts Press, 2014).

Wald, Alan, *American Night: The Literary Left in the Era of the Cold War* (Chapel Hill: University of North Carolina Press, 2012).

———, *Trinity of Passion: The Literary Left and the Antifascist Crusade* (Chapel Hill: University of North Carolina Press, 2007).

Contemporary Fascist Currents and the Neoliberal Moment

Belew, Kathleen, *Bring the War Home: The White Power Movement and Paramilitary America* (Cambridge, MA: Harvard University Press, 2018).

Berlet, Chip, "What Is the Third Position?," *Political Research Associates*, December 19, 2016, politicalresearch.org.

Berlet, Chip and Matthew Lyons, *Right-Wing Populism in America: Too Close for Comfort* (New York: Guilford, 2000).

Bhattacharya, Tithi, "Donald Trump: The Unanticipated Apotheosis of Neoliberalism," *Cultural Dynamics* 29 (2017), 108–16.

Jayasuriya, Kanishka, "Nationalism Marries Neoliberalism to Fuel Rise of Asia's New Right," *Conversation*, March 20, 2014, theconversation.org.

Lowndes, Joe, "White Populism and the Transformation of the Silent Majority," *Forum* 14:1 (2016).

Lyons, Matthew N., "Ctrl-Alt-Delete: The Origins and History of the Alt-Right," *Political Research Associates*, January 20, 2017, politicalresesarch.org.

Panitch, Leo and Gregory Albo, eds., *Socialist Register 2016: The Politics of the Right* (New York: Monthly Review Press, 2015).

Penny, Daniel, "#Milosexual and the Aesthetics of Fascism," *Boston Review*, February 24, 2017, bostonreview.org.

Prowe, Diethelm, "'Classic' Fascism and the New Radical Right in Western Europe: Comparisons and Contrasts," *Contemporary European History* 3:3 (1994), 289–313.

Singh, Nikhil Pal, "The Afterlife of Fascism," *South Atlantic Quarterly* 105:1 (2006), 71–93.

Tamás, G. M., "On Post-Fascism," *Boston Review*, June 1, 2000, bostonreview. org.

Toscano, Alberto, "Notes on Late Fascism," *Historical Materialism* blog, 2017, historicalmaterialism.org.

Traverso, Enzo, *Left Wing Melancholia: Marxism, History, and Memory* (New York: Columbia University Press, 2017).

———, *The New Faces of Fascism: Populism and the Far Right* (London: Verso, 2019).

Index